DIVINE
REASON & RHYME

Access Higher Guidance
And Nature's Wisdom

Volume 1 of the "Wisdom of the Ages" Series

By Sundae Merrick

Order this book online at www.trafford.com
or email orders@trafford.com

Most Trafford titles are also available at major online book retailers.

Print information available on the last page.

ISBN: 978-1-4120-1403-8 (sc)
ISBN: 978-1-4122-1795-8 (e)

Trafford rev. 05/30/2019

Trafford PUBLISHING® **www.trafford.com**
North America & international
toll-free: 1 888 232 4444 (USA & Canada)
fax: 812 355 4082

Dedication

This book is dedicated to all who desire to learn how to access Higher Guidance as their Source and those who already use the Art of Divination. Also, I wish to extend this dedication to our ancestors and everyone who has preserved and utilized the knowledge of Nature's Wisdom.

Acknowledgments

I wish to acknowledge and express gratitude first to my Inner Self, the greatest teacher I have ever had the opportunity and good fortune to experience. I also wish to acknowledge the encouragement and typing support of Peg Hoefer and Sheila Miles. Jim Berenholtz gave me assistance with amakua and sounds for which I am grateful. My appreciation for some of the editing of this book goes to Sara Levine and Lisa Galloway. I thank you all, my dear friends, for your inspiration and feedback.

I would like to mention my mother, Lois, who gave me some of my first reference books and guided me toward these subjects, thanks, Mom!

I want to thank my clients and students who have given me the platform on which I can share the wisdom of Guidance.

In closing, I acknowledge all the courageous and beautiful souls who desire to experience the awareness of their Inner Selves more. The aspiration to create a richer realization in our lives by understanding and applying Nature's Wisdom and Divine Reason & Rhyme more profoundly will reap rewards.

DIVINE REASON & RHYME
Access Higher Guidance and Nature's Wisdom

CONTENTS

Chapter 3
KARMA & THE GIFT OF FREE WILL 45

Chapter 4
INTUITION, OUR CONSCIENCE & CONSCIOUSNESS 55

Chapter 5
CLEARING & PREPARING FOR RECEIVING GUIDANCE 69

NATURE'S REFLECTION OF DIVINE ORDER (cont.)

Chapter 9
ASTROLOGY, NUMBERS & OTHER DIVINATION ARTS 143

Chapter 10
GUIDELINES FOR GUIDANCE 167

Introduction

Divine Reason & Rhyme is a guide to living Divine Plan in this Millennium. It is an essential resource manual on how to get back to the proverbial "Garden" as in the Garden of Eden, wherein everything was provided. The better we are connected to our Spiritual Self[1], our Inner Guidance, the better we flourish. We can learn how to be our own psychic, minister, doctor, and psychologist[2] and how to be trained to find our own Inner Guidance[3].

This book was written with the intention that trusting and acting on the idea that Divine Guidance will bring us back to a state of grace and harmony, which most of us seek. I will reveal and share my process of coming to trust Inner Guidance.

Through the years with clients and loved ones, I have been disseminating the vital importance of the wisdom of Guidance. People from all over the world call on me for assistance in understanding their life cycles, relationships, the best possible direction, choices, etc. I learned to listen, see, and experience Divine Guidance through the symbology of Divine Creation and Inner knowing.

In the course of this book I will include my personal experiences, as well as those of others who practice Divine Guidance, the art of Divination. It is possible that you will recognize some of your own experiences, which you may not have reflected on as being Divinely guided. This will give you the opportunity to see the instances and situations in which you can use the techniques in this book to receive and/or enrich your own Guidance. You may discover that you have been accessing your own Guidance without realizing it consciously.

The Higher Power wants the best for all of us. I want to inspire and to encourage the manifestation of our Highest expression through the wisdom of Divine Guidance.

It is not the purpose of this book to attempt to teach you to foretell the future. By teaching you to describe the energy, and to understand the opportunities and the challenges that present themselves in your life, you will be able to make the Highest and best possible choices from your own Guidance, rather than from habitual patterns.

I always pray for my Highest and best and allow the Divine to do the rest. I pray for others in this manner, too. It is my purpose to show you how to feel guided in each moment by your Spiritual awareness, to make the right choices for yourself. Listen to Guidance, let

[1] I choose to capitalize "Self" when it comes from Inner, Higher, etc.
[2] Always seek assistance from qualified health care practitioners as well!
[3] I choose to capitalize "Guidance" when it comes from Divine Source.

go, and allow the Divine Plan to unfold. This takes away the burden and pain of trying to control people and situations.

Choices, choices and more choices! This book is an opportunity to learn to HONOR Divine Will through asking for, receiving and acting on Divine Guidance. We will explore how you can actually do it yourself and learn to understand it. It is difficult if not impossible to live a more enlightened and fulfilled life without lighting our way through the darkness. Divine Source is the Light and Space and the results obtained from acting on it are completely fulfilling, because it is the Divine plan for us.

We will look at all of the wonderful ways in which we can receive Guidance, so we can discover Divine Will for us personally. In life, there are so many options; this is the best way we can choose appropriately without limiting ourselves with our narrow human perspective and reasoning skills. I am sharing the knowledge of knowing. We can know and understand more about Divine plan for us and make better choices in our life.

We have the opportunity to become Self-empowered by accessing this great power from within. Let's "surf" our own Inner energy channels. We can experience our authentic Sacred Self. We can cultivate a relationship with that Self by creating our own personal daily Self-ritual time. It is possible to learn how to move through life in a Higher and better way by accessing Divine Plan.

Changes in Our World

We have all noticed great changes in weather and natural disasters as we approached the year 2000. Usually, there are about 700 natural disasters per decade on the average. We have seen a remarkably high incidence, 2400 in the 1990's alone. This is the most frequent and most severe, about 3 times greater than any decade in the past. We have had a 700% increase in floods and 600% increase in hurricanes and tornadoes, 4 times the volcanic eruptions and 2 times the amount of landslides. Instead of 1000 tornadoes in 30 years, we had 1000 tornadoes in the 1990's already.[4]

There was a television show, "Signs from God" that brought to light these natural disaster statistics. It also indicated that there were many apparitions of the Virgin Mary appearing and a statue of Jesus Christ bleeding. When the blood was analyzed, it was found to be female blood. This can be interpreted as a return of the feminine Spirit in the new Millennium. Remember that Christ was pierced on his left side, again making a statement about the feminine side. I interpret the feminine side as being our Spiritual and emotional expression. The left side of the body is connected to the right brain and the

[4] From the video, "Signs From God."

intuitive and subconscious function. These phenomena can be interpreted that it is time to discover and embrace our intuition, heal the contents of the unconscious and to turn back to our Spirituality and the Spirit within. We need to honor and resolve our emotional selves and to learn to act on our intuitive Guidance from the Inner Self, our "Spiritual connection" with the Divine.

Father Peter Stravinkas, editor of "The Catholic Answer" and publisher of many books, says "These extraordinary phenomena are not normally the way God works to communicate his will or his way." "God is the Lord of Nature, and as the Lord of Nature he can suspend the laws of nature to communicate an extraordinary message or get mankind's attention." Many believe that the predictions about natural disasters were foretold. We are now fully aware of the damage, destruction and loss of life that have occurred. It is bringing people together. More people are praying and paying attention to their Spirit. Others are selfishly invested in power and money and not getting the message of Spirit.

In a situation where our environment, our lives and other things seem out of our control, we need a "Soul-u-tion" which comes from our Soul. We can't seem to fully figure it out with our limited intellectual perspective. We need to tune into the deepest and Highest level of our being to get a more Spiritual solution. The best "Soul-u-tion" is to go inside, pray for our self, as well as everybody, and receive our Guidance. Pray for the Highest and best for all; follow your Guidance and watch it unfold. It will unfold in its perfect kaleidoscope-like way. Everything falls into perfect order with Divine plan and Divine time. We can relax, breathe and pray. How nice to have permission to relax and just be.

It is important to find our Spiritual center every day. We will learn how to find it together. Make it part of our daily rituals, along with prayer and gratitude. We can only control our life to a certain degree with our ego in charge. One can learn more, have a Higher experience and do all the things one does for one's self through the Guidance of our own Spirit. We can choose to break dysfunctional patterns, choosing to replace them with beautiful loving patterns. The patterns that set an example for our young ones are the ones that we embody. Then they can embody and demonstrate the same loving patterns to the incoming generations.

We are ready for the new Millennium, if we have been giving attention to and practicing having a foundation of physical, mental, Spiritual and emotional balance in our lives. This book will give us the opportunity to assess our wholeness and connection to our Spirit. If we have been lacking masculine values, we will learn how to balance them. At this time, most of us need to pay attention to the feminine values of our Spiritual and emotional selves. We need to honor the feminine as a stronger focus in order to be balanced, personally and within society.

What many of us need are some Heart and Soul classes. Singing, dancing, all arts, intuitive opening, having a relationship with the Divine, flowing and releasing emotions are some of the feminine skills for men and women. Many women are not aware of the importance of this development, as it really has not been encouraged in modern times. Some men and women don't necessarily know they have a feminine side yet or know what their right brain is all about. We have developed our left brain and masculine skills so extensively that many have forgotten about our other talents and skills. We need to care more about our loved ones and ourselves. I believe we collectively want to possess a Higher knowing and to express it fully.

We need to know the Divine Plan for us, by learning to use the right brain and intuition, again! It is important to encourage everybody that desires it, in this way. By our example, our loved ones will have an opportunity to experience it and embody it more. Imagine how life would be with more love, fulfillment, sensitivity, peace, harmony and compassion!

This balance of masculine and feminine is going to be the new workout for the Millennium. We all have four bodies: physical, mental, Spiritual and emotional. This workout requires us to be equally pumped up with awareness physically, mentally, Spiritually and emotionally and fully centered within this 4-corner foundation. This training for the Millennium is strength training for our feminine side, for some of us. For others, it is strength training for the masculine side. The desired result is to have wholeness, balance and choice. Our 4-corner foundation training, our balance of masculine and feminine values and expression within our self, is the wisdom

It is my belief that we can become mystical artists in our own lives, as we align more and more with our own Spiritual awareness through our intuitive or Inner knowing. This has been my path and area of service for most of my life. I have been assisting others in discovering their own Guidance.

We no longer need to be banished from the Garden. We do not have to feel lost and disconnected from our true Divine heritage. We can recreate the Garden of Eden on this earth by choosing Divine Will and Plan. It is only through this channel of Divine Guidance that we can become aware enough of Divine Reason and Rhyme to choose appropriately. When we choose this, life is much more rewarding; everything falls into place in its perfect order.

This book is to encourage us to become a mystical artist in our own life by noticing, accepting and acting on our own Divine Guidance. I call Divine Guidance my compass in life. Just as a compass uses magnetic north as a guidance tool, we can too. Understanding the signposts and our place in the Universe makes this journey more inspiring. To be on track, we need to know Divine magnetic north. Life can be richer, deeper and more fulfilling. We can experience the harmony and melody of our Universe, with Source as our Guide!

This book and this message can open us more to our own Inner knowing, which is unique and perfect. We can learn how to access this Guidance through understanding and connecting with our Spiritual or Inner Self, intuition, energy, dreams, nature's reflections, polarity, elements, emotions, colors and the messages they reflect. There is Divine design and order in nature and life. We will discover it with the Divine as our Guide, through our own intuitive Inner knowing and the messages it perceives. We can fulfill our Highest evolution and expression by knowing Divine Reason and Rhyme in our own lives!

Chapter 1

Divine Guidance, Our Best Source

It was a rainy, dreary afternoon and the visibility was limited. A fog had permeated the countryside. The bridal party, some guests and me, were motoring together in a long white stretch limousine to a distant chapel for my Goddaughter, Cynthia's nuptials. I was seated next to the bride-to-be, at her request. Prior to the wedding, she had made many long distance calls, requesting my counsel and support. The bride's mother had determined the wedding date and she had not consulted with me about the astrological significance of this most auspicious occasion. I recognized that this was not the best time. I also knew that it was not a great period for me to be traveling; I was experiencing several challenging cycles myself. At first, I had considered not going to the wedding; however, I felt guided to be there to support her and share in the joy of her special day.

We had nestled together peacefully in the backseat, as we journeyed to the chapel. Just as I was adjusting the bride's gown and remarking on how nice it was to see her calm and relaxed, our limo rear-ended the car in front of us. In a flash, we were catapulted out of our sweet reverie. As we were propelled through the air, I experienced a sense of Superconsciousness; each millisecond in flight seemed like an eternity. When I flew across the length of the stretch limo, my right hip struck the corner of the TV console. I plunged to the floor on my right side; my neck whipped side to side. My body took the brunt of the accident and it also cushioned Cynthia's fall, protecting her from serious injury, as well as her unborn child. She was shaken but not injured. As her Godmother, I was definitely there for the bride!

For a time, I lay dazed and crumpled on the floor. I gradually became aware of the red flashing lights of the emergency vehicle reflected on the interior of the car. I was in shock. My body had frozen into position and it wasn't moving. I knew I was hurt, but I didn't know the extent of the damage. Paramedics surrounded me as they cradled my head and neck in a brace. I was being persuaded to be transported to the hospital by ambulance, so I could be x-rayed. I felt bewildered and confused about what to do.

I had tenaciously flown over ten hours from Hawaii and driven resolutely two more hours from the airport to get to the Pennsylvania farmlands, to support my Goddaughter's marriage. Fully committed, Cynthia desired to go ahead with the ceremony and left in another vehicle. Undaunted, I lifted my eyes upward and heard my Inner Guidance, through a flash of intuition, suggesting the use of a pendulum. I asked the Maid of honor, Sara, for her necklace and proceeded to pray for the Highest Guidance. Sara, a dear friend, kept the emergency crew at bay while I focused, prayed and asked for Divine Guidance. In the process of asking if I should go to the wedding, I saw the familiar counterclockwise pattern of the necklace, giving me a positive response. It was wonderful to have Sara intervene for me with the well-intentioned Paramedics, while I waited to see the direction of the swing. I asked twice, because I knew I was not in my normal state of mind. Two times, I got the same unfaltering answer, "go to the wedding!"

Even though I was traumatized, in pain and visibly stunned, my choice was affirmed. The ceremony was delayed until I arrived at the chapel. I was met by a massage therapist/Reiki Healer who assisted me in releasing my emotions and getting out of shock. My muscles were tightly contracted in a protective manner and I had not cried up until that point. I emitted a torrent of tears. My whole body shook as I began to release my painful posture.

During the ceremony, I sat comfortably sandwiched between two Reiki healers while they sent me loving, balancing and healing energy. I was elated that I did not miss the opportunity to experience the marriage. It was much more fulfilling to be in the energy of love and union. Had I chosen out of fear or logic, I would have missed out on this beautiful experience.

The next morning, I went to a caring chiropractor and received wonderful treatment and x-rays in a warm environment. He helped to relieve some of the pain. Ill-starred, my neck and lower back sustained excruciating soft tissue damage and I would have to undergo neck and back therapy for several years. Although painful and uncomfortable, I learned and grew so much from the experience. It has given me time and substance to meditate on; to heal and prepare myself for what was to be next.

Looking back, I have contemplated on how the "accident" portended and mirrored the nature of the bride and groom's relationship, as well as what I needed to balance and transform in my own life. I had counseled them about reconciling any erratic emotions, rebelliousness or instability in their conduct. They chose to be married during this volatile cycle and were unfortunately unable to heal their differences. They separated within their first year. This unpredictability is indicative of Uranus energy. I have had other loving friends who have married during this same vacillating energy and have also separated.

It takes an incredible amount of energy, attention and healing to create a foundation for a marriage or business during a challenging Uranian cycle. It is much more effortless to commence a union during a more stable, mature Saturn cycle or perhaps a Neptunian cycle of unconditional love. We have a choice, if we know the reflections of those cycles. There is great importance regarding the date of initiation for any enterprise. It sets up or originates the energy for the foundation of the endeavor.

For myself, I looked at the deeper meaning in my life. I recognized that I needed to heal, balance and create a new foundation. This was my second accident in less than two years. Earlier, I had been struck forcefully from behind, in the left hip, by the corner of a metal stock cart in a store/warehouse. Intriguingly, this impact had synchronistically damaged my right hip area at the same level. My pelvic girdle was upset for the second time in the lumbar-sacral area of the second energy center. This portended a time of great introspection for the initiation of a new foundation of creativity and material success.

I could have chosen to feel depressed and abandoned by the Universe, writing the whole thing off as two unlucky misfortunes. Instead, I gave it penetrating, symbolic scrutiny. The right side of my body represents my masculine sphere, the physical and mental arena. Since my neck was also injured on the right side, I recognized I was moving in a new direction in my life, physically and in my career, mentally. Since then, I have learned so much more about therapeutic stretching and it has enhanced my Yoga teaching and personal practice. I have acquired more information and experience to create a better foundation for myself and to share with others. I recognized it was time to embark on a new objective into another area of expression, writing about Guidance. My experiences required depth within myself, to contemplate the meaning of the Divine Reason and Rhyme of my existence.

When we are lost, stressed out, in shock or have pain, it is difficult to assess the situation or the damages. Ask for Guidance and then choose appropriately. Without Guidance, we may make the wrong choice, endanger our self or not have a very fulfilling experience. Through Guidance we can understand the profound meaning in our life that is essential to comprehend for our maturation and evolution. We can make better choices, if we have the knowledge of how to access our Guidance in any situation.

Divine Reason and Rhyme

It is important to our health and well being to listen to, understand and utilize Divine Guidance, which comprehends fully the Divine reason and rhyme in our life. When we don't, many of us go through life feeling anxious, unclear, and confused. We feel separate, lonely, depressed and derailed. It is not always in our best interest to make choices based on our limited ego and personality self, our fallible human reason.

Dis-empowered choices frequently feel in conflict with our hearts and we become unhappy with our existence. It is then that our experience of life does not feel like a gift and a blessing. We have separated ourselves from Divine Source and our Inner Self, that part of Source that is in each and every one of us. The original meaning of the word sin is "acting without". Some have forgotten our connection with the Divine and the wisdom of acting on this Guidance. Others have lost the understanding of Divine Order and the reflections of it, in nature. This is the reason we experience being dis-empowered, isolated and aimless in our life. It is not fulfilling to be clueless about our process and our purpose.

The Higher Power continues to communicate with us through our natural and supernatural experiences. All we have to do is open our hearts, minds, ears and eyes to Divine Guidance. In our daily experience, Guidance is being revealed to us continuously. When we learn to understand the symbology, we become empowered with it.

"Knowing" arises from reflecting on our experiences and our Inner awareness. It is our Guidance. It speaks to us through our conscience, our dreams and our intuition or through the many reflections of nature. As we learn to identify our Guidance and to act on it, we feel more fulfilled in our life than we have ever been. This wisdom has transformed my life and it will recreate yours, if you choose to learn about it.

We have alternatives, unless we are not conscious of all the possibilities. We can act on Divine Will through our Inner Guidance, which is an enlightened, unlimited choice. We can choose according to our reason and intellect, which is limited in perspective. The last is usually not a preference, reacting from the unconscious mind. The same patterns of thoughts, emotions and behaviors are played over and over. In this case, we are not truly free to choose. Why be imprisoned by our self-limiting patterns, when the possibilities are infinite?

Some of us have overlooked acting in partnership with Source. The story of Adam and Eve in the Garden of Eden clearly demonstrates our separation from Divine Guidance. It was truly the "original sin," when they decided to act their intellect alone. Adam and Eve did not listen to Divine Guidance and alienated themselves from paradise. Our Divine Source is a Creative Intelligence that wants good for us. We can choose to learn how to listen and act on this Divine Guidance.

The lesson in the story of "The Garden of Eden," was to listen to and honor Divine Will to remain in a state of grace, living in bliss. Adam and Eve thought they could have more wisdom than Source, by eating from the Tree of the Knowledge of Good and Evil. This tree represents our option to use the gifts of our intellect and reason, which are incomplete in perception. Divine Source wants us to be connected to our Inner knowing to determine what is good and evil for ourselves, according to our own values and conscience.

We are to look inside, into our own heart and soul, to hear the wisdom our Divine parent has especially for us.

Each one of us has a perspective of the truth; not one of us is totally unlimited in our vision without Divine Intelligence. Our human reason and intellect are not that vast, acting on our own. Divine Insight is infinite and we can access it through our Inner knowing and our intuition. Divine Guidance and the reflections of nature can assist us. We can learn how to understand this wisdom. We can be shown the way, the direction that was intended for us, to fulfill our purpose in the Divine Plan.

What is Divination?

Webster's Dictionary defines divination as "the act or practice of foretelling the future or unknown by mystical arts; a prophecy; a successful guess; clever conjecture."[5] I prefer the definitions of mysticism and guidance. Webster's mystical means "something that is spiritually significant or symbolic and relating to intuition, contemplation or meditation of a spiritual nature." Webster characterizes guidance as "advise or assistance, the act of guiding; direction; leadership."[6] Our lives can be Spiritually significant, if we desire it. It is possible to learn to interpret the cycles, to identify the opportunities and get direction in our life.

In my experience, Divination is our ability to access the Divine for assistance in making choices and understanding our process with unlimited insight. More simply expressed, it is talking to Source and getting an answer. It is a way of tuning into our Highest and best and obtaining the truth for us, so our choices are inspired. I define "inspired" as "coming from Spirit." It is the perfect Soul-u-tion for us!

Divination or Guidance can be an intuitive flash or symbolic, like seeing something significant in nature or through dreams. We can utilize mysticism, as it relates to intuition and awareness of symbolic representation. Our lives can be guided and Spiritually significant, if we desire it. It is possible to learn to interpret nature, cycles, dreams and our intuition, to identify the opportunities and get direction in our life.

It is up to us to discern the most excellent potential for our lives from our own Guidance, rather than from habitual patterns. Otherwise, our life will be a repeating pattern with the same theme. The characters, locations and the situations may change, but it can be the same old story. I want to inspire and to encourage the manifestation of our Highest expression through the wisdom of Divine Guidance.

---

[5] Webster's New World Dictionary, 2nd edition (Cleveland: William Collins Publishers, 1979) p. 412.
[6] Webster's New World Dictionary, 2nd edition (Cleveland: William Collins Publishers, 1979) p. 621.

Using Divine Guidance

We can heal that sense of separation and balance our ego selves, when we hear, understand and utilize the wisdom of Divine Mind. This healing is reflected in the clarity of our Inner knowing, the wisdom of our choices and a sense of being one with Divine Order. When we make choices that cherish all of life fully; our life feels more magical, loving and light-hearted, no matter what the appearances are. We feel a sense of oneness and unity with Source and all of creation. We realize that what hurts one part of creation, in turn, hurts us too. We are all connected.

To discover the Divine Reason and Rhyme of Divine Order in our lives, we need to feel more connected to our Divine Inner Self, which was fashioned from part of the Divine Consciousness of Source. We are Divine children; it is our true nature. We need to understand and practice how to make this connection for more fulfillment and satisfaction in our lives. It is wise to understand and honor this Spiritual relationship for more fulfillment and the perfect "Soul-u-tion" in our lives.

We can learn how to listen to our Inner Self, access our Inner knowing and how to tune into and experience the wisdom of Source. To do this, we need to develop our intuition and devotion. In this way we are living Divine Will in each moment. This is true maturity and Higher Self-development. Why live in a destructive way, with immature ego separation concepts, when we can become a co-creator with Source in a constructive way? We can all be mystical artists of Divine Mind and Will through our Inner Self and our intuitive Inner knowing.

Choices in the Garden

Acting on Reason

As Divine children, we were blessed with the gift of reason. At various times, we have been tempted to use our human reasoning skills to figure out our own lives, the lives of others and all of creation. We have been attempting to discover, from our limited perspective, the reason and rhyme in Divine plan. This is an impossible task. We do not have the capacity of consciousness that Source has, "all knowing and all seeing". Many of us have wanted to know as much as we can of the full scope of the Divine plan, which is unrealizable for humans. We can be very invested in our "personality plan" (personal ego survival pattern) and desire others to follow that as well.

In the story of Adam and Eve (the first children), they had their personal ego plan and used their free will. They were curious as to what they would experience if they ate the forbidden fruit of "the Tree of the Knowledge of Good and Evil." This is similar to and reflects the behavior of children and some adults today. They are inquisitive and want to know why and why not. They apparently wanted to discover for themselves. I don't think Adam and Eve shared that fruit to spite Source. I feel that they wanted to know, discover and experience and not just to be told by their Parent. Just as our children disobey us, to learn from their own experience and develop their own truth. We were born with the ability to reason, an incredible capacity for curiosity and a thirst for experience. That is how Source created us; it is not wrong or bad. Many times we suffer the consequences of our intellectual reasoning abilities; they are not always infallible.

When Adam and Eve were forbidden to eat the "fruits" of the Tree of the Knowledge of Good and Evil, there was a Divine reason why they were forbidden this fruit. Maybe Source did not want us to think we "knew it all," or to learn to judge and blame others. It is not our role to play a Higher Power in another's life's experiences. In judgment of others, we have a false sense of righteousness and separate ourselves from each other and from unconditional love. We demonstrate a selfish, limited ego perspective without Spiritual and emotional values. This is what can come to pass when we think we "know it all" and act only on mental reason and physical evidence.

An example of this is that many of our wars have been a battle of ideologies, blame or a false sense of responsibility or guilt. We want to force others to honor our values, which we determine are factual, orderly and reasonable or what our culture and our religion tell us. We have attempted to justify our wars with our limited human reason and the dogma we have been programmed with. We have attempted to create a world in which everyone shares the same ideas regarding philosophies, religions, race, etc.; regardless of the costs of death and destruction. There is so much diversity in creation, that this only causes conflict. No one point of view or personality is the only way. What is good for one culture or person may be evil to another.

Acting with Free Will

In the allegory of Eden, the first children had an opportunity and a choice to eat of the "fruits" of the Tree of the Knowledge, Good and Evil. This tree was available in the garden. If it were not there, there would be no choice. They were specifically told not to eat of that tree and they did anyway! Adam and Eve utilized their free will to learn and experience; they chose their own course of learning. Source allowed them to do their own will, just as we are permitted to use our free will.

The incredible part of creation is the gift of free will! We get to use our free will and reason, in any way we wish. We can express it positively or negatively, creatively or destructively. Source has so much love and acceptance for us; we can do what we will. Source knew the consequences of the misuse of free will and still we were blessed with the opportunity to choose. What a loving, accepting Parent we have!

Through us, Divinity can express and experience everything including the dualities of our existence. In truth, Source wants to be, to love and experience through us. We are all a part of Source. The Creator experiences through the created. Creation is an opportunity for that to happen! Source loves all of creation, all of the creatures. The Higher Power has created the Divine reason and rhyme of this Divine design. All we need to do is to learn how to discover it for our self.

Why is Divine Guidance Important?

Many times we have experiences that we either don't understand or don't take the time to reflect on. Everything that happens in our lives has a deeper and more meaningful insight than we might have thought. If we truly want to understand and be aware of our life's messages, we need to look at each experience more deeply. Contemplate and meditate and write about it. Before long, we can understand and be able to act on the wisdom that the experience reflects to us.

This is an example of the theory and my belief that there are no "accidents," and how it affected my life for the better! Remember that there is a constructive and a destructive interpretation for all experiences. There is an empowering or a dis-empowering version of every story in our lives. We need to determine which is viable and resonates for us. It is very personal and is determined by our evolution.

This incident was about ten months after the last one. I had three painful "accidents" in three years. Many might feel victimized by the misfortune of having so much suffering, discomfort and financial loss to deal with. The question always seems to come up, "Why me?" Rather than stay in an intellectual lament, it is possible to get a more significant and penetrating look at the situation.

Only 13 (representing the 13 moons of the year, the Divine Feminine) days after the dawn of the new millennium (Year 2000 representing balance of the polarities of masculine and feminine), I was driving toward Bishop Street and changed my mind. I stopped to make a left turn to go to Queen Emma Street. I was facilitating a man exiting a parking lot by waving him through, so I could enter. Milliseconds later, while I was waiting for my turn, I was rear-ended by the driver behind me. My neck was turned to the left (the feminine side) and snapped to thc right (the masculine side) on impact, damaging and hurting my body at the base of the spine (the foundation) as well.

I was moving on one path, attempting to play cautiously by the "rules" of the powers that be, represented by the name "Bishop St." As I changed my direction, I was facilitating the masculine again (waving the man through.) I realized later that I was changing directions in my life as well. As the millennium was progressing, I was devoted (represented by the neck) to the currently neglected "Spiritual and emotional values" and moving more toward sharing the feminine principles in balance with the masculine, through my writing and teaching (as the street name "Queen Emma" suggests.) I was progressing in my leadership (represented by the 1 in the 13,) away from the fear of the patriarchal, controlling, profit-oriented masculine (represented to me by the name "Bishop Street.") (Note: someone else might have a completely different interpretation, it is very personal!) I recognized the feelings of fear from some distant lifetime about being persecuted for sharing these feminine values.

I pondered the reverberations that this fear had affected my ability to come forward (masculine) into the public arena, instead of keeping my practice and myself, "personal and small." I have in the past, been cautious about challenging the powers that be in this patriarchal society (represented by the Bishop.)

I knew that I still felt vulnerable going more with my creative expression (represented by the 3 in 13) of my feminine side and facilitating more feminine knowledge and balanced masculine values, with the public. (The three also represents freedom from worry and more optimism.) While changing directions I was at a standstill, I was exposed and vulnerable, and the impact brought pain to my body. Because my neck was involved, I realized it was about direction and about devotion to my path.

Within two hours of the accident I was in treatment with a dedicated and caring male (balanced male and female values) practitioner of acupuncture and network chiropractic. I did not experience the extreme trauma that other accidents had provided. What I did experience was the awareness that I was getting a new network of energy in my body so that I could be more effective and safe in my vulnerability with sharing the "positive feminine process and balance with positive masculine values." I realized that I could risk being a leader and facilitator of a new direction (represented by Queen Emma and the new millennium) and even add to my overall health and well being. I was healing in ways that would take me in new directions.

The 19-year old young man, who rear-ended me, said he "just wasn't paying attention." This is a great example of following the status quo, a culture that doesn't seem to care about the health, feelings and well being of others or our planet. What was rewarding was that he was willing to admit and take responsibility for his actions. This gave me great hope for the future of younger generations.

We can see how I have taken an "accident" and used it to give more meaning to my life's process. It has empowered my path and has continued to strengthen me as I go through my therapy and healing. I have taken the time to process the fears and limitations from the past. It has given me time to slow down and see my path more clearly. I realize that I am on track with my personal Divine Plan and evolution, because it is being reflected back to me so perfectly. I feel positive and empowered, and I have joy in my life and peace of mind whether I have suffering or not! I know I have chosen my appropriate path.

I truly believe that we were meant to enjoy our lives in the garden of this beautiful planet, Earth. When our choices are guided from Divine Love and Light, life becomes more enjoyable and delightful. We are living the most beneficial physical, mental, Spiritual and emotional values because they come from Source's own Love and Wisdom. When we are fully expressing all that Source has intended for us, we manifest our Highest and Best. As we live according to Divine Guidance and Will, we recreate the original concept the Higher Power had for us in the story of the Garden of Eden, a Divinely inspired and physically experienced, Heaven on Earth!

Reasons for Acting on Divine Guidance:

- *To clear up the confusion in our lives and get on track with our Higher Self*
- *To live more peacefully and lovingly*
- *To awaken our higher Spiritual faculties and open our hearts*
- *To open the perceptual center or third eye to see and act in a Higher way*
- *To see more clearly in our life and make better choices*
- *To live as a conscious co-creator with Source*
- *To be more multi-dimensional in our perceptual abilities*
- *To exercise our free will in its Highest expression*
- *To make better business and financial decisions with a win-win philosophy*
- *To invest more wisely with our time, energy and money*
- *To communicate with others beyond space and time*
- *To be more insightful and conscious in life*
- *To be more considerate and compassionate*
- *To be more devoted to balanced values*
- *To possess a bigger and Higher vision and perspective*
- *To live a healthier life on a healthy planet by honoring nature*
- *To give a legacy of love and wisdom to our children*
- *To give our descendants a clean environment*
- *To experience personal growth and evolution*

- *To manifest our Highest and Best expression on Earth*

Life can be painful and confusing, which is the biggest reason I know of to inspire us to follow Divine Guidance. It can perfectly guide us. It can actually save our life. It has literally saved my life several times. (See chapter on Guidance Though Intuition & Dreams) Angels, nature or loved ones can be messengers of Divine Guidance in our life. Many of we have read stories of angels, dolphins, dogs, strangers, etc., arriving at just the right time to assist people who have been praying and asking for help. Guidance and assistance will come if we ask.

When I first became an entrepreneur, I needed Guidance and assistance. I was fearful and constantly worried about the source of my income. I did not initially utilize Guidance. I did not realize that worrying is a dissipation of energy, it pushes away what we want and it is a disconnection from our true Source. My earthly parents were not able to be there for me. I did not learn how to trust that I was cared for. I learned that if I wanted something, it was all up to me. It was all on my shoulders. I felt so alone in life.

Worrying is not trusting that our Divine Parents are there for us and will show us the way. In the past, I was not feeling Guided and connected. I am sure that many entrepreneurs experience similar feelings. Those of us who have traditional jobs may worry about being fired or losing our job. All of this changed as I began to recognize where the genuine Source of my income really came from.

Divine Guidance has been essential in my life. It has allowed me to set a true course for my life and assisted me in making the right choices to stay on that path. It has allowed me to choose to heal, grow and move on a path of Higher Self-destination. Worthiness is a factor. When I felt more connected to Source, I felt more worthy. I realized that I was a Divine child, worthy of everything good.

Guidance has enabled me to identify and develop the professional skills that I needed for right livelihood. My services are in alignment with my true Soul purpose and I have the opportunity to receive income to provide for myself and be my own "boss." I like having autonomy with my Higher Self. Through Divine Guidance, my primary authority is from within. It is not necessary to report to any authority outside of myself for my income. I rarely, if ever, feel worried or fearful that I can't make it as an entrepreneur. I feel in alignment with Source's plan. I ask for and act on Guidance and I know that I will be provided for. THE DIVINE IS MY SOURCE!

What is Divination?

Divination is our ability to access Divine Guidance for assistance to answer questions and to make choices. More simply expressed, it is talking to Source and getting an answer. It can be intuitive from within, or symbolic as seeing something significant in nature or through dreams. It is our way of tuning into our Highest and best and obtaining the truth for us, so our choices are inspired ones. I define "Inspired" as "coming from Spirit" and inspired can mean the "Spirit within".

Webster's Dictionary defines divination as "the act or practice of foretelling the future or unknown by mystical arts; a prophecy; a successful guess; clever conjecture."[7] As I stated in the introduction, it is not the purpose of this book to attempt to teach we to foretell the future. I relate Divination to the word, Guidance. Webster defines guidance as "advise or assistance, the act of guiding; direction; leadership."[8] I can show you how to describe the energy and understand the opportunities and the challenges that may present themselves in your life. It is up to you to make the Highest and best possible choices for yourself from your own Guidance rather than from habitual patterns. Otherwise, our life will be a repeating pattern with the same theme. The characters, locations and the situations may change, but it can be the same old story. Source wants the best for all of us. I want to inspire and to encourage the manifestation of our Highest expression through the wisdom of Divine guidance.

Some examples of habitual patterns would be: the person who continues to marry an alcoholic like their parent, the theme of co-dependency or the person who never experiences true success based on poor self-esteem. Another example is the unfulfilled person who puts money and success in the world ahead of love and family. There is an attempt to fill the hole of loneliness and separation with material goods, power, and recognition, which is never truly fulfilling. Addictions are the attempt to fill ourselves with something, so we don't feel pain. This can be the pain of emptiness, separation, unfulfillment, low self-esteem, or other types of pain resulting from our experience and karma. All of these patterns can be healed. Only then, can we make truly Divinely inspired choices.

For a lot of people, life is so painful, lonely and unhappy, they can't continue to live. I saw that in my own family. They made self-destructive choices that ended their life prematurely. I learned that it is important to make the appropriate choices as we develop. I knew that if I did not make wise choices, I too, would die prematurely. When we make Guided choices, life is not so painful and unfulfilling that we don't want to be here. It is my

---

[7] Webster's New World Dictionary, 2nd edition (Cleveland: William Collins Publishers, 1979) p. 412.
[8] Webster's New World Dictionary, 2nd edition (Cleveland: William Collins Publishers, 1979) p. 621.

desire for all of us to grow, heal and learn in our lives. Life becomes more satisfying, peaceful, loving, and harmonious with Divine Guidance. It is my aspiration to show us how to feel guided in each moment by our Spiritual awareness, to make the right choices for ourselves.

Our lives are constantly changing and evolving. I know we have the 'free will' to grow, expand and embrace all that is Higher and better. I have done this to the best of my ability, in my own life. I no longer feel the pain, the restrictions and the unfulfillment of my earlier experiences. It is up to us to change our destiny. Let's turn off uninspiring entertainment, get out of the "easy chair" or our "lazy boy" recliner and wake up! No one else will or can do it for us. We can be truly free. We do not have to be limited to any way of being or outcome. Our life and the lives of others can be as fulfilling, expressive and loving as we want it to be.

Philosophy of Divination

My philosophy of Divination is about becoming more aware of the Divine in the reflections of Creation all around us and inside us. It allows us to tune into our Highest and best choices through our Inner knowing and intuition. All of Creation reflects Divine Order. It is only necessary to learn to perceive that order, feel it and see it on a deep Spiritual level and act according to that Guidance.

It is my belief that we can become mystical artists in our lives, as we align more and more with our own Spiritual awareness. It is only then that we can become aware enough to choose Divine Will. When we choose it, life is much more rewarding, and everything falls into place in its perfect order. This book is to encourage us to become "all we can be" (our Highest and best expression) as a mystical artist in our life.

A Brief History of Divination

It is historically recorded that the astrologers of Babylon were able to predict many things by observing and utilizing the wisdom of the cycles of the stars and the planets. They realized that these heavenly bodies reflected certain energies. They employed that information to advise and make choices.

In the Old Testament of the Bible, there are indications that Divining was not restricted to certain professional groups, but was a normal part of everyday life and in widespread usage.[9] It is interesting that presently, Christianity does not have good things to say about Astrologers and people of Divination. Some say it is a tool of the Devil. When

[9]Michael Loewe and Carmen Blacker, ed. *Oracles and Divination* (New York: Random house, 1981), 195.

Divination power is misused, by taking away another's free will or attempting to control the outcome of situations or people; it is not good.[10]

Our ancestors were far more connected to nature. Since their eyes were not glued to the TV set, they observed nature, the cycles, seasons and the skies as a part of their everyday life experience. They passed more time outside in nature than most of us typically do. They were in telepathic communication with their animal brothers and sisters and heard the wind whispering messages to them. They could feel changes in the atmospheric pressure that foretold rain. Time was determined by the placement of the sun in the sky. The phases of the moon were observed and utilized. Large stone circles, pyramids, temples and other structures that designated the equinoxes and solstices were erected. A solar or lunar eclipse was a major event in their lives. They were mystics, naturally.

The story of Moses was an example of a prophet or man of Divination. There was destruction of life and prohibition of free will in early Egypt during the time of Moses. The Hebrew people were held captive and used as slaves to build monuments at the will of the Pharaoh, Ramses. The Pharaoh had usurped their free will. Moses was Divinely guided to ask the Pharaoh to set the Hebrew people free and to lead them out of Egypt. When the Pharaoh disobeyed Divine Will, there were repercussions. There was death and destruction. Was this death and destruction commensurate with the suffering of the Hebrew people? To take away another's adults' free will is a grave injustice and has the dire results of karmic repercussion. (This is discussed in the chapter on Karma and the Gift of Free Will.) There are consequences for making immoral choices.

It is the Homeric poems that provide us with one of the earliest recorded documentation for the usage of oracles and Divination in antiquity. At the shrine of Athena Pronaia in Delphi, near the cleft of Castalian, there is continuity of worship of Athena from pre-Hellenic times.[11] She was the Goddess of wisdom and truth. The oracles of Delphi were representatives of the wisdom of Athena, able to tune into a Higher knowing to answer questions by those seeking greater understanding and wisdom.

It was much more accepted in the early days of Christianity to have prophets. John the Baptist was another man who experienced Divination. In this story, he foretold the coming of the Messiah. How did he know this? He was accessing his Guidance through an angel.

In the story of the Nativity, the Wise Men found baby Jesus by being directed by the stars. Astrology was a highly developed science and art among the Magi. The Magi were learned instructors and high representatives of the great academies and mystery schools of

[10] See chapter on Karma & the Gift of Free Will

[11] Michael Loewe and Carmen Blacker, ed. *Oracles and Divination* (New York: Random House, 1981), 98.

the Orient. According to ancient records, the symbolic star had been observed for many months prior to the birth of the Holy Infant; symbolizing that something very special and fortuitous was about to happen. Close and careful tabulations had been made regarding the movement of the star.[12] (Author's note: it was actually the conjunction of planets appearing as bright as a star.)

Nostrodamus predicted many things that have happened in the modern world much earlier than they actually happened. We can read it in his first book of prophetic work published in 1555, called Centuries. It is in the opening lines of the Centuries that he gives a clear, specific description of having engaged in the ancient rite of Divination by water.[13] Here is an example of using nature's elements to gain Higher wisdom.[14]

Benjamin Franklin, one of our country's earliest leaders and inventors, was an astrologer. He published an almanac of natural cycles. In addition, some of the world's oldest, wealthiest, and most powerful families have utilized and continue to seek the services of astrologers and other varieties of mystics. John Pierpont Morgan consulted with Evangeline Adams regarding his investments. He said, "Astrology is not for millionaires, but (for) billionaires."[15] Prominent leaders of countries and some world religions would not think of taking action without consulting Guidance.

These leaders, rulers and politicians know that Divination can guide them in their decision making. One of the reasons Ronald Reagan's term in office went as well as it did had to do with astrological Guidance. He engaged the services of a professional astrologer for all public experiences and major timing of events and meetings. Astrology, with its Divine reflection, has been the guiding light of many courts and kings. During the Renaissance, there was no monarch of importance without his court astrologer.[16] Queen Elizabeth II consults her astrologer on a regular basis, continuing this age-old royal tradition.[17]

Edgar Cayce was called the "sleeping prophet" because his predictions came through during a dream state. It was Cayce who was able to determine that the placement of the great pyramids of Egypt coordinated geographically in space with the Belt of Orion. This came through one of his dream state realizations. He did not physically measure it. He saw in his dream, that these three pyramids were aligned with the constellation of Orion. Astronomers have measured and confirmed the accuracy of his information. Edgar Cayce

[12]H. Spencer Lewis, *The Mystical Life of Jesus* (San Jose: Supreme Grand Lodge of Amorc, 1953), 124.
[13]Lee McCann, *Nostradamus, the Man who Saw through Time* (New York: Farrar, Staus, Girouz, 1941), 159.
[14] See chapter on Nature's Refection
[15]Jeanne Avery, *The Rising Sign: Wer Astrological Mark* (Garden City: Doubleday, 1982), 346
[16]Lee McCann, *Nostradamus, the Man who saw through Time* (New York: Farrar, Staus, Giroux, 1941), 144
[17]Jeanne Avery, *The Rising Sign: Wer Astrological Mark* (Garden City: Doubleday, 1982), 346

predicted that they would find the temple of Osiris in chambers beneath the Sphinx and they did. He also made medical diagnosis and developed treatments based on his trance state. His ability to access information and medical jargon that he was unfamiliar with in his waking state, was amazing to many.

Most of the choices that we will be making in our own lives will not have as many far-reaching consequences as it does for world leaders. Yet, the more we take responsibility for choosing Guidance on an individual basis, the more we impact all of humanity in a positive way. There will be more love, peace and harmony individually and globally. We will experience a sense of greater freedom. This can and will be a healthier, safer and more fulfilling environment for our existence when we include Divine Will. Divine Guidance is the key to experiencing Heaven on Earth, the Original Divine Plan, like in the Garden of Eden!

Divine Reason and Rhyme is about becoming more present with the Divine in the reflections of Creation all around us and acting on the wisdom inside us. All of Creation reflects Divine order. Divine insight is seen in polarity, elements, emotions, colors, numbers, energy centers, body parts, planets, stars, animals and sounds. There is a symbolic language that represents that order. It is empowering to learn the language, perceive the messages on a deep Spiritual level and act accordingly.

Presently, mystical behavior has been relegated to psychics and saints. It is believed by the general populace that you must be born with the gift and very few can understand the mysteries of life. As we align more with our Spiritual awareness, everyone can become more mystical. Then, we can recognize and choose Divine Will.

Let's be receptive to our insights, allowing the Divine Plan to unfold. It takes away the burden and pain of trying to control people and situations. When we choose it, life is much more rewarding; everything falls into place in its perfect order. I want to encourage and inspire everyone to become a mystical artist. Let's discover and manifest our Highest expression through the wisdom of Divine Reason and Rhyme.

Chapter 2

Who Is The Source Of Your Guidance?

Society

As parents and caregivers, are we teaching the outdated survival patterns of our parents and their dysfunction to our children, or personal growth and evolution? Most people do not know how to receive Higher guidance or have not learned how to access it from their parents, family, friends and community. Most likely they are receiving opinions: ideas or behaviors that they learned that are 'ego survival' patterns, points of view or belief systems based on security or identity. Rather than teaching personal growth and evolution through listening to our intuition and conscience, we are learning dysfunction. Our objective, should we choose it, is to learn about and heal our own family karmic patterns. We need to learn for ourselves what mom and dad could not teach us.

It is difficult to teach what we do not know. Many parents did not learn healthy patterns from their parents and therefore do not know how to teach them. Conversely, they probably thought they were doing a good job passing on what they learned. They did do the best that they could. They did not have the most advanced therapists, tools and techniques that are available today. We learned to give our power away, instead of learning Higher Self-Empowerment, connection to Source, Self-Determination and a Higher sense of responsibility.

Occasionally, we will have a few outstanding teachers and parents that know how to inspire their students and children with how to find their answers inside themselves. Some are taught to listen to their Inner wisdom. Unfortunately, most people don't talk about Higher truth and where to find it.

In my case, my parents were not emotionally available due to their dysfunction and they left early in my life. First my mother moved away from my father when I was six, and I never saw him again. I assumed more responsibility for my younger brothers and myself. We were informed that Dad died from heart disease. One of my brothers disappeared and died at about the same time. My mother and brother passed away after suffering from cancer a little while later. I learned to pray to a Divine Mother/Father God for assistance, and I received it. Many others have reported the same kind of experience. We needed to look beyond our earthly mother and father (because some of us didn't have them any longer) to something much greater, our Divine Mother/Father.

Mom and Dad

When we were children we always asked Mom and Dad to answer all of our "why and how come" questions. As children, we relied on and trusted their answers. As parents, we gave the responsibility for education and learning to our children's teachers. We trusted them to know the answers and assumed they knew how to teach our children. Most of us were taught and accustomed to getting answers from outside of us, from an authority. Many are still hoping to obtain answers from experts, loved ones, bosses, government officials, religious representatives, psychics and other authority figures.

If we are from dysfunctional families, orphaned or had any other major challenges, we have had to learn to rely more on our Inner Self. Out of necessity, we were forced to exercise our own Divination muscles. We learned to listen to our Inner Self in the stillness, in our pain, in our sadness, or loneliness.

In the 90's, the massacre and bloodshed of our children in Arkansas, Colorado and elsewhere have made a blatant statement about the need for better Guidance and wisdom from parents, role models and the media. Many children don't feel connected to a Higher Power and especially aren't connected with their Inner Selves. These children have had no healthy Inner inspiration to guide them, only their experiences of disconnection, aggression, destruction, dysfunction and addictive behavior. How did our children become violent and aggressive? The mass media is and has been a strong force, presenting negative role models and programming our children and civilization. In our educational experience, history is mostly about war. Our sacred icons have become "the almighty dollar", the stock portfolio, and material acquisition. Life experiences mold certain beliefs like "my color is better than your color" and "might makes right". This is what is being programmed into our children.

The following is a poem that one of the parents, Darrell Scott, father of two victims of the Columbine High School shooting in Littleton Colorado, presented to the subcommittee on crime in the House Judiciary.

A Poem by Darrell Scott

Our laws ignore our deepest needs.
Our words are empty air.
We've stripped away our heritage.
We've outlawed simple prayer.

Now gunshots fill our classrooms and precious children die.
We seek for answers everywhere and ask the question why.
We regulate restrictive laws through legislative creed
And yet we fail to understand that God is what we need.

The New School Prayer

(This was written by an unknown teen in Bagdad, Arizona)

Now I sit me down in school
Where praying is against the rule
For this great nation under God
Finds mention of Him very odd.
If Scripture now the class recites,
It violates the Bill of Rights.
And anytime my head I bow
Becomes a Federal matter now.
Our hair can be purple, orange or green,
That's no offense; it's a freedom scene.
The law is specific, the law is precise.
Prayers spoken aloud are a serious vice.
For praying in a public hall
Might offend someone with no faith at all.
In silence alone we must meditate,
God's name is prohibited by the state.
We're allowed to cuss and dress like freaks,
And pierce our noses, tongues and cheeks.
They've outlawed guns, but FIRST the Bible.
To quote the Good Book makes me liable.
We can elect a pregnant Senior Queen,
And the 'unwed daddy', our Senior King.
It's "inappropriate" to teach right from wrong,
We're taught that such "judgments" do not belong.
We can get our condoms and birth controls,
Study witchcraft, vampires and totem poles.
But the Ten Commandments are not allowed,
No word of God must reach this crowd.
It's scary here I must confess,

When chaos reigns the school's a mess.
So, Lord, this silent plea I make:
Should I be shot; My soul please take! AMEN

Parents, don't wait until tragedy happens, resulting in a broken heart. Stay in communication with your children; teach values and how to be good role models. Look at our own dysfunction! They do what we do. Demonstrate loving and kind relating to your self and others. That is how they will learn to love themselves and others. Participate in activities that they enjoy in an enthusiastic manner. Include them in things we enjoy so they feel a part of our life.

Please do not pressure or push children, encourage them to succeed in the outer world in a balanced manner. Do not teach the patterns that dad learned from his father, like "working long hours is the most important value for success," "that doing and having is everything." We teach children our "overworking" ethic, to be overly responsible for others "enablers," to be duty bound "people who love too much" and to deny the Higher Self "martyrdom." We are labeled selfish if we attempt to fulfill our own needs. These family patterns are passed on from one generation to the next, creating more dysfunction.

Every negative and unhealthy family pattern that is not healed gets passed on to the next generation. Our children are attracted to us in this life in order to heal specific kinds of family patterns or karma. As we role model these behaviors, they become more deeply etched in our children's personality "self." This is the small self. As the small self is fed on a diet of dysfunction, it leads to feelings of disempowerment and low self-esteem. This perpetuates the control games and the put-downs because we try to feel better than others by trying to make them feel less. Our children do it to other children. The patterns that we learned from our mother and father will be passed on to our children if we do not take responsibility to heal them in ourselves.

We refer to ourselves as the "human race." Many people live life with the stress of competing and being rivals, as if we were in a competitive race. The preoccupation with doing and worldly accomplishment is not only supported by parents, it is supported by education, science, government and corporate America. I don't believe I have ever heard a "mission statement" about Being. We are human Beings and we have the right to Be. Many don't teach children "to Be." They do not know how to be with their feelings, hear the wisdom of the heart and Soul and express their Spirit.

When our children feel disconnected, depressed with pain, lonely, afraid, isolated, shamed, or put down, they need us more than ever! Do not allow them to withdraw completely from the family experience. Encourage them to share and not keep it to themselves. Inspire them with stories from our own experience. When our son is teased and put down for having emotions or is called a "wuss, mamma's boy, gay, baby, wimp or sissy", acknowledge him and affirm that he is courageous and well balanced in his emotional expression. If the daughter excels at sports, science and math, it is not wise to tell her she'll "never get a husband." Acknowledge her strengths and affirm that she can be whatever she wants to be; that was my mother's gift to me.

The danger is to not pay attention. It is important to notice what is going on with our children and us. Encourage masculine and feminine values. It is the unconditional love, acceptance and compassion of the mother they need to know from one or both parents. It is the father's wisdom, structure and problem solving skills they need to know from one or both parents. Develop both values in our own consciousness. That will reflect wholeness and today's children need to learn wholeness (even if we may not have when we where a child). Let them know they are loved just for who they are and just by their Being. When our children are feeling attacked and teased by their peers, teach them to go inside for their own love. Show them our love by not working long hours and by being good to ourselves and our family. Demonstrate love in action by being available to them for their projects, interests and relationships. Have a family night every week, for games, communication and celebration. Teach them to be a human Being instead of a human doing. Be in nature and show what relaxation, peace and contentment look like. Allow them to learn the value of Higher Self.

If they don't know what Higher Self is, they may never develop it. The Self is called many names, the Spiritual Self, the Inner Self, the Higher Self, the Divine Self, the God Self, the Sacred Self, the Soul, etc. Encourage them to put the Self back in Self-esteem. They need to learn to connect to a Higher part of themselves so they will always feel good inside no matter what is happening on the outside. They will know true Self-empowerment and their own conscience. They will not have to play power and control games, endangering themselves and others.

It is our responsibility as representatives of Mother/Father Divinity to be vigilant in our awareness, and we can't do that if we are always busy. Cut out some of the unnecessary activities and downsize our expenses so we don't use the excuse that we have to work to pay the bills. We can work for Higher Self-expression, Soul purpose and love and not work just for the money. Share with them our own growth process so they can see everyone needs to heal and grow. Be their guide, their facilitator, and not their dictator. Teach and demonstrate the value of their "Inner Guidance." Be aware of what they are doing with their time, especially for entertainment. When relaxing with television, movies, video games, they are in an alpha state of hypnosis and totally receptive to all input. It is crucial what is going into our unconscious mind. We all need healthy boundaries, especially from the media and violence.

Some experts say that media has absolutely no impact on our young people. Our action heroes use force and aggression to take control and to have power over others. They are extremely violent and encourage violence. Our children are even dressing like their favorite violent movie icon. How can experts, in their good conscience, believe that it has no effect, when children are acting out the violence they see? If we don't pay for it, then writers, producers, and directors won't make it. It is up to us to refuse permission to our children to see violent movies. We as well as our children need to learn to say "no." We need to show them the boundaries by our example.

Parents, who respect each other's personal space, set an example for their children. By respecting our child's personal space, we can assist them in developing more Self-confidence. A child can best access their intuition if they come from feeling grounded in their sense of Self. The child feels safe and feels that he deserves to be. Also, allowing the children to come up with their own insights and answers supports their Self-empowerment and their ability to utilize Guidance in their own lives. Being a coach and a dictator are two different things. When space and the opportunity to listen to their Inner Self are given, the child recognizes and learns how nurturing and instructive they can be with themselves. This leads to more Higher Self-fulfillment!

Our country and our families are facing a crisis of feeling dis-connected, hopeless, without values and suffering from poor self-esteem. The media and every family in America are discussing this subject, perhaps even around the world. The tragedies of mass murders have been an unfortunate wake-up call for all of us. Every negative and unhealthy family pattern that is not healed gets passed on to the next generation. This perpetuates the control games and the put-downs. Our children do it to other children. We tell them to listen to and obey authority, some of whom have not been setting very good examples and not listening to their own conscience. We teach dis-empowerment, disconnection, separation and control. We pressure and push our children to excel and succeed in the world. We work long hours, teaching them it is more important to make money than to develop good relationships.

Numerous parents force children to believe the religion they were brought up with and they themselves do not honor it. They guide them to do as they say rather than follow what they do. Many kids today do not relate to what they may consider outdated religious experience. More mothers and fathers are working and have little time to grow emotionally and Spiritually, to connect, empower, nurture and be good role models for our children.

Healthy Values for Children and Adults:

- *Having a relationship with Spirit, our Higher Selves, family and the community.*
- *Loving ourselves and all our brothers and sisters in Our Divine family*

- *True Inner Self-empowerment and conscience.*
- *Honoring our fathers, mothers and others*
- *The Spirit of sharing, cooperation and courtesy.*
- *The power of speaking our truth with diplomacy.*
- *The value of communing, communicating, processing emotions and Spirituality.*
- *The importance of Self-growth and how to heal unhealthy mental and emotional patterns.*
- *Developing mind and heart harmony, for better integration.*
- *Balancing masculine and feminine values and qualities for wholeness.*
- *Hearing our Inner Guidance and know we deserve love.*
- *The value of Being (not doing: TV, video, etc), we need to have a healthy Inner world.*

Parents, we can learn the values and Spiritual principles that are necessary for a well-balanced life. We can demonstrate Divine family by honoring our relationship to our spouse and/or children. Express understanding, compassion and the Spirit of sharing and cooperation. Allow our children the opportunity to see the two of us in the peace making process, so they will know how to do it. Share our techniques of communication and communing together. If we don't know how, learn. Reveal how Inner guidance works by our example and experiences. Teach them to look into the mirror, to contemplate, "what is my message?" by doing it ourselves. Exhibit the power of speaking our truth with diplomacy. Display the power of cherishing love and teach our children how to protect and honor themselves. Inspire them with the wisdom that we are all brothers and sisters. That includes our neighbors, all races, all religions, and all ages. Teach by our example; our children will do what we do or the exact opposite, especially if the energy is out of balance. Show them what Self-empowerment looks like and empower our children to be there for themselves, knowing that we can't always be there for them.

Teachers and Religious Affiliations

When we come through our primary, secondary and higher educational experiences, we were and still are taught rote memory. Memory was the way to succeed in school. Students are not taught to think deeply and question. If we memorize the facts we are given, we will succeed. In most cases, we were not taught how to access our own Inner wisdom, to understand the mechanics of energy, how the Divine is reflected in everything and how it all worked together.

The educational experience, for the most part, is totally based on the left-brain experience of linear sequential knowledge. We were conditioned to use our logic, our memory and other kinds of mental skills suited for left-brain function. Some children are forced to use their right hand to write (controlled by the left brain) when they are actually left-handed (controlled by the right brain). We were led to believe that these skills were more important, more valuable and even superior to right-brain function, which required imagination and intuition. We were taught to use those skills in art, dance and creative writing, which are the first to be eliminated if there are budget cuts.

We were not encouraged to use our intuition or Inner knowing, unless we were given the gift of a very insightful educator. We were not prepared to use our intuitive powers and abilities. Our educational system has left out the importance of being able to perceive and develop with the right side of the brain as well as the left, in most instances.

We are training people to be robotic worker bees for the workplace, followers instead of independent, Self-fulfilled and Self-empowered beings. We are not preparing them for life or life's challenges. We are not teaching them to develop emotionally and Spiritually. We are developing a society of half-brained citizens instead of whole-brained balanced individuals. They are not learning balance with brain function, Inner Self-development and to be able to take advantage of the wonders of intuition and accessing Inner Self. If people are aware enough, they search out this training or therapy on their own time. Usually, it will happen when they are in enough pain that they become dysfunctional in the workplace or act out extremely in the schools. These empowering skills give us the kind of wisdom and information to which our rational mind does not have access.

This kind of focus in education develops people who lack a good balanced foundation. It is like having a table with only two legs, the mental and the physical. An effective person has all four-corners of their foundation in place: emotional and Spiritual, as well as the mental and physical. To train people in left-brained functions predominately is ludicrous. There is too much stress in life, relationships and in the work place. The result is a nation of people that are dysfunctional and not prepared adequately for life. Everyone loses.

When we don't know how to access our intuition to know what we want or need to do, some of us were taught to go for advice and counsel with our religious representatives. It was assumed they would be able to tell us what Divinity wants for us. Unless we were gifted with a truly Divinely inspired person who could give love, compassion, good feedback and acknowledgement, we were likely to get dogma, rules, rhetoric and biblical references. If it did not make sense to us, or our personal experience, we would be unable to apply it.

Good Guidance touches us deeply and resonates in our mind, heart, body and soul. It fits perfectly for us personally. In most cases, there is not likely going to be a "general rule of thumb" for everyone, unless it is Love and Truth, which are synonymous with the Divine.

Other Authority Figures: Scientific, Corporate, Medical and Legal Systems

It is not wise to accept any and all authority. Different authorities or organizations are directed by different motivations. Many times it is a commercial or biased interest that is being advocated rather than for the greater good of all. This is especially true in many "Scientific studies." Statistics can be manipulated to show whatever "truth" one is advocating. This is another opportunity to check in with our own Inner guidance. Find out your own truth and act on that. Do not assume that authority figures know better than we do.[18]

Our government and corporate interest have been working together, one supporting the other either, financially or legislatively. Corporations claim money and jobs are more important than effectively managing our natural national resources. They buy lobbyists to influence legislature. It is common practice to invest in "Scientific studies," that have favorable results. They also make huge contributions for the executive and legislative departments. This is why it has been difficult to obtain and enforce good legislation for the protection of our environment. Multinational corporations wield incredible power, maintain potent governmental relationships and possess enormous resources.

In the course of writing this book, I had the opportunity to experience what is happening in the medical and legal fields. Please understand that I do realize that some of these organizations are providing a great service. Yet, I am shocked by the lack of values and the disregard for the "Golden Rule," demonstrated to me during this time, by these institutions. Instead of "do unto others as you would have them do unto you" it seems to be, "those who have the most gold, rule." I don't feel it was a coincidence that they happened during this period. I truly feel they reflect the disrespect, the indifference and the neglect that some people are receiving by the larger institutions, especially the insurance companies. It demonstrated to me that some values have been disregarded in order for ego survival mechanisms and greed to continue.

The Ego Survival Values Are:

- *"Being right", strategy and winning are more important than the truth, responsibility or accountability.*
- *It is OK to damage someone and try to get out of it with lack of responsibility, dishonesty, and denial of financial retribution.*

[18] See chapter on Karma & the Gift of Free Will, Misuse.

- *If we have money, connections or power behind us, it is possible to manipulate the system and not have to honor and pay for someone we have hurt or provided poor services to.*
- *It is about winning at all costs and a profitable bottom line, even if it was really about our own negligence. It is not about reparation & healing.*
- *Get angry and punitive towards the injured party; deny their injuries and hurt them some more. It doesn't matter if they have to pay for the injuries we caused, the doctor's bills, attorney fees, and loss of their business investment capital and savings. (I now realize that many people are in so much pain that they feel it is only fair to take it out on others.)*
- *Be professional, agreeable and pleasant yet deny reasonable claims, because we have the power. "Because we can!"*

The traditional values of, "what we do to others, we do to ourselves;" "do unto our brother as we would do unto our self" have been forgotten in some instances. Anger and guilt can turn back in on us and cause disease and disharmony in all of our personal and business relationships. If we are angry because someone has boundaries and wants them honored, it is probably a result of the times when our boundaries were pushed and we were powerless to do anything about it. Remember that chronic anger is toxic and we are poisoning ourselves. I have observed behaviors that remind me of dysfunctional children, crying out for help. We can learn from healthy children to process anger quickly and move on with our lives.

In contemplating about this, I realized that I could have been a very angry, uncaring person in the past, to draw those kinds of experiences; or a light that drew the dark for transformation, or both. I knew I had things to heal in me. I needed to take responsibility for wrongs I had instigated in the past and do the right thing in the present.

In the long run, it's going to cost so much more if we don't speak our truth, take responsibility and heal our own anger. It is less expensive on all levels. Divine Guidance will assist us in doing the right thing, if we will take the time to listen and surrender our negative ego survival mechanisms. Divine justice takes care of the rest!

Health Maintenance Organization

I have experienced good results with different types of medical insurance at other times in my life. During different cycles, we may have different experiences. The following represents my experience of a major medical institution, at the time of writing this book. One of my closest of friends, Michael, appreciated the care he received with the same organization at a different location. As I mentioned previously, every system has good in it as well as that which needs improvement.

This was my first encounter with an H.M.O. I have always chosen my medical practitioners in the past. I chose this organization because of the high ranking it received nationally. I was most disappointed with the total lack of care and caring I received. I felt totally disregarded and demeaned. There was little compassion or dignity with my treatment in my experience. Later, I realized that this was another opportunity for me to heal my past.

I was shocked to see that it took about a month to get an appointment with a physician. On my initial visit, the nurse examiner was brusque and hurried during an intimate, internal gynecological exam. I felt very uncomfortable and not safe. I asked for a complete blood work-up and I didn't receive all of the tests. She and her assistant couldn't get me out of the clinic fast enough. It was a very poor first impression.

However, more offensive treatment came when I wanted to discuss my blood tests and get to know my new "primary care" doctor. In the 3 minute time period he spent with me, he assumed I was there for something else. I had to ask him in the hall, as he was rushing off, about my blood tests. That was the end of the discussion.

I went in to get an eye exam. I spent $100 filling the prescription on new eyeglasses. I experienced pain while wearing the glasses. It was necessary to go back and have my eyes re-examined by another eye doctor in the organization. The exam results were quite different than that of the first. I did not trust this prescription. I decided to get an outside optometrist for another exam, at additional expense. I received another totally different prescription. I had the glasses made and this time it was accurate.

I finally got an appointment to see the dermatologist at this organization, (again, not in a timely basis). I was very concerned about a mole that had increased in size on my face and I wanted it to be removed. Since it was the "wrong kind of cells", she refused to do anything about it, even though it could have been removed easily. She gave me the card of another doctor outside of this H.M.O. to get the work done. Then she removed some other cells from my forehead that were the "right kind" of cells which were not a big concern to me. She got most of it, but not all of it. I pleaded with her about the mole. I didn't have the extra money to go to an outside doctor, as I was injured and not able to work. It was difficult enough to pay my monthly premium. It was heard on deaf ears. Their policy about what they thought was "cosmetic" was more important than the patient's needs and desires.

After six months, I quit the HMO. There was not one service I wanted, that was even satisfactory, much less, "caring and like family," as the HMO advertising claims. The family that I experienced would be considered neglectful, disrespectful, abusive and emotionally and physically unavailable. It appeared to me that some of these "caregivers" did not have people skills and treated people like cattle, just moving them through as fast as possible. I did not receive what was published as the "member's rights and responsibilities."

I felt that I wasted my money, paying the monthly premium for this HMO. I wanted to recover the entire sum. I filed an appeal within their system. I requested reimbursement for my paid insurance premiums in addition to the cost of my prescription eyeglasses. I was shocked and appalled that my appeal was denied. It was denied on the basis that I received a variety of medical services during my enrollment. It did not matter that the services were unsatisfactory and sub-standard.

Perhaps I was wrong not to take this case immediately to Action Line (local TV consumer alert). I care about others, including their reputation. I thought I would give them the opportunity to make things right. It was interesting to see how justice works with their Appeals Committee.

I must say that I felt angry, outraged and shocked about how this organization handled disputes as well as services. It was a parody. It was my experience that this organization was out of integrity with advertising claims, services and members. The Regional Appeals Committee process was a waste of my time and energy and a travesty of justice.

I wrote to the organization again, "I do not know how people can sleep peacefully at night when they do not take responsibility or accountability for their poor services and mistreatment of members. How can we feel good about ourselves to think that our "members" should pay for inferior services? It is dishonest. I am not responsible to pay for our staff's training in "good provider care". That is basically where our Appeal Committee is leaving it. They said that they have "informed the staff." They said, "They are attempting to decrease the wait time." This was not responsible or acceptable to me.

There was consistently something inherently wrong with each service I requested, beside the long wait time. This organization was responsible and accountable for this. They had those words on the wall of the conference/training area during the appeal process. Yet, I saw a total disregard for these principals. Perhaps it is management, pushing the staff to rush to save time and money, pressuring them in some way that makes them irritated and abrupt. Perhaps their own staff feels badly about the quality of services they are providing. There are obviously some serious problems at some HMOs.

I have heard more and more negative personal experiences by other ex-members who had more serious complaints than I, who did not bother to go through the appeal system. They just quit. I am probably one of the few; foolish enough to think I could get justice within their system. I can only take solace in that there is a Higher Authority. What goes around comes around. These practices will ultimately fail. The energy will come back.

Perhaps one day their wife or daughter will have the sense of violation that I did, when a brusque and irritated person gives them a pelvic exam. How would we like that kind of energy inside of us? How would we feel about our eyes hurting, because we were given the wrong prescription for new glasses? Or be pulled out of the exam room before we could discuss what we wanted? Or be told that everything was "in range" when it wasn't.

Not only did I not get reimbursed, I lost time and travel for appointments, letters, and appearance at the Appeals Committee. I suffered physical, mental, Spiritual and emotional distress throughout this miserable and disturbingly outrageous experience. I received no satisfaction other than having spoken my truth to the people who could have made a difference.

Legal System

I had the unfortunate experience of being injured by an employee in a warehouse/retail outlet. At the time, I was in the best shape of my life; physically, mentally, emotionally, financially and Spiritually. I was inside the building, looking at the merchandise of the shelf, when a metal stock cart loaded with boxes struck me from behind. The boxes were stacked so high, it was impossible to see where she was going. The sharp corner went deeply into my left buttock. I doubled over in intense pain, realizing I was injured. I had no idea to what extent I was wounded. I was in shock.

The following are from notes and letters to my doctor:

I am experiencing intense pain that saps my energy. I have shooting pains up my back and down my buttocks on the left side. There is a constant aching on the left side where the sharp edge of the cart hit my lower back. It is difficult to fall asleep without medication because I am so uncomfortable. I cannot move my bowels without assistance. Even then, I am constipated most of the time. (The MRI showed that I had disc damage, two bulging discs, on the left, lower lumber 3-4, 4-5.)

I have been paying for massage therapy, heavy housekeeping and light office work. I have exhausted all of my savings. Since I have not been able to work, I have no income. I am forced to go back to work in this injured state. I have applied for rental assistance, food stamps and will be making use of the food bank in Kailua. Financially, I am completely stressed out.

I experienced complete physical exhaustion and emotional break down. I was trying to work a partial schedule with great pain and minimal energy. As I write this letter, I am taking turns sitting, kneeling and standing. I can only sit for a few minutes. Even the small things in life are more difficult to accomplish. I feel unsuccessful with my current level of performance in everything I do. I feel like an invalid and not the vibrant, attractive, energetic and healthy person I was. It affected me on so many levels:

Professionally:

- *It is painful and difficult to sit for an hour consultation, impossible to sit or stand longer. I have to use an ergonomically correct chair to sit for an hour. It is essential to use my lumbar traction unit immediately after.*
- *There is difficulty in demonstrating certain sitting postures in Yoga (I am a Yoga instructor) and I can no longer balance well for the standing postures.*
- *Sometimes my back locks up and I have to crawl to the music controls when I teach.*
- *I am no longer a good example of total fitness.*
- *I can no longer lie supine without discomfort on an exercise mat. This is important during the relaxation and meditation segments.*
- *I am backlogged with my accounting, business planning and marketing efforts.*

Socially:

- *My social life is extremely limited. I have to carry a pillow with me wherever I go.*
- *I can't sit for dinner, parties, concerts, movies, and theatre without being totally uncomfortable and in pain.*
- *Most of my focus is on the healing process. I don't feel as if I have energy for much else.*
- *I can no longer do the things I love that help me keep in shape and the endorphins pumping: swimming, snorkeling, kayaking, hiking, bicycling, roller-skating, dancing*
- *A sexually intimate life is impossible.*

Spiritually:

- *I could not feel the Ultrasonic core energy current that travels up and down the spine to sustain health, vitality and connection with Divine Source. (See Chapter 4 on Intuition, Our Conscience and Consciousness.)*
- *My connection was broken and fragmented, so was I.*

This business did have premise insurance of $10,000 at the time of my injury. They paid about $5000 of my $16,000 medical bills. They refused to pay for any more. It was necessary for me to obtain legal representation to sue for damages.

We went to arbitration. The arbitrator knew the lawyer from the insurance company. They brought in a completely different cart (plastic, rounded edges instead of sharp metal) and a different employee. I was appalled that the cart and the employee were totally misrepresented. I informed my attorney of my observations, and he said not to say anything or they may try to discredit my testimony. He said it would only serve to antagonize them. We received a shockingly low "award" of $12,000. The insurance company claimed they already paid $5000 and was only willing to pay $7000 more. This would not be nearly enough for all of my medical, legal, household and office expenses, loss of income, much less for all the pain and suffering.

My options were limited. I could settle for less or take the case to trial. I was not willing to risk more financial loss. In this particular state, we need to improve our position or award, by 30% in a trial, or we are responsible for all court fees and the attorney fees for both parties. These fees can be considerable. It is an effective deterrent to keep the number of cases out of the court system. It is not necessarily justice.

The business partners, who had secured the insurance company and their lawyers, did not want their insurance company to pay all of the $10,000 medical bills that were part of their policy. It wouldn't have come out of their pockets. They were angry with me. I can only speculate that I was an outsider and the adversary to them. Obviously, if it were themselves, their wives or daughters who were injured, there would have been a completely different attitude regarding the situation. I am pretty sure that they had no thoughts about the "Golden Rule." I don't think they ever considered doing "the right thing." It was more important to win the competition, not to take responsibility.

They had the resources of a large insurance company behind them. They could treat me any way they wanted. My resources were exhausted. I couldn't take the chance of going to trial. I chose to accept financial responsibility for their negligence and the damages it had caused me.

In our experience of modern life, we are taught to have big insurance companies behind us, hire good lawyers, hide information and truth in an effort to avoid responsibility and "get away with it." We are taught the principal of "CYA" (cover your ass.) From television, our children learn that "high profile role models" can get away with murder if they have enough money and power. This is a sad statement regarding our dysfunction as "a nation under God." As citizens, many are not willing to tune into Guidance to do the right thing. This can create the demise of our country and our civilization.

It is not worth avoiding the responsibility. It will come back around to us, maybe not immediately. "What goes around comes around" is a Universal Law. If we don't follow our conscience and treat people the way we want to be treated, we will receive the same back to us. No one can truly "get away with" anything. The Higher Power knows, we know and our conscience will not let us forget it. The whole world and our experience will reflect it back to us!

Our Spiritual Family

Spiritual family is the best source of Guidance and protection. It is our Divine heritage. It is our origin; it is our Source of love, peace and harmony and true wisdom. We forget that we have Spiritual family available to us while living on the Earth. It is my intention to remind us all that we have the ability to access our Spiritual family, those beyond our Earthly perspective.

Our Divine Mother/Father

We have Divine Parents. We are their Divine Children and our Divine Parents want to provide for us, just like earthly parents do. "As above, so it is below." Our Divine Parents deny us nothing. We have their permission to ask for what we want and need, and to ask for our Highest good. We even have permission to ask for and receive what may not be for our Highest, although we may not receive it!

The real truth is that there are no "true orphans," even if we do not have an earthly family or have been taught dysfunctional patterns and behaviors. We truly have a Divine family if we care enough to nurture our relationship with them.

When we want unconditional love, forgiveness, compassion, it is easy to go to the Divine Mother. When we want wisdom, understanding and insight, we can go to the Divine Father. Or we can pray to them as One, our Divine Parents. Masculine and Feminine principals are not an issue. Divinity is about Unity. If Divinity is not well balanced and integrated, then who is?

Good or bad, happy or sad, we are loved unconditionally by our Divine Parents. They don't administer punishment or bad karma to us. We do it to ourselves by our choices. It is how we use our free will and reason that develops our karma. We are responsible for our choices and the consequences that come from those choices.

Our Angelic Family

There absolutely are angels and they are willing to assist us in every moment. All we need to do is ask for and pray for assistance, and to let them know we need their help. They are our etheric brothers and sisters in light bodies. They are beautiful and radiant, and we can have a relationship with them too.

My first conscious experience of an angel was right after surgery. I was scheduled to go on a journey around the world for my preparation in my work. I felt weak and incapable. My head told me I had no right to begin my journey. I prayed passionately for guidance and assistance late one night in my bed. As I lay there, I heard the rustling of angelic wings next to my body and I could feel currents of air and energy surrounding me and enveloping me. I knew in that moment that I was destined to go on that journey and that I would have all of the support that I needed. That night I rested in deep peace.

Another Angel experience happened during the 1986 Harmonic Convergence. An Angel appeared on an unplugged television set in Mt. Shasta California. We were invited to view this miracle. I walked in the door and was overcome with awe at the spectacle I saw. There was the most beautiful, radiant light-being emanating from the television screen. I couldn't believe my eyes! There before me was the most incredible celestial experience I have ever felt prior to that time.

One of the most astonishing experience with angels happened to me my first time on the beach in Lanikai, Hawaii in 1989. I lay down on my towel and looked up at the clouds, contemplating what a beautiful experience I was having being in Hawaii. After a while, the clouds above me started to swirl in a clockwise direction forming an incredible vortex of energy right above me. As I looked up, I began to see a multitude of beautiful pastel light-bodies circling overhead. I felt an incredible, peace and contentment and knowingness that this was a very special place for me to be. It is interesting to note that the name Lanikai literally means, 'heavenly water.' I truly did experience it as a Heavenly environment for me. Eventually, I moved to this awe-inspiring place in 1992.

More and more people are sharing stories of Angelic visitations. More and more people are experiencing it firsthand. If we realize that it is possible to have an Angelic experience, it is more likely to manifest in our reality. There are magazines, books, and special Angelic message cards about Angels. Read them, become inspired. Open our heart and be receptive to our own Angelic visitation.

Our Spirit Guides, Ancestors & Elders

Some intuitive people prefer to relate to Spirit guides. They receive perceptions from guides regarding what they need to know. Spirit guides are our allies who have accepted the responsibility to guide us through our lifetime. They do not interfere with our free will, much like the Angels; they are only there to assist us when we are open to receive it. Some people have more talent with reading spirit energy. These people are called Spiritual channels or mediums. They can channel beings from other dimensions and from different cultures.

Some of our ancestors are our loved ones who have departed and are accessible by our intuition. Some people feel more comfortable associating with people they have known from the past. Those people usually have a strong psychic ability and can feel see and or hear spirits that have entered the room. If we have a strong connection with a dearly departed family member, we can ask that person for assistance and guidance.

We can gain great wisdom from learning more about the roots of our Native traditions and their Teachings: *"Our Native Nations are gathering the Teachings and preparing the way for the Fifth World of Peace by returning to ceremony, ritual, and using the wisdom of the Ancestors to heal any old wounds and bitterness.*[19] *We are also reminded that the ancestors who rode the Wind before us are a part of our roots and that we are here to respect the value of their gifts and their lives by living in a balanced manner. "...humankind is the bridge between Earth and the Sky Nation and like the Standing People (meaning the trees with roots in the earth and branches in the sky), we are of both worlds. To accomplish this balance, we must live in harmony with All Our Relations, be rooted in this world through our Mother Earth, and allow our spirits to fly through the other worlds and be at one with those realities as well.* [20] *...there are in truth over 387 Tribes and Traditions on Turtle Island (United States of America). These Traditions are finally beginning to trade information and teach others outside of the Tribes the Medicines, rituals, customs, and understandings of their Ancestors. Honoring all abilities in the Self and in others marks the pathway of peace.*[21]

Spiritual Advisors

There are a plethora of wonderful people who are truly dedicated to advancing our Spiritual nature in a balanced manner. Most will support us in listening to our own hearts and souls. These people provide the kind of advice and wisdom that can assist in directing us until we have clear and consistent communication with our Inner Self. These people may take the form of ministers, psychics, psychologists, counselors, mentors, coaches, spiritual astrologers, mediums, psychologists, teachers, healers, and supportive friends. If we hear these advisors say something to us that feels right, feels familiar, and makes us want to take action, do it! They also may give us some opportunities to contemplate more deeply our own process and come up with our own insights. By giving their assessment, support and their experience of what our process is, we can gain valuable insight. They can act as a mirror in which we can see our self so much more clearly and completely.

Books, tapes, videos, classes and television shows are wonderful opportunities to explore the ways to find our own Inner Guidance. At this time, these resources are readily available and are abundant in the marketplace. Many self-help books have become best sellers. If we don't like to read, we can buy the same information on tape/CD and listen as

---

[19] Jamie Sams, *Sacred Path Cards: The Discovery of Self Through Native Teachings* (Harper Collins Publishers, 1990) 87.
[20] Jamie Sams, *Sacred Path Cards: The Discovery of Self Through Native Teachings* (Harper Collins Publishers, 1990) 72.
[21] Jamie Sams, *Sacred Path Cards: The Discovery of Self Through Native Teachings* (Harper Collins Publishers, 1990) 67

we commute. Many will be drawn to classes that develop intuition and Spiritual awareness. Some will learn by sharing with others in groups.

The serious student on the path to Higher Self-awareness will find the metaphysical, self-help and health sections in the major bookstores or in the smaller metaphysical book stores. There are some wonderful programs on television that support our healing process. One of my favorites is the Oprah Winfrey show. I feel that this show has made an incredible impact on millions of people in seeing areas in themselves that need to be healed.

The most important guideline to remember is that it needs to feel right in our being. If it doesn't feel right, let it go. If it feels right, go deeper with it, explore it. Learn to draw on the experiences of others to facilitate our own learning. Discover a way to understand our self and expand our awareness so we can hear our own Guidance better.

Divine Children/Divine Inner Self

As children of Divinity, we have many names for that part of our heritage. Some of these names are the Sacred Self, the Authentic Self, the God Self, the Soul, the Spirit, the Divine Inner Child, Divine Inner Self, Spiritual Self and the Higher Self.

According to my Guidance, "God/Goddess" or "our Divine Mother/Father God," made us each as an individual Divine Ray of their Love and Light. This perfectly balanced Creation, their Divine Child; many call the Divine Inner Self. The Divine Inner Self is free of all karma and blemish, it simply is. It is the "I Am" principle inside of us. It is the Spirit of Divinity within us. This is how the Higher Power experiences through us.

Many people continue to search for Divinity, strength, etc., outside of themselves. As a result of not feeling a personal experience with Source, many people feel empty, separated, disconnected, and needy. It creates a sense of an insatiable addiction. They attempt to fill that hole with whatever they can use to distract themselves from the feeling of emptiness. We choose whatever addiction we have a proclivity to base on our emptiness. These addictions can manifest as addictions to love, overwork, substances, violence, horror, sex, shopping, food and other self-destructive habits. They are so destructive with their personality self because there is no connection with their Inner Self. For some it is the only way to feel.

However, there is a more personal way to experience our Divinity and that is to know intimately and personally our Divine Inner Self. If we teach our children to find that Source within them, they will have more Self-confidence, Self-esteem, and Inner peace than they have known before. This is our true Source of personal harmony, fulfillment and love.

When our children misbehave, it is better to allow them some alone time to hear the voice of their Inner Self in the silence, rather than to send them to their room to play with distractions of radio, television, or video games. After time has passed, ask them to relate and share what they heard from the voice within them. Get them into the practice of hearing that voice before they make a decision and after they have made a poor decision. They will then learn to be more accountable to that part of themselves and more in harmony with their own Guidance. We cannot be with them 24 hours a day. Their Inner Self is always available and needs to be developed for the child to have good conscious Guidance, to know their own conscience instead of just what we tell them. Webster's Dictionary defines conscience as "a knowledge or sense of right and wrong, with the compulsion to do right; inner thoughts or feelings, consciousness."[22] Remember, it is important for them to find it out on their own just as Adam and Eve did, then learn to accept the ramifications of their choices. They will learn to make better and better decisions and choices.

Personality Self vs. Inner Self

We want to distinguish the personality self from our Spiritual Self. The personality self is how we express our personality traits in the outer world. It is comprised of our defense mechanisms and ego survival patterns. It is what we want the public to see and experience about what we want them to know about us. Usually, it is based on our ego, fears, insecurities, victimization and inadequacies. It has a lot to do with the kind of difficulties, challenges and abuses we have suffered or witnessed. It is the part of us that "acts out or reacts." The tendency is to gloss over our imperfections with our personality persona to show others that we are okay. By the same token, if we received acceptance and a sense of being loved by being a victim or a martyr, this may be the face we show to the world. The personality self is invested in what is "familiar," what we have experienced in our families and in family patterns.

I was very angry and extremely sad and lonely from the experiences of the past. No one seemed to know it. I was described as a very self-confident person. I put on a bright, yet false smile for the world to see to hide my shame and denial about being abused and being in a family that was so dysfunctional. Through much evolution and learning, I became more and more real with myself. I realized that I was much more than my personality and my history. This is true for you as well. We are not our personality self. Our truest essence is

[22] Webster's New World Dictionary, 2nd edition (Cleveland: William Collins Publishers, Inc. 1979) p. 302.

our Spiritual Self, our Divine Inner Self. This is our most personal and available Source of Divine Guidance.

Trust and Unconditional Love

In over-protecting our children, we teach them not to feel safe and not to learn to trust themselves and Divinity. The result is that they rely more on us, the Earthly parents, rather than the Divine Parents. This practice perpetuates "enabling" and no one has to grow. We continue to repeat the same errors. This may be the single biggest mistake we make as parents and caregivers. We are dis-empowering them by not affirming their love connection with Divinity and their Inner Self. We need to teach and demonstrate trusting their ability. Let them make mistakes and contemplate how they could have handled it better. Let them come up with their own answers. This is how they develop true Self-confidence.

Our responsibility to our Selves and others is to be an example of trust, compassion, balance, and the most important of all, love. When in doubt, learn to go inside our Self. We will find our own answers and we will know that they are right for us. They will resonate with love and truth. Learn and put into practice the foundation and importance of utilizing all of our abilities; sensing with our bodies, feeling with our emotions, thinking with our minds, and intuiting the wisdom of our Spirit. They are all equally important!

Chapter 3
Karma & the Gift of Free Will

What is Karma?

Most people know the law of Karma as the "Golden Rule." That rule is "Do unto others as you would have others do unto you." "You reap what you sow." "What goes around comes around." There is a law of cause and effect; it is a Spiritual and Universal Law. It is the consequences of our choices and our acts. If we don't want the same thing to happen to us, we best not do it to someone else. It's that simple. In the various religions, many say the same message with similar words. The essence of karma is to value yourself, others, and all of creation with devotion and right action. Right action is Divinely inspired.

When we choose to be destructive, controlling, and hurtful or wish harm on someone or something, we create that same karma and response to our actions. Let us refer to this as negative karma; this is not the most desirable for most of us. By the same token, when we choose to be constructive, empower others, and take responsibility when we have hurt or harmed someone accidentally, we produce more desirable results for ourselves. We can refer to this as positive karma. As we can see, karma is both positive and negative. Our good acts and wishes produce good responses, and they are a wise investment. The energy of positive thought and action always balances the negative, so our karma is neutral or better.

An example of this principal would be reflected in international sports competition. One ice skater intentionally caused injury, hurt and harm to another in order to win a title. She ended up barred from competition and dishonored. The other competitor healed and went on to win a 2nd place honor in world skating. In this case, karma was demonstrated rather quickly.

The Universal law of Karma may be too complex to comprehend in its magnitude. We do not always know what is being balanced and from when, as it plays out in our life and the lives of our loved ones. It is difficult to know when we are being in service to one another to balance energies brought about by the law of Karma. It takes great wisdom and diligence to persevere, give retribution, and stay positive and loving. We can choose to stop creating negative karma by using Divine Guidance. When we draw on Guidance to the best of our ability, the choices are wise and the karma is positive.

We all are born with limiting, negative, unconscious patterns that hold us captive by continually drawing on the same familiar circumstances and behavioral patterns. We make the same unconscious choices over and over. We seem to magnetize that energy. This is part of our suffering. Our minds and hearts are not free because we are making unconscious choices. They merely reflect and draw our negative patterns.

In addition, we are born with wonderful talents and abilities to use wisely and to Self-actualize. By using Guidance, we can identify these talents and find the right path of expression. In this way, more people can get up and out of their "lazy boy" recliners and start to make a constructive difference in their own lives and that of others.

We can commit to learn and evolve. When we heal these negative patterns by learning to love better and more honestly, we have positively transformed our negative karmic patterns. We can make wiser, conscious choices that are inspired Spiritually and lovingly.

When bad things happen to good people, it does not necessarily mean that we deserve punishment or that we are working out negative karma. A loved one may need our assistance and they may be "acting out" with us. This requires a great deal of love, compassion and patience. We may need that. We may have accumulated too much stress and dis-ease and have neglected to care for ourselves. It is possible that something in our life needs to change radically, structurally, or we are in the wrong situation and need to realign. We have the responsibility to our Self to change for our Self. We need to consult our own Guidance for greater understanding.

When one goes through an accident that involves the spine, it can indicate a change within their life structure. Their foundation, literally, may require strengthening or restructuring. It can release old emotional energies. When the neck is involved, it can indicate new directions. This releasing, processing and restructuring can happen in post accident treatment and therapy. What you strengthen on the physical level with the appropriate attitude can restore you on other levels, if that is your intention. It is important to remember that there are truly "no accidents," only opportunities to heal and grow in whatever form it manifests.

It is interesting to note that karmic consequences happen during certain cycles (see section on Guidance Groupings, Capricorn). It may not happen immediately following our action. It does happen at the perfect time in our life when we need the redirection, the healing, or different results. Karma is a wonderful instrument of change in our life, even if it is sometimes uncomfortable.

Positive karma is about more blessings, love, abundance, and happiness. We feel more like living on this earth when we are a magnet for those results. We have more loving relationships, we feel more fulfilled. Wise choices and wise actions are a wise investment.

Responsibility of Karma

We are responsible for our Karma and all the consequences that happen in our lives. We manifested it through our choices. If it is not obvious that we created it in the present, we produced it in the past. If we were destructive, deceitful or hurtful with our actions, we are accountable. It will come back to us in some form; we can count on it, maybe not immediately, which leads people to believe that they might have gotten away with something. We do not get away with anything. It is foolish to think that we are not responsible for our actions.

When we do not feel we deserve something unpleasant, it may be for our Highest and best. Sometimes that is difficult to see without Guidance. The most important thing to remember is that no matter how painful or uncomfortable a situation, an accident, a disease or injury is, it is about our need to release, grow and change. It is our responsibility to choose our Highest and best. Remember that it is a choice to view ourselves as an empowered person, not the victim. When we are hurt, it is easy to choose being a victim. In our recovery time, we have the opportunity to contemplate our lives and whatever changes we need to make. Identify those required changes. Actualize and make those changes happen in our life. Few people like pain and will do anything to avoid pain. Pain is a great motivator to realize one's Self and realign one's Self. Few people change for the fun or love of it. Yet many will change to avoid pain. If there is a fear of change, we can move through it by processing it so it does not have to result in dire consequences for not changing according to Divine Plan.

Our Divine Parents are not foolish. They give us a lot of space to learn and grow. Yet they do not remove the Universal law of cause and effect, without it we may not choose to take responsibility. We have a responsibility to our Self (soul/Spirit) to free our self, to grow and learn to choose wisely.

A good idea to keep in mind is to make every attempt to harm no living thing. This is the philosophy of vegetarians. They will not eat animals. There is a difference between creating harm and utilizing the gifts of Creation for nurturing and sustaining our lives. It is important to honor our food as a sacred sacrament of life and be grateful to the plants and animals that are becoming one with us by our communing with them. It truly is the sacrament of communion. The Native American people and other native peoples were very much aware of this principle and each time they went on a hunt, they would pray over the quarry and to the spirit of the animal. This is honoring all life, and it is what we need to do.

We do have a right to claim a space for ourselves to experience freedom from insects and larger animals. When my space is invaded, I attempt to release the critters outdoors. If they have become a dominating feature and threaten the home, of course, you want to protect your space and fumigate. Say a little prayer as they are released from their earthly existence. Some people have actually been successful using telepathy asking the intruders to leave. My friend, Michael, talks to cockroaches and gets them to leave voluntarily!

It is difficult to make wise choices and decisions coming from our unconscious patterns and our human intellect, in their limited perspective. Our ability to reason and comprehend on a Cosmic and Universal level cannot encompass the breadth and dimension of Divine Mind. Since our choices and decisions affect us all, a Higher responsibility can be assumed. We can actually have much better results by tuning into Divine Guidance, in which all life is cherished. This is our Highest and best Source. We need to understand karma and the lessons and situations it provides.

Learning the Lessons of Karma

In the biblical story, it was a difficult lesson and the cost was high, to be banished from the Garden of Eden. Adam and Eve suffered the repercussions and consequences of their choices. They didn't know what they had (paradise) since they had never experienced anything else. According to this story, Adam and Eve learned about suffering and making their own living without the benefits afforded, by living Divine will.

Most of us suffer, as we live outside of knowing and living Divine will. That is the main source of karma. We have an opportunity to heal this. When we are listening, trusting, acting and communing with our Higher Self, we are honoring Divine will.

Listening to the Guidance of our Higher Self will give us the opportunity to understand and comprehend the lessons we are learning. When we understand what is happening and why, it is somehow much more comforting. It gives meaning to our experience and the knowledge of right action. It brings more conscious awareness to our process. Knowing what to do frees us from worry, anxiety and stress. We sleep better and live healthier. It has really assisted me in being more positive when times are tough!

By trusting what we hear and knowing that it is for our Highest and best, we can endure more comfortably. It gives us the courage to change, grow and go on when things seem their darkest and most insufferable. When we feel our suffering is meaningless, blame others and make it their fault, we miss the mark. It is only by trusting completely that everything truly is for our Highest that we can accept responsibility and learn.

By acting on the wisdom of Guidance, we accrue no new negative karma. We can stay free of negative karma by right action in the present and healing the negative karma of the past. We all have the opportunity to heal the "sins of the past" (acting without a Higher Power) by healing whatever life presents us with. That may take the form of addiction, illness, accident, injury, financial or emotional misfortune, etc. All of these "opportunities" give us the arena in which to heal old patterns and Spiritual disconnection. It can also bring Higher and stronger connections with Spirit.

By utilizing our Higher Self to understand better, we can be more conscious of our process and make some incredible progress in this life. Less focus can be placed on striving for outer, material success. More concentration can be available to create our own Inner Garden, which will bear fruit naturally and less stressfully as it manifests in our physical world.

When we create in our "Inner Garden," we are capable of producing a more inspiring, peaceful and loving experience. By communing with our Higher Self, we have the ability to experience Heaven on earth and incredible joy and bliss. This is the way back to the Garden. We can all co-create it together. What we plant on the Inner, we will reap the harvest of in our physical, tangible experience on earth.

It is only through our own direct experience that we come to fully know something. We need to know that each choice that we make is important and each choice has consequences. Our children need to know that there are consequences to their actions. We need to be good role models and a good example with how we make our own choices. When I learned to stop reacting to people and situations and contemplate and meditate about it, life began to change for me. I looked for and found the truth in the situation for me and stopped blaming and acting like a victim. I was able to listen to Guidance and make a choice for a more positive, constructive mode of action or being. I began reprogramming my responses in life. When our children and others see that new behavior, they begin to open to a new way of being and acting. This affords new opportunities for all of us to use the gift of free will.

The Gift of Free Will

We are Divinely gifted with free will. As Divine Children, Divine Mother/Father gives us the gift and the responsibility to make our own choices. When making our choices, we can choose to learn, grow and love better. We can also continue making choices that causes pain and suffering.

During my earlier years in life, I experienced so much pain, anger and sadness. It was a way of life for me. I felt victimized by situations and people in my career arena and in my personal life. Life wasn't fulfilling or rewarding for me. I kept wondering, "When am I going to get mine?" "When is my ship coming in?" I rarely got the accolades, rewards and distinction that I really wanted. Life got so painful, I wasn't sure if it was worth being here.

I knew I needed a different kind of life to stay. I explored as many healing modalities as I could. I knew I needed to change and heal my negative thoughts and feelings.

We have the power to change our negative patterns and our destiny to become our Highest Expression. We need to be daring enough to discover and be our unique and authentic Self. We need to honor others who are courageous enough to express themselves and their truths, instead of ridiculing them for being different or having different ideas or philosophies. It requires Divinely guided, wise choices, mental and emotional growth and Spiritual practice, transcending the separation of the personality ego self.

We are staying in our small self when we are focused only on the ego and what the poorly programmed personality wants. The ego developed as we were children, to assist us in coping, surviving and attempting to get whatever we wanted. At times, the personality self adapted to dysfunctional situations. We developed ego survival mechanisms that can play out through our lives and in other lifetimes. These negative patterns are stored in our unconscious mind. It represents our immature self. This ego self chooses poorly. Unless we choose to heal, this is our option, it happens automatically, and can be unconscious.

Many psychics make predictions based on our emotional baggage and negative thought patterns from childhood. They are telepathically picking up what is in our consciousness. These patterns keep repeating and they are easy to discern. We believe what the psychic says, feel helpless, fearful, hopeless, powerless, etc. and it becomes a self-fulfilling prophecy. We give our power away. We attract the very thing we are trying to avoid. If we don't heal that pattern, it will continue to repeat in our lives. We are not free. We have become enslaved as a society and a civilization to our patterns. We have not earned the right to use our free will.

Earning the Right

We have to earn the right to have free will. Otherwise, we are reacting instead of acting freely. If we are unconscious about our actions and patterns, we remain enslaved, imprisoned and unhappy. (See the chapter on Clearing and Preparing for Receiving Our Guidance.) Learn how to earn that right.

Earning free will is part of our ability to choose. If we are operating from old programs and patterns, we will not have a free will choice. We may think we have a preference, yet we are simply choosing that which we have selected before.

Sometimes, we don't realize that we have the power of our free will to choose transformation and healing. We feel like a victim with a person or circumstance. That is when we are not applying our personal Self-empowerment. Choose to connect with your Highest Guidance through your free will and your intuition. Do not just cross your fingers and hope for the best. Make wise choices based upon what is for your Highest and Best expression, Spiritually. Your life can unfold in magical and unique ways beyond your wildest comprehension.

Misuse

It is our right to misuse our free will. It can bring, (what we may consider to be) undesirable consequences. We do not have to choose to be Divinely Guided. In this way we can learn and experience many things. Unfortunately, many times we hurt ourselves or others in the process, not to mention the effects it might have on our Earth. This is learning the hard way; many of us are good at that. We were truly gifted with free will and personal Self-empowerment much more than most people know or use. (Just as I was writing this, a bird landed on my louvered window directly in front of me as if it were bringing that message or validating how truly great our gifts are!)

Ignoring Guidance

I had the opportunity to misuse my free will regarding my career. My Guidance was directing me towards a profession facilitating personal growth and entertainment. I felt insecure and fearful about making such a dramatic change. Would I be able to make enough to support myself, did I have the talent and ability, would I be successful? These were difficult questions at the time. I chose with my free will to make money with corporate America. I knew from the past I could be successful and it seemed to be the easiest route with guaranteed income. I made my choice based on fear and insecurity.

Consequentially, extenuating circumstances prevented me, after only one week in my corporate position, from continuing on my wrong path. I ended up injured and bedridden for ten months with plenty of time to listen to my Inner Guidance. I developed my love and respect for Guidance to the extent that I couldn't let myself misuse it consciously any more.

I am not alone in the misuse of free will. Scientists, employing their unique ingenuity, desire to create a better product, perhaps a better lifestyle, and more health for all of us. Their corporate sponsors want a commercial product. Sometimes, they have created other, negative effects that they were unaware of. They didn't think to or know how to attune and align with Divine Will. Many of us take the easiest or least costly route, to meet a deadline or because it seems to be the path of least resistance. Many products have had to be recalled because they were released prematurely and were unsafe.

Our planet is suffering and it will take much contemplation and meditation on Divine Will to restore it to its natural state of balance. Some of the damage is humanly irreparable. We have discovered holes in the ozone layer around the Earth, which is now being linked to cancer of the skin, the green house effect, global warming and changing weather patterns. We have poisoned our soil, water, and our bodies with toxic chemicals. There are many species of plants and animals that we will never see or be able to reproduce again. We are responsible as a civilization for bringing about the demise and destruction of these species by our unwise free will choices.

Unconscious Control Games

Another misuse of our free will is forcing others to see and do things according to our perceptions or our will. This behavior constitutes control and manipulation. We are taking away their freedom of expression and their choices. When we do that, we are playing tyrant, dictator or oppressor. This happens in many control games. By using control games, the dysfunctional person hopes to create what they desire. It is a dishonest approach to getting what you want. Control games usually end up attracting only more havoc and distrust. Watch any soap opera type drama. They present some excellent examples of control and manipulation.

Control games are usually unconscious and played by people who have learned them from their parents. Those who play them feel powerless, insecure, victimized, abused, fearful, angry, sad and lonely, hurt, betrayed and have low self-esteem. They have no or little Spiritual connection, no trust in a Higher Power and no relationship with their Inner Self. The more dysfunctional they are, the more oppressive their behavior is. Some are not even aware of their behavior; it is so programmed into their subconscious mind, it has become unconscious.

These are some of the manipulative behaviors that are most common: jealousy, possessiveness, intimidation, inferiority/superiority, victim/victimizer or martyrdom, seduction, guilt, deception, withholding, worry, criticism, righteousness and judgmental attitudes. It is important to understand that these coping behaviors have consequences. When we act in these ways toward others, it will come back to us. Many of us are working through the control games we learned in our early family experience. We want control of others so they will need us and won't leave us. Notice when you are using these behaviors. What we really want is love, acceptance, attention, appreciation, validation, and/or security. Be willing to be honest and ask for it!

Conscious Manipulation Results in Karma

To block the free will of others is to misuse our personal power. The use of black magic or sorcery to control and manipulate is a conscious, more serious misuse. Any time we choose to take power from someone to get what we want, we are abusing his or her free will and there will be a karmic repercussion. Karma is a Law of the Universe in which what is sent out comes back. Some people take their choices too lightly, without looking deeply into their net effect and the final outcome. By reading and studying this book, we can have a better and deeper understanding and relationship with our Inner Self and learn how to make wiser choices.

Appropriate Use

The appropriate use of free will is making choices in which no one or no thing is hurt in any way. It is simply impossible to do this on our own. Life in the Universe is too complex for human reason and intellect to figure out how each choice affects other life.

In order to achieve positive, wise, life supporting decisions, we must tune into Divine Mind. That is our only guarantee that we will not be destructive in any way. To use free will constructively is a sacred, devotional practice. Nothing is done or created without the Divine as our partner.

Life is so much better and healthier for us and others when we use free will in concert with Divine Mind. My prayer and affirmation is, "Divine Will is my will." Decisions and choices are easier and wiser.

When I finally fully honored my life direction through my intuition, Guidance and free will, my professional life became so much more fulfilling. I felt on track with my purpose. I used my intuitive Guidance to create a non-profit health educational corporation called Universal Health. In that way, I was able to learn from some of the best health educators and healing arts professionals. In the past, dysfunction, emotional baggage and a negative belief system had blocked me. I was able to clear my heart and mind and achieve harmony. I reprogrammed my subconscious mind, which allowed me to heal at deeper levels. I learned to access my own love, my Inner Self and Divine Mind, so much more. In addition, my personal healing has educated me about many of the things I need to know to facilitate personal growth for others. Healing, discovering my Inner Self and Divine Guidance have been a blessing in my life and can be in yours!

Chapter 4

Intuition, Our Conscience & Consciousness

Definition of Intuition

Intuition is the immediate knowing of something without the conscious use of reasoning. We don't have to figure it out or contemplate on it, it's just there, readily available. It is direct knowing. We can feel it in our gut, thus the term "gut feelings". Intuition gives us an opportunity to see a picture, hear a message, or get a feeling from a higher part of ourselves. It originates in the unconscious right brain and is many times referred to as our "Inner Knowing" hence the term "insight."

Intuition allows us to maintain a connection with Creation through observation, listening or feeling to gain insight. Our insight is expanded when we understand symbology. In the Guidance Groupings in Chapter 11, we can perceive the different elements, body parts, animals, etc. that symbolize our Earth connection and the messages that they represent. There are also stars and planets which connect us with more of Creation. *"Anytime anyone seeks the Silence of the balanced heart, the intuitive process can allow the truth to come forward. Truth is the final destination of any seeker's path. When the truth is found inside of the self, there is no need to look further."*[23]

There are certain people who are extremely gifted with their ability to access their intuition. Many times these people are professional clairvoyants, psychics or intuitives. Not everyone has the same talent, although everyone is born with intuition. It is part of our ability to connect with each other and our Creator.

> *"Intuitive knowing without precedent can also be called psychic intuition. The difference between this type of intuitive knowing and psychic knowing is a question of degree. We believe that psychic knowing is a stronger, finely honed intuitive sense. But it is nonetheless a natural mental ability. In fact, the two types of intuition, with and*

---

[23]Jamie Sams, *Sacred Path Cards: Discovery of Self Through Native Teachings* (Harper Collins Publishers, 1990), 60.

without precedent, are so closely aligned that it is often hard to tell for sure which one you have experienced."[24]

Intuition can present itself in many ways. Sometimes we will see a flash of a picture in our head, hear an Inner voice or get a strong feeling. Many people do not honor their experience. They dismiss it or do not recognize it. In our Divination experience, we pay attention to everything in our awareness. We develop greater awareness by learning how to see, hear and feel more and by focusing on intuition.

Our children are asked to learn by seeing and memorizing. We have relied generally on the kind of primary and secondary school systems that suppress our intuitive and creative Self in favor of a purely mental experience. Art and physical education programs have been diminished within school budgets.

For the most part, many have not learned to honor, trust and act on their Inner voice or to have a relationship with their Inner Self. It is the missing piece in our development. This is a primary means in which to discover the truth and our educational system does not teach it. This is beginning to change at the University level. We can take responsibility to learn it on our own until the educational system stays abreast with learning research.

Changes in Attitudes of the Scientific & Business Community

Science has been enthusiastically researching the results of the intuitive process and defining ways of learning for the education system. They are finding so many more ways of learning than what we have been utilizing. They are validating the result of the intuitive process.

Upon discovery of the value of the benefit of intuition in dollars and cents, the business community is changing how they view obtaining results. They are working with new tools or paradigms, they are seeing more creative solutions to business problems and bigger payoffs for that creativity, and the bottom line speaks loudly.

"The following are other indications that the climate of opinion toward intuition is changing:

- *Stanford University's School of Business teaches intuition as part of its "Creativity in Business" course taught by Michael Ray and Rochelle Myers.*
- *In Stanford's Graduate School of Business different kinds of meditation, dream analysis, Aikido, I-Ching, Tarot cards, trance dancing, and shadow masks are part of the curriculum.*

---

[24] Laurie Nadel with Judy Haims and Robert Stempson, *Sixth Sense: The Whole-Brain Book of Intuition, Hunches, Gut Feelings, and Their Place in Your Everyday Life* (Prentice Hall Press, 1990)

- *Surveys show that many chief executive officers rate intuition as one of their most prized creative assets.*
- *Government experiments on intuition show that intuitive skills can be learned.*
- *The scientific community is beginning to change its views on the roles of intuition and consciousness. Cognitive psychologists, behavioral scientists, and biologists are starting to accept that mind, or consciousness, is a valid starting point for scientific research."*[25]

Even though all persons can not or will not embrace new ways of thinking and learning, there will be those who will adopt these techniques and use them for the betterment of their lives and those of the ones they love. The top 5 – 10% is the achievers, who literally act on their dreams and their gut level feelings while the rest respond negatively or neutrally. We can choose to be in the top 10% by developing our intuition.

Practice Intuition

Anyone can develop their intuitive skills. It is necessary to believe it is possible and then practice, practice, practice. My first experience at recognizing my intuitive talents was during a course of EST training. I was amazed at my ability to share with my partner all of the things that he had projected to me telepathically. I had never attempted to test my intuition prior to that time. After that experience and the experiences I had with accidents, I began paying very close attention to my intuition. I began to honor it more and more. The more I honored it, the stronger it came.

The time my intuition saved my life, (see page 89, "Picture Example") I still didn't give it much thought or credence. I took it for granted. I don't know if I even thanked Divine Source for the intuition. I am sure many of us have had experiences of guidance and not realized that we could develop our intuition even more with our focus, awareness and gratitude.

I do know that from grade school on, I was spending an enormous amount of time on the telephone answering questions and counseling my classmates. I had no idea where the answers were coming from. I did not think anything of it. It is interesting that I end up becoming a counselor and giving guidance to people in their lives. Now I consciously use my intuitive gifts to assist others and their choices.

---

[25] Nadel with Haims and Stempson

Making a Decision or a Choice

Many of us do not have the courage or knowledge about how to participate in life in an active manner. Many of us just allow the circumstances around us to determine our fate. We do not take responsibility in the co-creation of our life with Divine Source by listening. Many do not know that it is possible to sense Divine Will or how to do it.

When we need to make a quick decision or a choice, we are under a lot of pressure. It is essential to find a quiet place where we feel safe. Tell yourself that your intention is to hear Divine Source speak to you through your intuition and then just contemplate, be aware and notice as you are running the situation through your consciousness. Feel any sensations, any emotions, see any images or pictures or hear any sounds that come into your consciousness. Be with them, acknowledge them and be grateful for these sensations and experiences. All of a sudden, you will have a sense of knowing what those pictures, sounds and feelings mean for you and your life. It will come to you clearly and resonate through you. If you don't experience clarity, you have not accessed your intuition. Wait and try again and continue to try until you get clear.

In psychology it is Carl Jung who valued intuition as the most natural way of obtaining useful information regarding a person's healing process. Because the unconscious is not readily accessible, we can not get it from personality and intellectual observation alone. Our intuitive perception can reveal the onset of emotional dysfunction.

According to Jung's theory, "there are four psychological functions: thinking, feeling, sensing, and intuition."[26] We usually go with our strongest suit. If we are gifted mentally, we will lead with our mental skills without developing our other functions. Our perceptions can be limited without utilizing all four functions. *"His four functions correspond to the predominant intellectual skills of the reptilian brain (sensing), limbic system (feelings), left neo-cortex (thinking), right neo-cortex (intuition)."*[27]

In the past, Jung has been criticized in our country for his mystical association, use of symbology and application of the psychic and intuitive process. Why should we be limited in time and space if we are truly listening to the wisdom of Source speaking through us? Animals are capable of sensing danger and have predicted earth changes like earthquakes, hurricanes. In Jung's book called *Synchronicity*, he makes a clear case for how all things are inter-related and inter-connected in time and space. We only have to open our eyes to see this inter-connection and relate it to what is going on in our life.

---

[26] Carl Jung, *Structure and Dynamics of the Psyche*
[27] Nadel with Haims and Stempson

We all know of someone who has dreamed about the death of another. In reference to the notorious O.J. Simpson trial, an interesting thing may have happened with regard to the sister of Ron Goldman, Nicole Simpson's friend. It was reported that Ron's sister had a very strong dream that Ron was not to go to Nicole's house and he went anyway. It is possible his sister could have saved his life had he listened to the wisdom in her guidance.

"Drive by" intuition occurs when we are driving on the street and something draws our immediate attention. It can be a person or a building. One day, while driving down Keeaumoku Boulevard, the HMSA building captivated my attention. Later that day, I received a call to deliver a birthday telegram to a doctor in that building. The same thing happened while driving by the Shriner's club not long after.

Life is so synchronistic, we can have a question on our mind and turn on the radio and a song comes on the radio or the announcer says something that can connect us to our own Guidance. We can realize that we needed to hear that very message at that specific time. Many of us are moving too fast through life and we miss life's synchronicities. This is a big loss and sometimes we don't even realize it. We may have missed many opportunities to solve problems, connect with a certain person or just to understand the cycles and processes in our life or the lives of our loved ones. There are so many ways in which the Divine communicates with us. Imagine how our lives would be it we were listening fully!

Our Intuition Rhythm

Teachers and students can be as aware as business people that we have a natural rhythm. Every 90 minutes we have an ultralian rest response. Drowsiness and loss of attention mark it. Students may be more receptive during this period, even though they look like they are not paying attention. This response makes us more receptive to conceptualizing information although it may not be effective for details and facts.

When we feel that state of drowsiness and the need to close our eyes, let's give ourselves an intuition break. We may solve a problem or challenge, just by taking a short break to be with it in our consciousness. We are allowing that part of us that knows the answer to come through in its own rhythmic timing. This is especially important in business and in creative situations where we need inspiration and Guidance.

Dominant Style

Each one of us has a dominant thinking style. Some of us are more emotional; some are more mental. Many of us are very attached to our thinking style. It becomes habitual and easy to replay. It is natural to want to go with our strengths. Unfortunately, we have difficulty communicating and relating with those whose style of thinking is opposite of ours. When we use our minds or our feelings to try to control people or circumstances, it restricts our ability to receive the fullest potential of what is available with our Divination practice. If we are caught up in our head and the logical functions of the linear mind, it limits our ability to be open to Divine Guidance. If we are too emotionally charged, we are no longer receptive to it because we are too filled with emotional tension.

When we use both, we put our sensing and intellectual ability together with our feelings and the intuitive nature of our Spirit. It takes awareness and patience to become proficient at maintaining equilibrium once we create it. It is necessary to make an effort to achieve that balance for our life to fulfill its greatest potential. The more balanced mentally and emotionally we become, the more expansive our ability to receive Guidance.

Frequently, reason is the valued way of using intelligence. There is a new developing paradigm. Reason and intuition utilized together create more wholeness and whole brain activity. Letting go of too much reasoning activity allows very mentally motivated people to find Guidance easier and quicker.

With expanded awareness we can connect on a soul level. I experienced this when my brother, who lived in Arizona, left his body due to his illness. At 6:30 am in Hawaii, I awoke suddenly and I was aware of his passing. I felt as if I was truly there with him; as if I were experiencing it at the same time. I wasn't surprised when the telephone call came, that he had passed. I had truly sensed the exact moment of his death. I would have missed this moment completely if I had not been open to this kind of sensory awareness. It was beyond time and space. It was truly a beautifully shared soul experience.

All the way through high school and college, I used to think that my left brain dominance was superior to the right brain. It really worked well for me in memorizing and regurgitating all the information on paper for tests. I kind of felt sorry for the more creative types who couldn't seem to do what I was doing. It gave me the feeling of being superior. I never took an art course. I never attempted to balance my dominant style. My impression was *left is better, right is only for drawing and painting, it has very little value.*

When I finally included the right brain conceptual, artistic side of me, I loved it. I changed from business to an artistic expression in entertainment. I got into costuming and choreography. I created performances with a dance company and musicians. I began to realize it was much more fun to utilize the right brain and that I could make money while having fun. It became very valuable for me to use the right brain in my career. I developed an entertainment company in Los Angeles. I proved to myself that right brain expression truly can pay off.

We can change the dominant style that we use in our life. We do not need to be exclusively left or right brained. By practicing the attributes of the other side of the brain, we can change our style and way of being. We can become integrated and whole.

Corpus Callosum

People who are born left-handed, and most females, have the advantage when it comes to intuition. What is common in both of these groups is a more developed corpus callosum. This is the connection between the left and right brain and it has a larger cross section of numerous fibers. There are multiple axon connections in the cerebral cortex and limbic system that are more numerous in the female brain. It allows faster response time for the interaction of the right and left brain, first by access to the intuition, and then by utilizing that intuition in productive ways with the logical mind. Females and left handed males are natural whole brain thinkers, more open and sensitive. They are more spontaneous and can change more easily. As more men develop their feminine side, they can develop and strengthen their own intuitive feeling, cognition and creative ability. I recommend using the left hand more. For example, I use my left hand for mouse function while using the computer.

What is Our Conscience?

Our conscience is that part of us that assists us in making choices. It is a resonance that we feel in our heart and soul. The more we feel the harmony of our ultrasonic core current, (see p. 65) the easier it is to decide if the selection is a harmonious choice or not. If we do not know or feel the harmony of this current, it is difficult to choose. We do not get the validation of feeling at peace with our decision. When our core current is fully available and functional, it corresponds or resonates with our core set of values. How we interpret our values and move into action choosing or declining is based on how those values resonate with our Inner harmony.

The healthy soul values all equally. It inherently knows what to value in any situation and how to honor and respect all parties. It supports empowering everyone to be a winner and to honor him or herself. When we hear our conscience speak to us, it is usually a sense of intuition coming through our gut feeling to guide us with respect to our Inner values. Divine Source speaks to us through our conscience. It is important to be able to feel the unrestricted expression of our harmony current in order to have an effective and healthy conscience.

If we value all of life and ourselves equally, our conscience will not keep us up at night. When we do not value others or ourselves, we feel the pull of our conscience nagging us and demanding our attention. It will not allow us to eat or sleep without uncomfortable thoughts constantly churning in our mind. We may even get an uneasy feeling in our gut. We may feel guilt or anger about the perceived injustice. These are the moments for us to sit down, and write out all of the thoughts and feelings, that are going on. See them on paper. Read it out loud. Notice our reaction. Sit, contemplate and be with them. It will become very clear.

Make a choice to honor yourself and whoever is involved in a way that resonates with our highest values. Then and only then can we get a peaceful, restful sleep. Be sure to make good with retribution. When we make things better, our body and mind will feel better. We will not harbor anymore emotional or Spiritual negativity.

When we ignore our conscience or our intuition, there is a great build up of tension. It becomes overwhelming as it becomes stronger and stronger in our dreams and in our interactions, attempting to get our attention. "If you don't feel your intuition, this could be a sign that you have been ignoring it or denigrating it for a long time" says author and psychoanalyst Ernest Rossi. When you hear your conscience reminding you to choose wisely, honor it instead of calling it "that nagging little voice".

For example, in the past, I had a neighbor lived on rented property with fruit trees and the landlord left on vacation when a banana tree yielded ripe bananas. My neighbor cut the bananas down and used the bananas. When the landlord returned and asked about the bananas this person felt uncomfortable with the fact that he had used them for his consumption. He couldn't let the thought go that he had done something unfair, uncaring and not sharing; that he could have shown more generosity. His conscience told him that he needed to make it up the landlord. He went out and bought bananas to share with the landlord to feel comfortable with himself and honor that little voice inside. Only then could he feel comfortable with that situation and his relationship with the landlord. He resolved the issue.

This is a very simple example of the conscience in operation. Many of us deal with very simple opportunities to listen to the conscience. Some of us have really complicated and complex situations in our professional arena and with other people. By listening to our conscience, we strengthen our connection to our Inner Self. We make better choices and decisions.

Intuition and Nature

"Vision Quests are a tool used by those seeking direction in life. Any time anyone seeks the silence of the balanced heart, the intuitive process can allow the truth to come forward. Truth is the final

destination of any seeker's path. When the truth is found inside the Self, there is no need to look forward."[28]

When we apply our intuition we can connect with all living things. This is particularly fun when we are with our pets. When I first got my newest little kitty, I didn't know what to name her. A friend came over to see her and asked me what her name was. I said I didn't know and in that moment she yawned very big and I heard her say her name is Venus. Indeed she has evolved into the most loving, little kitty I've ever experienced. She rubs her little head on my leg constantly, rubbing me and showing her undying love and affection. Our pets can tell us what they want to be called, they know intuitively when to comfort us, they have a connection with us that is more natural to them. It is appropriate to develop an intuitive connection with them. This can be a wonderful exercise before we attempt to connect with animals and plants in nature. Once we have that connection with our pet, we can realize a greater connection with all of nature. When we take time to be in nature, we can feel, see and hear nature talking to us and that will be covered in the chapter on Nature's Reflection of Divine Order.

Three Areas of Human Consciousness

"Normal consciousness is not complete but is an exquisitely evolved, selective, personal construction with the primary purpose of insuring individual survival, but it is not necessarily the only manner in which consciousness can operate. The dominant Western paradigm has prevented us from clearly seeing the scientific import of the esoteric traditions."[29]

"Our ordinary consciousness is largely directed toward active manipulation of the external environment, for the most part we remain unaware of internal physiological processes, those phenomena, occurring "within our own house", from the dark. We each tune out subtle internal stimuli and direct attention outward, toward the external world, in order to survive."[30] This explains why many people don't hear their Guidance. They are looking outside of themselves for survival. If we direct our focus inward we can flourish instead of just survive.

During my travels through the Himalayas and Nepal, I encountered the Garungs, a local tribe. Some of them can go through the mountains regulating their own body temperature. They do not have to wear anything more than a shirt and part of their yoga meditation is to physiologically self-regulate so that they can survive the cold.

I have personally experienced walking on burning hot coals with motivational guru Anthony Robbins. When we did the fire walk, we altered our state of consciousness by

[28]Sams, 60.
[29]Robert Ornstein, *The Psychology of Consciousness* (W.H. Freeman and Co., 1972)
[30]Ornstein

lifting our eyes upward in order to transcend the normal state of consciousness. Our focus would not allow our feet to be burned. It was a miracle for me to see that we can transcend physical laws with our ability to focus inward and upward to a different kind of reality.

Learning to make changes in our focus and internal physiological processes could save our life. By using bio-feedback methods, in fact, we are influencing the internal controls of the body that have been referred to as automatic or autonomic. It could some day save our life to have that conscious control through our own meditative states.

There are many ways to alter a consciousness. It can happen when there is a major crisis going on in our life, sometimes by a spontaneous realization and an intuitive flash. It can happen through fasting, through utilizing movement and dance or anything that interrupts the normal linear left brain functions. It is accessing that right brain and the Superconscious that with practice we experience that sense of Oneness, that sense of unity that gives us a more whole experience, more awareness, rather than just the little bits and pieces that the left brain gives us. We can see a fuller, a more whole picture. *In the Last Mysterious Darkness, Augustine Poulain said that "mystic consciousness" is described by many in almost every tradition—from the ancient Hindu to the contemporary European. It is described in the Bible, in the Koran; it is a mysterious darkness a mode in which ordinary consciousness of a multiplicity of people and objects disappear to be replaced with an awareness of unity."*[31]

Freud's Theory of How the Mind Works

> *According to Freud, "the psyche consists of three mental domains; the unconscious, the pre-conscious, and the conscious mind. The unconscious, argued Freud, is the deepest, least accessible region of the mind, which contains hidden and seemingly forgotten memories and unacceptable thoughts, feelings and ideas. The preconscious contains information and memories just below the surface of consciousness, and in this respect, is part of the unconscious. Once information reaches the preconscious, it becomes relatively accessible to the conscious mind. However, the preconscious also contains information that is pushed out of consciousness.*
>
> *Human consciousness is divided into three areas. Most people are only accessing two of them, the conscious and subconscious. The more you direct your attention into the Spiritual centers located in the physical body, the more evolution you will experience. The more evolved your consciousness becomes the more contact it wants with the Superconscious."*[32]

[31] Ornstein
[32] Ornstein

It is our own innate Spiritual intelligence that is our direct line with Source or Divine Mind. In my experience of altering consciousness, I define the preconscious (the corridor, according to Freud, that connects the unconscious with the conscious) as an alpha brain wave state of complete mental relaxation of the conscious mind. This affords us the opportunity to access the Superconscious and the sub/unconscious.

Superconscious

I was guided not to use another person's definition of this concept. This is my experience of the Superconscious. The Superconscious is all of Divinity, the essence of all creation, all that is and ever will be past, present and future, eternity and space and all wisdom, love, harmony and truth including our Divine Inner Self (Spirit and Soul) as part of that Divinity.

When we access the Superconsciousness, everything manifests better. (It may not appear so at first.) Artists, athletes, performers, contestants, etc., have better results when connecting with this part of them. Many times we will hear winners thanking God, Spirit, Allah, Jesus or the Lord. It is no accident!

When we ask for Inner Guidance from our Divine Inner Self, we are accessing that part of us that is connected to our Divine Mother/Father, our Source. Intuition is our connection with our Divine Inner Self. The alpha brain wave state of mental and physical relaxation supports our intuition and connects us with our Divine Inner Self and Source. It is a corridor to our Highest and best. It is essential to make that connection first. After that connection is made, we need to develop the ability to interpret our intuition and dreams through nature's symbols which requires some study.

Harmonics

Through the power of Divine Source, sound and light fashioned the Universe. The Universe radiates harmonious sound currents to manifest matter. In physics it is acknowledged as "particle theory." Even sound relates to different categories of meaning. A specific musical note as part of Universal sound, as well as a specific color, as part of Universal light, resonates with the seven energy centers of our bodies. (See the chapter on Guidance Groupings.) Our Core current is made up of these harmonious sound currents.

Our Harmony Current or Ultra-Sonic Core Current

The Harmony current or Ultra-Sonic Core current is our connection to Superconsciousness, the Universe, Divinity and everything. It is that sound current and our breath that connects us with our Source. How this sound current moves through us will determine our harmony within ourselves and with all life.

The Ultra-Sonic Core current comes down through the crown of our head spiraling like a helix, a double strand of DNA, to the base of the spine and goes back up in that same spiraling movement. The stronger this current is, the more we are able to tune into the Highest part of ourselves. If there are energy blockages, compressed areas, or muscular contractions in the spinal column area, it is difficult to receive the fullest expression of this energy. Many people are not experiencing the fullness of the gift of this current. For health and Guidance it is important to have a freely flowing core current.

When I was creating a healing audio recording called "Relaxation and Empowerment" (see page 197) for our energy centers, I found it necessary to use the notes that resonated in the various centers. It creates a better feeling for each of the energy centers and it is arithmetical in nature and progression. It creates our overall sense of harmony. (See Chapter 11 on Guidance Groupings, regarding musical notes.) Our energy centers respond favorably to these musical notes.

In many traditions, the spine represents "The Tree of Life." It rests on and is connected to the pelvic girdle. The nervous system is a network of branches going to all the parts of our body. It looks like an upside down tree when viewed in an illustration. When the sacrum and the spine are aligned well, the cranium opens up like a flower to receive our fullest reception of the Harmony current.

It is necessary to open up that channel of energy so that this current can move through us freely and fully. If we've had an accident or injury that has compromised our spine or sacrum in any way, we will not fully receive our Harmony current. It is essential to do healing therapies that assists us in realigning our spine and releasing the energy dams that create pain in our body. That may include various types of bodywork and energy therapy, such as Chiropractic, Heller work, Rolfing, Acupuncture, Polarity Therapy, Reiki, etc. to assist us in opening these channels. Physical movement can assist and keep these channels open, like Yoga, Tai Chi, and Chi Kung. The more open we are, the more we can receive Guidance and the more harmony we will experience in our life. Since this current emanates from our Source, it tunes us more precisely to Divine Guidance.

Unconscious or Subconscious Mind

The unconscious reflects the most detailed storage of all of our life experiences from the past. It can and will affect the future because it magnetizes similar experiences so our life becomes a repeating pattern. It is necessary to become more aware of the content and function. When we become more aware, we then call this area the subconscious. We are now aware of what is programmed in this area.

The subconscious is no longer unconscious, because we have a slight perception about it. It comprises an accumulation of remembered incarnation memories, known patterns of ego and personality, recalled experiences, habits and reactions, as well as talents and abilities.

Most of us draw from the subconscious in an unconscious reactive way even when we are aware of it being an uncomfortable pattern. It is familiar and easy to repeat it. Until we observe that our behavior is limited and restricted we will continue to repeat the pattern unless personal growth work is done. It is then, that the content becomes very recognizable and we can stop the behavior and re-program new responses to experience more free will, love, peace, and harmony in our lives. The methods and techniques to achieve this state are covered extensively in *Volume II of the Wisdom of the Ages Series, "Mind Heart Harmony."*

The freer we are from limiting patterns and reactive habits, the more likely we will receive and recognize Guidance when it appears. To be truly in the "present" gives us an amazing ability to choose in each moment in a more positive way. Then we can use this ability to grow and evolve in Higher ways. As we advance individually, we create a shift in consciousness for the collective consciousness.

Collective Consciousness

The Collective consciousness represents everyone's unconscious contents. It gives certain groups a synergy of energy that is greater than the individual. It is indicated when gangs or other groups act out in a violent and destructive way. It was evident in groups like the Ku Klux Clan or the Nazi political party. People joining together around the world for global peace and in prayer, can also demonstrate the constructive power of collective consciousness. Many psychics draw impressions from the collective consciousness or the personal unconscious. It is possible to access that information.

It is important in our personal life to access our own unconscious and determine what is recorded there. We can then change what we don't want to keep. It is secondarily important that we be aware of what is going on with groups and their collective consciousness. We can choose to include ourselves in groups where the collective consciousness is constructive for growth, evolution, community and personal Self expression.

There is a global collective consciousness of all life on the planet. There is also a Universal collective consciousness. These represent the different levels and hierarchies of consciousness that are available for us to tune into in a positive and healing way. When the Universal level is reached, it becomes part of the Superconscious.

Conscious Mind

Our normal everyday consciousness, to those of us, who have not eliminated unconscious negative patterns and reprogrammed positive ones, is actually drawn more from the unconscious habits and reactions. It is not usually totally in the present moment. It is not fully aware unless it has been trained. Usually, it is scattered and unfocused, in the past or in the future, except in obvious moments in the demonstration of outstanding talents and abilities.

Those who have cleared a lot of unconscious patterns and practice disciplines of integration, like Yoga, Tai Chi, Chi Kung, etc. have a more unified focus. Their body, mind and breath are fully present in the moment, aware and open. They are truly conscious because they have trained for it and can access their Superconscious and subconscious in a conscious state. It is necessary to prepare for our Guidance like any athletic competition or test. We can train our body, mind and awareness for unified focus. This is the only way I know of to perceive fully beyond the five senses, short of Divine Intervention.

Eye Position for Specific Focus of Consciousness

Understanding and using appropriate eye position can be greatly beneficial. There is a science that has developed, to understand the numerous positions of the eyes. It is called Neurolinguistic Programming. It is good to research and study all of the positions. For Divine Guidance, it is important to comprehend the basics.

The position of our eyes determines how we direct our consciousness. When our eyes are focused downward, we are accessing our unconscious mind and can fall asleep easily. When our eyes are focused straight ahead, we are accessing our conscious mind and that allows us to stay more alert and present. It is easy to recognize the daydreamers and those who are not fully present, by looking at their eye position. When our eyes are focused directly inward and upward gently, we can access our Superconscious mind. It is essential to be aware of where our eyes are focused to go to the proper state of consciousness. The concept of eye position is to focus in the right direction, inward and upward gently, in order to connect more directly with the Superconscious level.

Chapter 5
Clearing and Preparing For Receiving Guidance

Develop Mind and Heart Harmony

Mind heart harmony is a peaceful, centered state of being in which we are fully free to recognize and value our own thoughts and feelings. We feel and act in harmony and in integrity with them. Our emotional response is in proportion and commensurate with the present situation, without emotional backlog or charge. We process our negative emotions on an ongoing basis with healthy venting techniques, which transmute all negativity. We take alone time for contemplation, meditation and reflection. Our thoughts are constantly refining in more positive and unlimited ways. We realize that a strong connection and relationship with a Higher Power is essential and the only true security we have on this earth.

It is the state in which we are aware of our Divine Inner Self and recognize that it is the power of Source acting through us. We don't give our power away to anyone or anything outside of our Selves. We feel Self-empowered. We do not postpone our happiness and peace. We are totally perceptive and responsible for our own love, fulfillment and actions. Everyone and everything else may then be a welcome addition to our lives.

Life continues to offer challenges and we are able to meet challenges and take responsibility for our growth. We notice that old self-limiting patterns and scripts are not blocking or limiting us anymore. Self-destructive behaviors are replaced with healthy, loving habits. We speak our own truth, not what others want us to say. We honor others and our Selves. We have healthy boundaries. We are free to choose wisely. We experience getting more of what we truly want and feel better and more balanced than ever before. We live healthy, creatively functional lives. We are now more prepared and able to achieve wholeness and Self-realization.

(Note: For more information on this subject, please read *Volume II of the Wisdom of the Ages Series, "Mind Heart Harmony."*)

Heal Dysfunction, Clear Emotional Baggage & Negative Mental Concepts

We all come into this world with patterns that we need to heal and grow from in order to love better. This is clearly a higher evolutionary path. It is possible to continue to stay in those patterns that cause pain by not choosing to grow. Our parents give us the opportunity to see these patterns and to possibly even reinforce them in us. Many times these patterns reflect family or "genetic" karma of the lineage of our ancestors. Many of us are not aware of our reactive behavior. It is programmed into our unconscious and in that way, continues and persists. This means that we are like a tape recorder operating on a "replay" mode. We need to clear the tape so that we can be fully present in each moment to choose appropriately.

When the pain of our patterns becomes strong enough, we either self-medicate, self-destruct or we learn to strengthen ourselves by healing these patterns. In this manner, pain serves us. It is a great motivator for transformation and healing.

Many of us are so filled up with emotional, mental and physical tension that remains unprocessed. There is no extra space inside of us to become more aware, more intuitive and more connected with ourselves. It is clearly difficult when we are blocked by emotional content and negative belief systems to receive to our guidance. When I was blocked and in denial of my feelings, I did not receive strong, clear intuitive messages. The more I emptied myself of negative emotions; the more I became open and receptive to my intuitive messages.

There are positive cycles when we spontaneously seem to open our consciousness to the best of our ability. During certain Neptune, Uranus, Pluto cycles, (see Astrology, Numbers & other Divination Arts) there is some degree of opening available. The more we are aware of this the more opening and clearing work we can do to maximize our potential. Guidance can give us clues as to what we need to do to heal ourselves.

I encountered a tremendous opening when I traveled around the world in 1979. Uranus was making a trine to Pluto. The energy that Uranus reflects is extremely spontaneous, intuitive, radical and a departure from the norm to experience new things in order to open and obtain more enlightenment. The energy of Pluto represents deep penetrating insight and the ability to psychically determine wisdom and energy and transform in Higher Ways.

One beautiful sunny California afternoon, I was sitting at an outdoor cafe with my friend Angelika, who was in the travel business. I had not done any extensive traveling prior to this time. She was expounding on her six week trip and all of the areas and countries she would be visiting on a Marco Polo-like expedition. This was to be an around the world adventure. Something inside of me said *that's for me!* I immediately said, "I'm going." It came out of nowhere; I didn't think about it, I just acted spontaneously. She was shocked by the immediacy of my decision and asked, "Don't you want to take the brochures home and think about it?" I replied, "I'll take the brochures and I'll go, I've already made up my mind." I was in a cycle which was completely spontaneous, intuitive and strong. It was not necessary to think, which was unusual for me at that time in my life. I had always planned things out very carefully. I was unaware at that time that I would be guided to travel around the world for six months!

In the past, I was always great at melodrama and I changed that for myself. I had been excellent at displaying temper tantrums and I was proficient at sadness and loneliness. When I cleared my heavy emotional baggage, it freed me up to be lighter and more humorous in my presentation. Part of my process of becoming an entertainer was healing my dysfunction and growing emotionally. Mind Heart Harmony gave me the confidence I needed to perform intuitively in front of others without worry, concern and fear of failure.

If we read books like *Think and Grow Rich, the Magic of Thinking Big,* etc., we see the repeating theme about growing up and getting rid of our negativity to become successful. There are so many books that encourage elimination of negative concepts and thoughts. These limitations impede our success and need to be purged.

Anyone Can Receive Guidance

Most people have not been taught to access their Guidance (or even know they have it) and have not even been aware that they can access it. The tendency is to think that only "special" people can access Guidance, and only these "special" people can hear or seek Divine Guidance. This is simply not true. Accessing Guidance is the same as exercising a muscle to strengthen that muscle and everyone can use these tools and methods to exercise and strengthen his/her access to Guidance. Anyone who is devoted and dedicated can.

Mystical Preparation

Many times people believe that mysticism is about the work of the devil or that they are not supposed to understand it because it is a great mystery. According to Webster's Dictionary, mystical means "something that is spiritually significant or symbolic and relating to intuition, contemplation or meditation of a spiritual nature."[33] Mystical behavior has been relegated to the saints in the past and not the general populace indicating that we have to be very, very special and very, very holy and pure to understand the mysteries of life.

[33] Webster's New World Dictionary, 2nd edition (Cleveland: William Collins Publishers, 1979) p. 942

Life can be a great mystery or we can choose to develop ourselves to understand our life better with contemplation, meditation and learning the symbols. We feel dis-empowered when we do not understand our life process; we feel victimized and we are easily controlled by others who say they have our best interest ate heart. We need to know through our own intuitive Guidance form our own higher Self what is best for us in the choices that we make.

There are many steps in doing this preparation work. It is vital to develop our intuition. It is necessary to be aware and feel our feelings. It is important to notice everything. It is essential to learn symbology. The more we understand the Guidance Groupings in Chapter 11, the more aware we can become of our own life's mysteries.

Develop Our Intuition

The more time we experience being still and consciously moving the breath through us, we will hear the voice of our intuition. Spend time listening for it, be patient, it takes time to develop this connection. The more empty we are, the more opportunity we have to hear and feel. By clearing the emotional and mental bodies, as I mentioned before, the more available we are to our own intuition.

I was gifted with intuition as a talent. I didn't realize that this was the case earlier in my life. It was after I cleared my mind and my emotions that I was able to feel it. I developed my intuition. I co-created and refined this aspect of myself as a party psychic. At first, as a beginner, I was so amazed each time the recipient would say, "Oh wow, how did you know that?" It seemed like a miracle every time. I began trusting it more and more. I became more and more creative in my expression of it. As a result of trusting and exercising these "muscles," my reputation as a party psychic mushroomed. The demand grew and so did my private counseling practice. It wasn't long before I was providing multi-cultural entertainment and talent, as well, to the studios, major corporations, special events and private parties.

Feel Our Feelings

Many of us are not able to perceive subtle feelings. Many of us have been conditioned to ignore them. For some, it is painful to feel their feelings so they ignore or deny them. In the practice of yoga, we breathe all the way down to abdomen completely before breathing into the chest. On the exhale, we squeeze the abdominal muscles to force the air out. The pelvic girdle rocks forward with the inhale and back with the exhale. This action moves cerebral spinal fluid up and down the spine. Consciousness travels on the breath and on that fluid. Our ability to feel inside our body and be perceptually aware of everything around us is enhanced by the breath. If we are a chest breather and we neglect to breathe all the way down to the abdomen, we will not be able to activate that pump as well.

These subtle feelings are clues to what is going on in our experience. Our body is important in its ability to relate what is going on in our life. Please do not ignore your feelings and your body. It will block your ability to obtain important sensory information.

As we open up our emotional body and release the stored emotions, we are ready to feel more deeply. Begin by becoming aware of your own energy field using the palms of your hands and moving through it. Feel in front of you around you, up and down. Feel close to your physical body and bring your hands out by degrees and notice the difference. When we become more energy sensitive we are able to perceive more subtle energy and feel it in our body. Notice if you feel the "psychic rush" when energy waves pulse up your body and you experience goose bumps and the hair standing up on the skin. This can indicate a validation of something spoken or thought.

We may notice a sensation in our heart when we are reading sadness in another individual. We may notice an uncomfortable feeling in our stomach when someone is having a problem with his or her emotional body. Our head may hurt as we read the energy of too much strain on the mental body. Our throat may have a sensation when someone has not learned to speak their truth or is holding anger or negativity, which they do not know how to vent in a healthy manner. In this way, we are able to interpret the feelings of others as well as our own feelings or wisdom. If we cannot feel, we cannot sense what is happening below the surface. Feeling is extremely important for our awareness.

While reading and interpreting others, it is important not to take on their energy or feelings. We feel and sense them and we release them. It is possible to become enmeshed in that energy, we need to shield ourselves with a prayer of protection. This is a prayer: "I take on nothing that is not my own". Those with more water element are especially permeable to other's feelings and need good boundaries. They need to watch who they spend time with because they can and will sometimes take on that energy.

Notice Everything

To enhance your awareness, be aware of and sense everything around the proximity, emotionally, physically and mentally. To access your Inner world, begin by closing the eyes; open the Inner eyes, the Inner ears and your feelings to all stimuli in your environment. This environment includes both your Inner world as well as the outer physical environment. We may see flashes of color, we may hear a thought or Guidance, or we may feel an experience or sensation. All of these things are important. We need to pay attention closely so we do not miss these signs.

When we are praying for answers, notice everything. One day I was contemplating and praying on how to deal with increased interest rates on my credit card, up to 13.99%. The very next day I received a pre-qualified credit card at 3.9%. Ordinarily, I throw advertising out automatically. This time, I stayed present and available for new opportunities. I would have missed this had I not reminded myself to stay open. Remember, I wasn't just contemplating; I was praying and noticing everything. Recall the expression, "Ask and you shall receive." Perceive everything and then act on the intuitive opportunities.

Learn Symbology

Symbology is the study of symbols. Symbols represent categories of information. Jung utilized symbology extensively. Our modern dream interpretation and analysis comes from his study of symbols. The tarot deck, astrology, colors, numbers, etc. are methods of Divination utilizing symbols.

Symbols and signs offer us an opportunity to perceive what meaning there is and can be correlated. They can be used together to create a greater meaning. Remember, that ancient civilizations drew symbols and representations of their life on cave walls, vases, rocks and other art forms. This is our link with the right brain, our intuitive process. These symbols and signs allow us to access the intuitive wisdom that is activated in our intuitive process. The following represent brief examples of some of the categories of symbols that we will be defining in greater detail in subsequent chapters.

We use color symbology everyday when we drive. Red means stop and emergency. Yellow means caution, slow down, things are changing. Green means go, we have the right of way. This ability to interpret meanings can be related to all the colors.

Animals are another source of symbology. Dolphins and whales indicate greater perception with their sonar and communication as they have been swimming in the oceans of consciousness on our planet for thousands of years. The owl points to higher wisdom as it sits and observes in the night. Birds reflect a message while talking birds represent communication. Lions and tigers can represent rulership, power and strength. The snake and phoenix designate transformation by the shedding of skin and the experience of death and rebirth. The goat, antelope and camel, which are amazingly sure-footed, can indicate being more grounded.

Number one represents unity and wholeness. Number two can represent balance. Number three can represent empowerment, generosity and humor. Number four can represent foundation and manifestation. These are examples of the meaning of numbers. Dates can have great significance. If a number continuously appears on a digital clock, it may have significance for us.

The planets, luminaries and the signs of the zodiac are symbols and representations of energies that can be interpreted in a manner that creates insight and understanding of our life process. This study is a little more complex and requires deeper contemplation and meditation on the meaning and inter-relatedness of each category: the heavenly bodies, the signs of the zodiac and the houses.

Each symbol represents a category that is more universal when we look at the properties of the signs and the symbols. The art of interpreting the symbols is to be able to attune specifically for an individual, including ourselves, based on the experiences and development of the Soul. Everything that Source created has Divine order and wisdom built into it. It is our opportunity to study it, understand it and act on it. (See the Guidance Groupings for categories and meanings.)

My Experience Following Guidance

In the early part of my life, I had no idea what my career path was to be about. I thought it was about making a lot of money, which is what I tried to do unsuccessfully for a while. I did not realize that I was actually preparing myself for exactly what I needed to do in order to get further on my path. I did not have a conscious understanding of what I was preparing for. Some friends suggested I see a tarot card reader. He told me that I would be writing, speaking and teaching. He said communications would be my focus. At the time, it seemed so unrealistic to me, I did not consciously follow that Guidance.

Even though I did not think about Guidance, somehow I was magnetically attracted to what I needed to do to prepare myself. I had no clue in my 20's where I was headed and what I was training for. At this time, I was using my logical, linear skills to learn about business, sales and connecting with the public. I was unaware of using any intuitive skills consciously. It was challenging and stressful to be working in a major corporation. It was necessary to be in denial of many of my own feelings in order to succeed.

I was aware of the cycle that created a tremendous opening for me and left the corporate world. During my time traveling around the world, I listened very carefully and closely. I wrote in my journal every single day. I noticed everything around me. I realized that I needed to change my career path from my contemplation and meditation on everything that I experienced. As a result of being away from the familiar people and things in my life, I felt a growing connection with a Higher Power and a Spiritual presence inside of me. I realized that I could not work for someone else and that I needed to be Inner directed to truly feel free.

Part of my Guidance was to use my entertainment and intuitive skills. I finally experienced what career fulfillment was about. I was able to consciously access my Spiritual

Guidance, entertain, assist others, and support myself. My unique talents were being applied successfully. I was an entrepreneur, my own boss. I never had to report to a career authority figure again. I only had to answer to a Higher Authority, my Inner Self and Divine Mind. I felt truly free on many levels, for the first time in my life. This would not have been possible without devotion and dedication to healing and learning how to access the Superconscious and interpret it.

Realization of Our Divination

How to Know When We Have the Right Answer, Right Place & Right Time

A commonly asked question is how do we recognize when something comes from Higher Guidance? What are the signs, feelings etc., which indicate we got it? When we truly get Guidance, there is clarity, a clear resonance and every cell in our body tingles and feels good about the Guidance. Our body feels so good to the point that goose bumps may rush up our body like an electric wave through us. There is an experience of complete confidence and trust in a successful outcome.

When I followed Guidance by relocating to Hawaii, all things were effortless, easy and just fell into place. I was blessed with the perfect home and found the exact kind of work I desired. I felt great and right on target. Things manifested even better than I imagined. There was magic and synchronicity.

When we don't experience actual Divination, there is a feeling of being incomplete and unsure. The reaction is more like a presence of uncertainty and insecurity. There are more questions instead of feeling like we have the answer. We keep asking. Things don't seem to come together well or at all.

A friend of mine decided she wanted to leave Chicago. The winters were just too cold for her. She decided to move back to Los Angeles. When she arrived, nothing seemed to go right or work out for her. She couldn't seem to find a good place to live. She felt blocked and frustrated when I received her call. Of course, I immediately asked if she had prayed for Guidance. She had not. I was not surprised, based on her results.

If we receive clear Guidance as to something that we have not anticipated, trust it and act on it anyway. It takes great courage to act on something the ego mind has not thought of or considered. It will produce the same positive results, regardless.

Many times we try to force things or try to make things happen with unsuccessful results. It is an indication that we are not in the right place for us or the cycle may not be right. If we go against our personal cycles, it's like attempting to swim against the current. We don't seem to get very far and we expend a lot of energy. We can do it, as we have the gift of free will. Another choice would be to go with the flow and with our cycles. It is okay just to be and wait until the cycle changes. One of the keys to success and happiness is having good timing.

Divine timing is our being on time with the Universal scheme and personal Self-Unfoldment. We are told "timing is everything" and this is really accurate. With the tools of Divination, our sense of timing is sure to be accentuated, confirmed and validated. We can experience a feeling of being in the right place at the right time. Everything can manifest with complete ease.

Resonation

When we feel at one with our intuition, there is an echo of validity in our body. We know it's the truth on the inside. There is a feeling of correctness and well being to the point of celebration. It feels good when the truth resonates. There can be the "psychic rush" up the body, which is created by an electromagnetic resonance to the truth. We may say something or hear an animal or bird, insect or reptile that validates it with their unique sound, like it's echoing our truth. We can hear it repeated on the radio or TV from the announcer, a song, a show or a commercial that is currently playing.

Ease

When everything falls into place perfectly, naturally with its own unique expression, there is ease. There is no struggle, no effort, frustration and impatience. It feels natural and easy. We may marvel at the simplicity and the beauty in which the experience is unfolding. It feels Divinely inspired. It feels like something that was beyond our human ability to create so perfectly. It is like slipping into something comfortable and having it fit perfectly and look great. When it has more ease, we know we have accessed our Guidance.

Validation - Reflection in Life

When we notice doors closing in our life, look for the open doors that present themselves. These new doors represent and validate where we need to go next. They reflect our new goal and direction. This is why it is important to notice everything. If we focus only on the doors that are closing, we will miss the ones that are opening.

When we make a choice that reflects our intuition and Guidance, we will see a positive reflection in our life that validates it. We may feel a confirming feeling or resonance that we spoke of previously and/or we may feel the ease as well. We will feel more on target with our goals. We will recognize a new level of experience entering into our life. Our life will seem better. We will see a direct reflection if we ask for it, that confirms or gives evidence which choice is the proper direction.[34]

An example was when I wanted to go hiking into a valley by accessing it on a very high ridge. It started raining and the trail was narrow, tenuous and muddy. I stopped to ask for Guidance because it was dangerous to continue. After my prayerful connection, I stood up and immediately about 25 bright green parrots came flying out of the valley, directly in front of me and then made a perfect U turn back into the valley. I knew my prayer had been answered. I got the "green" light from the Universe and proceeded, knowing I was safe.

[34] See Nature's Reflection of Divine Order

Chapter 6

Developing Our Spiritual Focus

Developing our Spiritual focus is essential for getting the most Spiritual Guidance. When we attune to our Spiritual Self with the correct body position, we have a much better opportunity to access Guidance. It is important that we understand we have a perceptual center, which is like a radio transmitter and receiver for communicating in a more multi-dimensional way. We can access our Spiritual Guidance and perceive the Guidance of our angels and guides through this transmitter. The alpha state allows us the opportunity to relax deeply enough to quiet the mind so that we are more receptive to whatever is coming through. When we develop our focus we will not be distracted from our quest.

The mind can become the master and take us away from our intuitive Guidance or it can become our servant with training. Only then are we free of the mind's hold on our consciousness. We will find that relaxing with conscious awareness of the breath will assist us in going deeper into the alpha state. It is there where we can commune and develop a relationship with our Divine Inner Self. Also essential to the process, is our intention and prayers for Guidance.

Body Position

Correct body alignment facilitates our ability to move energy and consciousness up and down the spine, to relax better and be more receptive for Guidance. The spine must be aligned so that the vertebrae stack one on top of the other in proper posture. With core stabilization, we can straighten the spine to receive more ultrasonic core current. We can lie down with our back flat on the floor or bed or we can sit in any yogic posture. A yogic posture is designed for proper spinal alignment.

Learn to sit, stand and lie in proper alignment. If we do not know how, take a class in yoga or postural training. The more we train for posture and alignment, the better our energy flows through us. As we expand and move our energy more consciously through us, the more our body and being are lighter. Our bodies will become a more comfortable place to live in. The more comfortable we are in our body, the easier it is to receive Guidance. Yogic postures and breathing can open our energy channels and awareness. There is an integration of body, mind and breath that enhances relaxation.

Another opportunity for self-care is foundation building, core stabilization and alignment training. In foundation building, we learn to strengthen the ankles, the calves, the thighs and the buttocks with the proper neutral pelvic position. With core stabilization, strengthening the muscles to support a neutral pelvic girdle allows the back to assume better alignment naturally. We can eliminate the curvature of the lower body when we strengthen our lower abdominals to push out gently for support and the upper abdominals to pull in at the belly button toward the spine. We create upper body alignment when we gently squeeze the rhomboids, the muscles between the shoulder blades which lift the chest, bringing the shoulders back and down. To honor and care for our body, we must be aware of the importance of our spinal alignment. If one of our vertebrae is out, or our muscles are tight, we will feel compression and contraction. It will take our awareness away from our breath and our focus.

The body may be used in an active meditation state for enhanced awareness and Guidance. It usually requires a repetitive movement. For example, Sufi dancers twirl around and around in the same direction. Runners receive Guidance in the repetitive movement of running. Dancers can access that state through ceremonial dance experiences.

The Perceptual Center

In order to direct ourselves to the Superconscious in the Spiritual centers, we must learn how to gain access through the doorway of the perceptual center. The perceptual center is sometimes referred to as our third eye. It is the gateway to the Spiritual center of Higher Knowing in the physical body. It is located between the eyebrows about two inches inside of the head.

To access this area, lift the eyes and the focus, inward and upward gently. Allow yourself to be in this state undisturbed and in a yogic position for proper breathing. Learn to be patient because it takes time to develop your ability to access this center. When we do, it is like having the Akashic Records or Hall of Libraries available to obtain answers and information with our Higher Knowing. We have a wealth of multi-dimensional resources within our perceptual center to be accessed at will, once we learn how.

When my dear friend Anya passed away, I had another opportunity to use my Guidance. All of her friends and family were gathered and it was remembered that Anya shared that she had some cash put away for her daughter in one of her books. The entire wall of the room was lined with books from floor to ceiling. It was going to be a difficult task to go through all of those books to find the money. Some people went over to the shelves and started to pull out books, leafing through the pages. I immediately turned my focus inward and upward for Guidance. When my eyes returned to the bookshelf, my attention went directly to a book that seemed to immediately jump out from the rest. I went straight to that book and opened the pages to the exact location of the money. This saved time and energy and was very beneficial to her daughter, Sara.

Be aware that in the course of our intuitive development, we will obtain results based on our own personal belief systems. The more we believe it is possible for us, the better our results will be. Everyone has intuition to some degree. We will be able to expand our intuition by using the tools and techniques in this book. We will experience much more success when we expand our Spiritual focus. It will give us more awareness on a multi-dimensional level. We will have a greater sense of the whole picture and find unity instead of feeling separate.

Utilizing these techniques does not necessarily require a Spiritual focus. Understand that Guidance can come from a variety of sources. Make sure that there is comfort with the source that is chosen. We have better results when we cultivate the Spiritual part of ourselves. We cannot rely solely on our mental logical, linear and rational mind. We already have the gift of intuition and if we want more, we must devote ourselves to that Higher Place in us. Our Spiritual birthright, as the Divine Child, needs to be accessed. We need to put our focus in this direction for the best results.

If we have not had a Spiritual focus in the past, this book will suggest how and what we can do to access our perceptual center and enhance our perceptions beyond the five senses. Everyone can become more multi-dimensional in his or her awareness. To be more multi-dimensional is being able to perceive beyond our third dimensional reality of time and space. There are 12 dimensions in total, according to many sources. We perceive only a small part with our logical linear minds. A Spiritual focus allows us to expand into so many more dimensions. We can fly with the Angels!

The Alpha State

The alpha state is a state of relaxation when the body is totally and completely relaxed to the point where all of the body parts feel warm and heavy, like they don't want to move. We are still consciously aware of everything inside of the room and yet we are open and able to hear our highest Guidance through our intuition and Superconsciouness. It is a most receptive state and happens naturally just before falling asleep and before waking. This time is particularly effective for prayers, reprogramming the subconscious or listening to hear the answers of any problem or dilemma we may have.

Many great inventors, philosophers and mathematicians have utilized the alpha state of relaxation. Thomas Edison and Albert Einstein were famous for their "naps." They utilized the alpha state quite frequently in their work. It was in their naptime, when solutions and creative ideas would come through, effortlessly. This enabled them to tap into Higher wisdom for physics, mathematics, and for inventions that had never been discovered previously, according to our history.

Daydreaming is an alpha state. It is a pleasant reverie and break from the mundane world. We can consciously direct our daydreams on subject matter and outcome. It is a visualization experience and may lead to intuitive insight. When students daydream during their classes, it may open their ability to learn the subject matter even more deeply. It is not good to assume that day dreaming is not an effective state for learning.

There are many tools that we can utilize to enhance the alpha state. Music enhances our ability to enter the alpha state; it affects our brain waves. Everyone has a different receptivity to different rhythms. Choose rhythms that stimulate relaxed awareness like environmental, easy listening music or stimulated awareness as in a tribal rhythmic beat. What ever takes you to that state is best for you.

Get comfortable in nature or any quiet place free from distraction. Nature is the closest we can get to perfection, since the Divine created it. It can promote the resonance of Divine order and our intuition to access it. Everyone loves to be in the beauty of nature, it is inspiring. We feel transformed. The air is clearer and cleaner and oxygen is more available. Many people go a nature spot to think or just to be and find answers without even knowing that they came there for Guidance.

In addition to music, listen to guided imagery meditation tapes or CD's. They can assist and teach us to get to deeper states of relaxation and awareness. We can buy or learn these concepts from books or seminars at most metaphysical bookstores, large bookstore chains or through your favorite authors and speakers.[35] Another idea is to create our own tapes/CD's. We can use the progressive relaxation from our feet up to our head or from the extremities to the interior. We can record questions to ourselves to be answered after the induction process. These can be specific questions accompanied by a long pause allowing our intuition to be activated.

I did not know any of this in the past. The alpha state of relaxation meant nothing to me. I was from a middle class family with no obvious intuitive gifts or strong psychic experiences that I was aware of. No one practiced yoga or understood the importance of the breath in my family. I only knew about altered states of consciousness that were reflected in

[35] See last page of book, "Relaxation & Empowerment."

the consumption of alcohol or mind altering drugs. This was self-medication, a way of avoiding the pain of our reality and not a sacred practice. Later, I realized that my Mother and I had many psychic experiences that I had not acknowledged because I was not familiar with the concept.

We can obtain a state of alpha by simply staring at one point. Focus on something like a candle or mandala[36] or a sound, like a waterfall. It is the lifting of the eyes inward and upward to access the actual Spiritual centers which give us a stronger link to our Guidance. Rather than getting just little intuitive flashes, we can feel a sense of connection, oneness and a sense of knowing more completely.

Repetitive movement is extremely helpful in accessing intuition. We can access intuition while walking, running or doing any aerobic exercise. In this state, endorphins are released that promote relaxation, feeling good in our body and the mind clears. It creates a more receptive state when we are doing something involving repetitive movement that does not require mental focus.

Art and artistic projects promote that same access to the right brain and intuition. We are relaxed, focused and yet not using the left brain. We achieve a sense of union just like we do with repetitive movement. If we like to paint, draw, doodle, do pottery, basket weaving, flower arranging, etc. this is another door of opportunity to access our Guidance.

How to Focus

We can become more creative and inventive in our own life by developing a Spiritual Focus. When we are posed with a question or at a crossroad in our life, remember to lift the eyes to the perceptual center. Ask in a prayer for Guidance and clarity. With proper eye position, patience and devotion; we can access our Superconscious.

To develop our Spiritual focus further, we need to practice finding the place of stillness inside our Self. Close your eyes, preferably in nature, and focus the eyes upward and inward. Lifting the eyes heavenwards gives us the opportunity to get a Higher response, from the Superconscious. Nature expands our connection with Guidance. In flotation tanks people feel the stillness, as sensory deprivation also enhances intuitive response.

When there is a mis-use of energy or poor choices that result in undesirable behavior, we need to learn to accept responsibility. The best way we can accept responsibility and develop a conscience is through contemplation in the stillness with sensory deprivation. Parents need to be aware that sending their children to their rooms equipped with radio,

[36] A mandala is a sacred geometric design created with the intention to produce a more multi-dimensional focus.

television, video games, etc. does not make an effective choice for contemplation and the development of their conscience.

In the past, parents and teachers used to make their misbehaving children stand in the corner with their backs facing outward. Their attention was directed at the seam of the walls only. This was a crude meditational experience with sensory deprivation and yet seemed to be very effective. Today, we have more space and can dedicate a room or an area as a meditational refuge with Spiritual accoutrements. This keeps us focused on a more Spiritual level and inspired, while we contemplate our conscience. Ask children and yourself to meditate about choices and to come up with a higher and better choice. We can make better choices when we devote contemplation time to them. We are allowing our children the experience of finding their focus and developing their conscience by our example and providing them with a space in which to facilitate it. We are not making them wrong; we are giving them the opportunity to learn how to make wiser choices. Express validation to your children when they come up with better choices. This develops their Self-confidence and Self-esteem. They will learn to look for answers inside themselves instead of being confused or relying on others.

In concert with accessing the Superconscious, trusting in the Guidance that does come through is fundamental for what we have prayed for and received. We don't want to trust in anybody else's guidance unless it resonates with our own. Two of the most significant aspects are to learn to hear, see or experience it; and then to totally rely on this Inner Guidance. Once we hear Guidance intuitively or symbolically, we need to act upon it and be devoted to it. Our acting upon this Guidance honors Spirit. It is how we make the access of our Guidance grow.

Perhaps the most difficult part of receiving Inner Guidance is the urge to deny or negate the Guidance in some manner. For example saying to yourself "oh, I didn't get it" or "oh, that can't be it". This urge to mis-trust is the single most difficult obstacle to overcome. However, by focus, practice, and trusting, then watching the results unfold, we will become proficient in receiving Guidance.

It was necessary for me to observe and record my astrological cycles like a scientist for two years before I was willing to admit what a perfect reflection they were. This will probably be true for those of us who are gifted in our mental and more scientific talents. This will be true for those who are more mental and linear. It will take convincing results before our mind can expand and open to Higher Guidance. We have to believe it is possible first.

The Breath

Inspiration happens as a result of the breath. It is the Spirit in 'inspiration' that we seek to experience through the breath. Guidance can be more easily achieved through breathing in yoga postures so that the energy moves through us unimpeded. We don't need to do anything complicated. Sit up or lie down so the spine is straight and the chest lifted by bringing the shoulder blades back and down, so consciousness can travel up and down the spine better in the cerebral spinal fluid. Then listen to our breath. For deep abdominal breathing, breathe into the abdomen filling it completely, then into the chest and exhale completely. The breath takes us to a more relaxed place.

The breath changes the actual physiology of our physical body with the increased levels of oxygen. It also changes our state of consciousness. We can achieve an alpha state of relaxation with the breath. Some yogis have achieved the state of theta through their breathing techniques. This has been scientifically measured. When we exhale with the sound of 'haaa', it assists us in releasing our tension, stress, and changing our level of relaxation.

The breath is inspiration, if you want more Spirit in you, practice using breathing techniques:

1. Deep abdominal breathing consists of filling the abdomen completely first, then filling the chest and then exhaling with the Haaaaaa breath. It releases tension and promotes relaxation; we receive more life force and create a stronger Spiritual connection.

2. Alternate nostril breathing consists of placing the index finger on the forehead and the thumb and middle finger on the cheeks, available to close one nostril. Pressing the thumb against one nostril, we breathe in through the open nostril filling the abdomen completely first, then filling the chest and then finally exhaling through the same nostril. We repeat the process with the middle finger on the other nostril. This balances the right and left hemispheres of the brain to achieve integration and clearing of the mind.

3. Breath of fire is achieved by placing the hands on the thighs bending forward slightly and forcefully exhaling through the nostrils. There is a natural inhalation that occurs from the vacuum of the exhalation. The abdominals are contracted upwards with each breath. It moves the energy of consciousness from the base of the spine and up with each breath. It also opens the Spiritual centers.

There are many different kinds of breathing techniques to achieve altered states of consciousness. I have just mentioned a few. I invite you to discover more.

Relationship with Our Divine Inner Self

Cultivating a relationship with our Divine Inner Self changes our world. It expands our consciousness beyond our third dimensional reality. We can know more and be wiser when we have this kind of relationship. We can know exactly what the best choices are for our Highest expression.

Self-knowing is the best kind. It comes from our Spiritual Self. It is important to be able to access it to give us enhanced perception beyond our five senses and then we can integrate it with our linear rational mode of thinking. The advantage is it to know and utilize our whole brain and have that perception. It has everything to do with knowing the Self. We can not get Self-knowledge anywhere else. It takes time and patience to cultivate this relationship. There is no other way to know Self.

The key is our relationship with our High Self. You can not develop true Self-confidence, Self-esteem, and Self-fulfillment in any other way that is absolutely fulfilling. Ask people who have become very, very successful and yet are depressed, or those who are very wealthy and are suicidal or artists that have been very creative and yet unfulfilled. It is a result of not having an integrated connection with the Self that exists within.

We are all a Ray of Divine Love and Light, it is our Spirit within us, our Soul, our Divine Inner Self. By making contact and having a relationship with that Divine Spirit within, we grow Spiritually. I have been and will be referring to that Spirit in a devotional way by capitalizing any reference to it, to honor Spirit.

Also the capitalization will distinguish the Spiritual Self from the small personality "self." This book presents techniques that teach us to access our Superconscious mind and our own Inner Self. The Superconscious is a Universal Collective Consciousness; whereas our Inner Self is more personal to us. We can gain entrance to the Superconscious by cultivating the relationship with the Inner Self. They both afford excellent Guidance.

Many people have difficulty accessing their own Inner Self and Superconscious. Most of the time, patience is the problem. Patience is positively a feminine virtue. The most difficult part of accessing my own Inner Self was the aspect of having patience. I am sure this may be true for many of us. Methods of becoming more integrated with our masculine and feminine will assist us and will be discussed in the following chapter.

Effective meditation and contemplation experiences and exercises can be utilized to help us get into the practice of "tuning in". Once the practice is established and exercised, "tuning in" occurs more naturally. It becomes a part of our everyday life experience without effort. The more open and receptive we are, the more we can receive.

As we honor our intuition and our Inner Self more, we will be able to tap into the Superconscious and acknowledge its Presence. It will naturally become more of a partner with our intuition and our conscious mind. The more we follow our intuition, the more clearly the Superconscious will speak through it in each moment of our life.

If we ignore or neglect the wisdom of the Superconscious, we will be presented with the consequences of impaired access and success. When the intuitive flashes are ignored, they diminish in intensity and frequency. Accessing our Higher Guidance is like exercising our muscles, so they can serve us better in life. If we don't, we lose tone and strength to the point that there is atrophy and we experience weakness. If we are willing to make important choices without our Superconscious, if we negate it, or ignore it, we risk suffering consequences.

Listening and honoring the intuition and our Divine Inner Self, which is where the Superconscious is accessed from, is like having the Divine whisper in our ear. Out of love for the Divine, act on that Guidance and achieve more success and fulfillment. Our life or the lives of our loved ones may one day depend on it.

The more time we spend with focus in this area, the more Spiritual evolution we will experience in our daily life and we will be reclaiming lost Spiritual and evolutionary perceptions and powers. We will know our Self more deeply and intimately as a being and a Divine Child of a Higher Power, than we have ever thought possible.

Learn to create the body, mind/emotions, and Spirit trinity synergy. Some of us have lost our 'Soul-fullness'. We need to regain that sense of "Spirit in residence" meaning within ourselves. We have been trained in our schooling to continue to learn new things, to develop our minds. In more recent years, we have become more active in terms of our physical fitness. Gyms, weight training, and cardio-vascular exercise are a part of many people's lives. We have a responsibility to develop ourselves on all levels. Anything that is going on with our body, mind or emotions is a clue as to how healthy and well balanced we are. Spiritual training is equally important. In our fast paced modern lives, our Spiritual body is easily neglected. We need to slow down and be still to feel our Spirit. When we have it all in balance, we feel more whole and Self-empowered. Our lives will reflect more harmony and success.

I was once lost to loneliness, sadness, grief, a sense of separation and a feeling of being unfulfilled in love. I did not enjoy or want to continue to live in this way. I really thought I might be better off dead. Through developing and cultivating a relationship with my Inner Self, I gained peace, contentment, love and fulfillment. My life became an experience worth living. I realized I truly was a Divine Child of a Loving Divine Mother/Father and I wanted to be here to fulfill my highest Self-expression.

In order to shift our focus, we need to redirect some of our preoccupation with technology and the outer world to our internal Self. This needs to be a part of our early educational experience. The growth that we achieve on an internal level will compliment and expand anything we do in the external environment. Both the internal and external worlds need to be developed equally.

> *Robert Ornstein says, "A medical endeavor is primarily directed toward the treatment of diseases, not toward individual responsibility for health. We attempt to control bodily problems from the "outside" with drugs, rather than to employ the individual built in capacity for self-regulation. As each new drug is developed, each new surgical procedure is perfected, less and less responsibility of the cure is delegated to the patient himself."*
>
> *He also admits "that it is an unbalanced practice in the development of Western medicine." He says "we have almost forgotten that it is possible for the patients themselves to learn directly to lower their blood pressure, to slow their heart to relax at will."* [37]

The more we know our Self, the healthier we can be. We can actually heal and balance ourselves with Self-regulation and we may need the assistance of great health professionals.

Devotional Prayer

The power of prayer is so profound in connecting with our Divine Inner Self and hearing our Guidance. Before doing any Divination activity, the prayer I utilize is "Divine Mother/Father please reveal to me or please tell me". I do this every time I can remember and I ask that it always be my prayer, for the times I forget to ask. My prayer is that simple. Make it your prayer that you are Divinely guided, always. The importance of prayer is our acknowledgement of our intention to connect with Source. Sound is important and saying it out loud can emphasize our determination. These elements in combination give power to our prayer.

The more we perform the lifting of our eyes to get into the Spiritual place, the more automatic the prayer is. The prayer is already there in that Sacred space. As we go into our Sacred place, we say our prayer for more ease in connecting with Divinity.

Learn to practice patience, it is essential. Sometimes the answers do not come right away. They do come in Divine time, though. I have prayed morning and night devotedly for six months, before receiving an answer. You will get an answer. It may not be the answer you had hoped for. It will be for your highest and best.

---

[37] Robert Ornstein, The Psychology of Conscious (W.H. Freeman & Co., 1972)

Chapter 7
Obtaining Guidance Through Intuition and Dreams

Our intuition works in magical ways. Utilizing the senses of seeing, hearing and feeling more consciously opens avenues of intuitive information to you. Get to know which ones you have a talent for.

With my eyes closed, utilizing my intuition, I perceive more multi-dimensional hearing, feeling and seeing, than I do in my normal conscious "eyes open" state. I hear things before people say them. I feel the area of their pain in my own body. I see more in a dream state than I hear or feel in my normal awareness without intuition.

Dreams are doorways to the unconscious mind and the Superconscious. They can reveal parts of ourselves we have hidden, suppressed or repressed. Dreams tell so me much about my own growth and development, as well as my clients'. Through the dream world. I experience great gifts of Guidance from the Superconsciousness, the all-knowing aspect of consciousness. You can too, as you learn to understand the messages in your dreams. We don't have to live in darkness, confusion and uncertainty. All we have to do is ask for clarity and be open to receive it.

See a Picture or Color through 'Clairvoyance'

Clairvoyance is the ability to see, perceive and understand things that cannot be seen by the sense of sight. It is seeing with our Inner eye. It is beyond time and space limitations.

Picture Example

One night I was deeply asleep having gone to bed late in the evening. All of a sudden, I saw a flash of red light in my dream state. I immediately jumped up out of bed to discover my apartment was on fire! My bedroom was filled with smoke. I could have died from smoke inhalation, according to the firemen who came to put out the fire in the living room. My intuitive flash literally saved my life and the life of my roommate. That red flash I interpreted to be an emergency which woke me up immediately.

Another time, I was sleeping and toward early morning I saw the same kind of red flash. I catapulted out of bed, feeling something on my back. I looked back on my bed to see a hundred legged, eight-inch centipede! The sting from this centipede is very painful and toxic. I was saved once again by acting upon the picture I saw.

Hear a Voice or Sound through 'Clairaudience'

Clairaudience is the ability to perceive and hear with our "Inner ears" so it is possible to be made aware of sounds that are not audible or perceived by the normal sense of hearing. It may be our Inner Self, guides, spirits or angels speaking to us.

Voice Example

I was traveling through Europe, the Mid-East, and Asia on a "Marco Polo" overland Journey. Unfortunately, I had not been able to get a visa in the United States to cross the border to travel through Iran. The Ayatollah Khomeini had just seized power and it was unwise as well as unsafe for Americans to pass through. I did not want to fly over Iran. I felt this would deprive me of the overland journey, which is one of the most famous overland experiences ever to be undertaken. The adventurer in me strongly related to the explorer in Marco Polo. I was really disappointed when I could not get a visa, so I began to tune into my Inner Guidance.

We were in the eastern part of Turkey close to the border of Iran. The rest of the group was able to get visas because they were from different countries. They were going to be able to cross over. While waiting for them to get their visas, I was sitting in a Turkish municipal office. I saw a man pass by and I heard my Guidance say, "this man can help you". I got up immediately and went after him to explain my dilemma. Not only did I get a visa for myself; I got visas for three other Americans. This man was wonderful and congenial. We were able to continue on our overland journey, just like Marco Polo! Following Guidance works like a charm. It's miraculous.

Another time I was on the Big Island of Hawaii with my friend Dharma. We had come to see Madam Pele, Goddess of the volcano, do her lava dance out to the ocean. We wanted to go at night for the best viewing. We were so excited and enthusiastic about this experience, we forgot to ask for Guidance prior to setting out. Lava flows can be extremely dangerous and unpredictable. The very evening we arrived, we prepared with flashlights and good shoes to walk the lava fields.

As we began driving toward our destination, a light rain began to fall. It began to increase in intensity until sheets of water were coming down in front of us minimizing our view almost completely. To make matters even more foreboding; the ocean waves began washing up on to the roadside. Suddenly, I heard a voice in my head saying strongly and firmly "Turn Back NOW!" My friend got the same message at the same time. We immediately turned the car around. All of a sudden, we noticed that it was completely clear in front of us, in the direction we were heading. Behind us it was dark, stormy, and frightening.

The calm and the peace were so shockingly different from the strong forces of nature we had just experienced. We sighed with relief and realized that we were not meant to visit that night. Maybe it was unsafe to go that night. We might have been warned about impending danger because it felt very dangerous as we drove toward it. The second night after checking our Guidance, we chose to go and felt completely trusting that it was the right time. The weather was perfect and we felt called to that place.

When things don't look good or feel good, it is important to listen, it might save your life. This brings up an important point that I like to remember. Before going into any nature adventure, I advise all to tune into their Guidance to ask for permission, safety and protection as well as formulating an intention or focus for the journey.

Get a Feeling or Information through 'Clairsentience'

Clair-sentience is the ability to perceive and understand information through feelings or sensations which are not felt by the normal sense of touch. Our bodies may respond to a situation or someone else's experience with a sensation. In dreams, our feelings about what's happening are one of the most important aspects in dream interpretation.

Feeling Example

While living in California, I experienced a deep foreboding feeling that my mother was going to die. This strong feeling occurred on a Monday. She resided in Arizona and although she had cancer, she was very active, and gave no clue that her death could be imminent. I immediately constructed an astrological chart and saw that the cycle she was in indicated that she may leave suddenly. The feeling was so strong; I packed up my bags promptly and flew to Arizona.

Meanwhile, my mother had been to the bank and the hairdresser, generally carrying on as normal. As soon as I arrived on Saturday, she took to her bed. I called all of her friends and said, "This might be the right time to say good-bye to Lois". They asked, "How could this be? She's been up and around and fine." I told them I was feeling strongly that if they wanted to say good-bye, this was the time. They came and we had a lovely good-bye party for her. I know that she was happy to have everyone there. She deteriorated quickly and by Monday evening her Soul left her body and passed into the Light of another dimension. She even waited until I returned from dinner to make her transition, while my brother and I were present and praying with her. I did not predict that she was "going to die." I responded to my feelings. I wanted to honor her free will.

Isn't it interesting that a week after the onset of the feeling, on a Monday, she left? She had all of her loved ones there for her. She had a great send off and I got to say good-bye as a result of following my feelings. More than telling her good-bye and that I loved her, I was even able to assist her with her transition, by guiding her into the Light.[38] This was a most incredible experience for me because I had not participated in a consciously assisted death process before that time.

Ask a Question

When we are unclear about a situation, a person, or a thing, ask Divine Mother/Father to show us the answer. There are many methods we can use to obtain our answers. I have listed various kinds of techniques for you to see what's available. (See Astrology, Numbers & Other Divination Arts.)

We can ask about relationships, job opportunities, talents, challenges, appointments, vacations, motives, actions, new locations, endings, beginnings, etc.; Anything that we truly need an answer about. It can be a major or a minor question. Sincerity is all that is required.

Be Devoted to Getting an Answer

Soon after being hired, I was suddenly fired as Director of Sales and Marketing for a subsidiary of a multimillion-dollar corporation. At first I thought it was a joke, as it happened on April 1st. When I realized it was for real, I was totally shocked. I had been on the job for only one month. In that time, I had done a promotional mailing and had successfully made a contact and appointment with one of the largest, most sought after accounts in Los Angeles.

I was scheduled to present our services and a proposal to one of the largest studios. Since my questions about my dismissal went unanswered, I consulted another manager in the firm I had become acquainted with. He replied, "Most people are just finding the restrooms and the water cooler, you have done so much in the short time you've been here. I don't know why."

[38]Read Stephen Levine, *Who Dies*

One of my friends suggested that we do a Tarot card reading about that situation. I sincerely wanted to know what had happened. We discovered that the Vice President's mistress, who had an office next to mine, got jealous and gave him an ultimatum. I had noticed her cool abruptness, yet I was too busy with my marketing campaign to give it much thought. It finally made great sense. It resulted in a wrongful discharge suit that was settled out of court in my favor.

If I had not consulted Guidance, I would have missed an opportunity. I would have continued to replay the events in an attempt to figure out what I had done wrong. The settlement money came just in time to save the family home from liens against it.

Be totally devoted to your quest for an answer. Say your prayers day and night. Trust completely that an answer will be realized. Never give up. You deserve an answer and your Divine Mother Father want to give it to you.

The Pendulum, a Tool for Guidance

The really interesting thing about pendulums is that you can use anything that can swing, like a necklace or a key on a chain. One of the easiest and most convenient methods of Divination is to use a pendulum. A pendulum is anything hung from a fixed point that can swing freely back and forth or in circles.

I believe that the pendulum can be used to detect a positive or negative answer in our energy field. My theory is that a pendulum's movement can interpret the electromagnetic waves of our Higher Knowing. I believe we can ask our Inner Self, the Superconscious and/or Divine Mother/Father to guide the motion of the pendulum.

Electromagnetic waves have a positive (electric) and a negative (magnetic) charge. We can ask for Guidance to show us the answer to our question through the swing of the pendulum. We can ask yes or no questions based on the direction of the positive swing and the negative swing.

How to Use a Pendulum

To begin, sit or stand with core stabilization and good posture. Get centered and focus your eyes inward and upward. This prevents you from guiding the pendulum. Use your breath to relax yourself. Say your prayer to Divine Mother/Father. At this point, ask your Guidance to show you a "yes", and then ask to be shown a "no". You can even ask to be shown a "maybe".

When I was new at working with the pendulum, I would ask every time to see yes and no. For me, the pendulum swinging clockwise shows the "no". A "yes" is the pendulum swinging counter-clockwise. A "maybe" is shown as the pendulum swinging vertically or horizontally. Some days it switches, so it is always best to ask if you can't "feel" that you are "switched." Some astrological cycles, up to 2-3 years, it is impossible to rely on the swing.

Some people don't get circles at all, only the linear swinging of the pendulum. There are no hard and fast rules for how the pendulum "should" swing. Rely upon your individual Superconscious to guide the motion of the pendulum in whatever direction it chooses. However, it is my theory that as a person becomes more comfortable with the pendulum method; circular motions will appear rather than linear motions.

If you are seeing small motions, you can ask to be shown bigger motions. Or, if you are seeing only small motions, the answer could be a little "no" rather than a big "NO". Remember to allow for better flow of energy, hold your hand out rather than resting your elbow on something. Pinch the chain or string between the index finger and thumb, allowing it to hang freely. Please understand that during some poor cycles, it doesn't work well at all!

In utilizing the pendulum, it is of utmost importance to phrase your questions very carefully and specifically. A question such as "is it a good idea to go workout?" would be not specific enough. A very specific question would be "is it a good idea to go workout today, this afternoon, for one hour, at my gym?"

You need to be very specific about time, place, person, and kind of activity when formulating your questions. Be as specific as possible or you may not get an accurate answer. It has been my experience that usage of this Divination tool is most challenging in terms of asking the specific question. It is very easy to leave out important details.

There are some people who get very good results by making a statement rather than asking a question. Take the "gym example". "I need to or it's in my best interest to go to workout today at the gym, this afternoon for one hour." There are many people who prefer to make statements. The choice is up to us, if we are more comfortable with questions, ask questions. If we are more comfortable making statements, make statements.

Without accessing our Superconscious, we are more likely to engage in ego mind play rather than being relaxed about our choices. I certainly recommend accessing the Superconscious for answers, especially on major purchases.

Opals are very important to me as a mystical stone in Guidance. I was shopping for opal earrings as my Guidance had directed me. I found some that "spoke to me" and they were priced out of my range. I used my necklace as a pendulum when I was considering if these were the right stones for me and if this was the right time to buy. I got a positive reading on both and received a 4-month, no interest credit plan to boot. I felt totally secure in the purchase I made and knew that I would be able to pay for it.

When making an important buying decision, pendulum for the right time and the right item. You will be much happier if you do and there will be no questions in your mind, "no buyer's remorse".

Vision Quest in Kahana Valley

A vision quest is a rite of passage for some Native Americans. It requires going out into nature without provisions to access the Spirits to get insight and messages. I want to share what I learned from my first uncomfortable, unscheduled vision quest; when I am lost, it is best listen to my own intuition.

One mid-afternoon, my friend Scott and I decided to take a pleasant short hike into the beautiful and pristine rainforests of Kahana Valley on the North shore of Oahu. We got a little map at the ranger station and set off for a 2-hour hike. What we didn't realize, was how numerous cross trails intersected the main trail and were not listed on the map.

We wanted to take a shorter hike because we had only a certain amount of daylight left. Within 2 hours we were hopelessly lost. Nothing looked familiar and the sun was resting lower in the sky. We climbed a nearby hill to see where we were. We gasped when we realized we were about 5 miles into the rainforest away from the ocean where our car was parked and the sun was rapidly sinking on the horizon.

We had no plan for how to get out of our predicament. I felt a rising sense of panic in my gut. I did not have a pendulum. Instead of listening to my intuition, I relied on my male friend's leadership. He suggested that we follow the stream out, reasoning "all streams must empty to the ocean." In my alarm, I agreed. Time was running out. Instead of being still and attuning to my Inner guidance, I trusted his intellect.

We began sprinting through the water, sometimes cutting and bruising ourselves on the rocks in the stream. At times we had to swim with our backpacks on our shoulders, submerging all of our trail food. We were feeling very exhilarated and high thinking we had discovered the solution as the sun was beginning to set. I didn't even feel the bruises and banging of the rocks on my ankles and lower legs. I didn't sense the scratches on my legs as the thorny bushes etched red designs upon them. Then lo and behold, the stream came to an unexpected barrier and ended. It did not go the ocean! We were shocked by our misfortune and we were out of light. We faced the reality with dread that we would be spending the night wet and unprepared in Kahana Valley.

This was an unexpected vision quest. Now we had no food, no water, our clothes were completely soaked and the only thing we had to lie on were the rocks in the center of the stream. The stream had separated, to create an island of rocks. We decided we better take off our clothes or we would freeze to death. We hung them on the bushes, put a wet beach towel down on the gravely stones and huddled together shivering. It seemed as though every insect danced on our bodies, including spiders and mosquitoes. I experienced every single rock that formed my makeshift mattress.

Reclining on our streambed of river rocks for the seemingly endless night, we watched the moon travel from one part of the sky all the way across to the other side. I prayed there would be no rain or flashflood, we were so vulnerable and exposed. There was no comfort and no sleep for me. About 2 a.m. my cotton pareau was dry. We attempted to share its meager warmth and shelter ourselves from the barrage of insect bites. The realization that I had neglected to ask for Guidance and had ended up in this dilemma became so apparent. I was so uncomfortable that I wanted to transcend my predicament. I felt my consciousness lifting out and over my body.

After watching the entire body of constellations move across the sky, finally the dawn arose. We jumped up, grabbed all of our things, we could not wait to get out. His body was covered from head to toes with mosquito bites, fortunately for me, they liked him better. We started back up the stream at a fast pace, when suddenly we spotted a trail marker on the bank of the water. When we got to marker, it did not indicate which way was out. Now, I was listening to my Guidance. My intuition said "use your pareau, tie a knot and make a pendulum." I did as guided and was able to, at each trail crossing, find the way out of the valley perfectly and rapidly.

Why didn't I tune in the afternoon before? I learned a very, very uncomfortable and major lesson. After having a long night of being with my Inner Self, I realized that I had honored someone else's logical deduction and relied on it for my safety and security rather than using my own intuition and asking my Inner Self.

Bruised, battered, bitten, bloodied, relieved and enlightened from spending the night in nature, we emerged basically unharmed from the valley. This example demonstrates very vividly for us, what can happen when we don't listen to our intuition or ask for Guidance. I have never made that mistake since in nature. Do you wonder why?

Ask to Be Shown in Your Dreams—Dream Guidance

Dreams are a wonderful method for accessing our Guidance. Everyone has the ability to sleep and dream. In a dream state, our intuition and the Superconscious can come through easily. All we have to do is ask to be shown or told the answer in our dream. Our feelings about what's happening in our dream are one of the most important aspects in interpretation.

Remember that we are all of the characters in our dreams. These characters represent different aspects of our masculine and feminine selves. A dream can be clairvoyant, in which case it is not necessarily just about us. The males in our dreams represent our masculine qualities. The females represent our feminine qualities. We can determine by our dream subject what qualities need to be enhanced, softened or mitigated.

Our dreams allow us to see what is happening in our personal process relating to the masculine principal of our self-development. Are we too aggressive with our energy or are we responsible? We also can see where we are with the female principal in our dreams. Are we too passive or are we patient? We can determine if we need strengthening of our masculine side or more receptivity of the feminine by the qualities that are exhibited in our dreams.

Dreams about Masculine and/or Feminine Qualities

In one dream, I was walking into a big fair or exhibit that seemed like an interesting place to be. I noticed that there a lot of men with the latest advance technology motorcycles. They were competitors vying for some kind of honor in a contest. I found it fascinating and noticed that a lot of the men were policemen, firemen, more aggressive types as well. As I walked around, it seemed like a safe place to be. There were high school bands playing music and cheerleaders which made it appear okay. I was carrying my cat, Angel, in a backpack as I walked around. Then I was suddenly alerted to danger, when an aggressive man tried to touch my cat. She didn't like it and she bit him. Then he made it apparent that he was going to try to kill my cat. I panicked and ran through the crowds attempting to elude him.

In this dream, the men remind me of my masculine competitive side. In many ways, it serves me. I am comfortable in competition and with technology. I enjoy the hero facet of my personality. I feel comfortable with my masculine action principle.

The music and the cheerleaders reminded me of my feminine side. I also enjoy my feminine side. I enjoy expressing it and feel comfortable in most situations. When there is an unwelcome action, the cat in my dream, was indicating my ability to establish a firm boundary when I felt uncomfortable. I was willing to protect my femininity by eluding the villain! It indicated that I still had some fears about male aggression and needed to learn to be more sensitive with others.

Dreams are another way of reinforcing the right timing. We hear it in business and we hear it in most everyone's success story. "I was at the right place at the right time." Having the ability to discern the right time is an incredible tool. Dreams telling us to take action or how to handle a situation come in perfect time. After observing many dreams, I recognized that they coincide with major planetary cycles. Knowing our perfect timing is everything!

There are three different ways of receiving our dream Guidance. One is very direct and easy to follow; the second one shows us the information clairvoyantly with a clear picture of what's to come. The last and most prevalent kind requires us to use our intuition and dream interpretation of symbols to understand and follow Guidance.

When we want our Guidance to come through our dreams:

1. Say a little prayer to your Divine Mother/Father before going to sleep and after waking, every day asking for your Guidance to come through your dreams.
2. Write a little letter to your Divine Inner Self to show you in a dream what you need to know.

Direct Messages

Sometimes you can obtain a clear, direct message that is free of symbology and interpretation and easy to understand. It is a real gift, be certain to act on it.

"Go to Hawaii and do your work"

My prayer for Guidance as to where to relocate was spoken at the war Heiau on the North shore of Oahu one warm July day, while visiting Hawaii. I prayed, if I am meant to be here, please call me back. After all, who wouldn't want to live in Hawaii?

After living in Los Angeles for eighteen years, I was getting an intuitive feeling it was time to move. I saw the same message in my astrology chart as well. I didn't want to mentally figure out where I should move. I wanted to be Divinely guided. After that July request, I prayed for six months, morning and night, about where I should move with no answer.

Finally on Christmas morning I awoke from a dream, having heard a distinct male voice saying with complete authority and certainty "go to Hawaii and do your work." I immediately took action and started making arrangements. By Valentine's Day, I was totally settled, living in beautiful Hawaii. That was the most direct and specific message I have ever received about locations.

When I arrived in Hawaii, everything fell into place perfectly. A beautiful home in the much desired community of Lanikai was reserved for me, overlooking the ocean. It had a million-dollar view with built in friends and family. My first opportunity, I went to a yoga class at the local gym; they offered me a job teaching yoga starting immediately. I knew I was Divinely guided.

We know when we are in alignment with Divine Guidance when everything unfolds perfectly and in Divine time. Divine time is the time that is Divinely inspired in the Universal scheme of things as opposed to ego time, which is right now! The ego survival mechanism and the personality self want things immediately. These parts of us do not realize Divine Timing. They cannot see the "Big Picture." They only see their small part. Divine Guidance sees omni potently and that is everything!

Clairvoyant Dreams

Clairvoyant dreams show us an exact picture or message of what's true, what's to come if we don't make new choices and what choices we can make that are wise. Sometimes we can even receive the message through the dreams of loved ones.

This dream came from a very dear friend, Bob Perry. Bob and I had been very close and felt like family to each other. Bob is an award winning, gifted writer, producer and director. He does not practice medicine and is not a trained doctor.

After my mother had passed, I was not feeling right or very energetic. I didn't think anything was wrong with me. One day, Bob called and told me he had a dream about me. In the dream, we were in a doctor's examination room. Bob was examining me and said I had a thyroid problem.

After reporting his dream to me, he told me I should have my thyroid checked out. We used to kiddingly call him "Dr. Bob" because he seemed to know about every physical ailment. He had experienced a lot of his own medical challenges. Based on his dream, I went to a thyroid specialist. Sure enough, I had a thyroid deficiency that was diagnosed as hypo-thyroidism. The doctor gave me a prescription and my energy levels seemed to balance out.

If I had not trusted Bob's dream, I would have continued to worsen in my condition. Thank goodness our loved ones can assist us when we don't know, through their dream Guidance. Be open and receptive and listen to your loved ones, they just might have an important message for you.

Dream Symbology

Sometimes answers come in the language of dreams that are symbolic rather than succinct and to the point. That is where we can look to our intuition and the recognition of what those symbols mean.

Carl Jung was well renowned for his insight into symbology. He wrote a great book, "Synchronicities" which relates great information about how all things are connected. It allows us to see the relationship of different aspects of ourselves in symbolic messages. He was a master of dream interpretation in his time. He was convinced that everything in our dreams means something.

Learn what your dreams are saying to you in dream language. It requires learning about the symbolic meaning of masculine and feminine, animals and beings, body parts, numbers, colors, and elements. We will learn more about these in the following chapters.

We can get answers in our dreams. A friend of mine decided to test seeking for Guidance through a dream. She prayed to Mother/Father God to be shown why she was resisting becoming closer to her husband. Upon the second night of asking to be shown the reason, she had the following dream.

In her dream, she was held captive by a monster. This monster was half hairy ogre and half human. The upper body was the ogre and the legs were human. She was not afraid of the monster, but he definitely held her captive. He spoke to her and said that in time she would become used to him. She met up with some other captives and decided they should escape. However, the only way she could escape was for her to make herself very, very small.

Her interpretation was that her relationship with her husband might be causing her harm; (at least the monster part of it). The upper body represents the Higher Self, the heart and the higher seeing. She had lived with him with reservation in the last few years and had grown accustomed to the situation. The other captives she met represented those parts of herself she had inhibited or not allowed their expression to be visible. The only way to stay in the relationship was to remain small; the only escape was her pattern of staying small. Perhaps she was limiting herself or him by forcing the relationship to continue.

After receiving this Guidance, she had the courage to re-structure her life. They decided to separate and divorce. Her husband was free to change his life, which he did with great success. My friend discovered the joy and contentment of more fully expressing her Higher Self. She could have attempted this earlier, but it was not the right time. It is interesting to note that her astrology cycle was Uranus opposite Uranus, indicating she needed to free herself to be who she truly was. The dream gave her the correct timing, everything unfolded perfectly, naturally and in Divine time. Eventually, they reunited and remarried.

Another example of Guidance came after a painful automobile accident in 1999. I was lying awake late at night contemplating and meditating on the significance of this accident. I had begun to doubt myself and my karma, thinking, "What did I do to deserve this?" My planetary cycle was Saturn squaring my natal Sun. This indicated some karmic restructuring, represented by Saturn especially in the area of expression and my finances as indicated by my natal Sun in the second house. When that happens, business and money slow down so a restructuring can happen. I was experiencing a shortage of income, energy, and enjoyment. As if things were not blocked enough already, there had been a pronounced shortage of appropriate romantic opportunities in my life. I was trying to discern if I had done something wrong, instead of trusting once again that everything happens for our Highest and best. The answer to the question of the significance of the accident was revealed clearly and beautifully in this next dream.

I dreamed I was with my friends and we were exercising. I felt a loose tooth and I pulled it out. It was old and damaged and only one-third of a full tooth. It also had a long root (this is something deeply rooted in the past). At first I was alarmed and one of my friends said "That's okay, you didn't need that anymore." Then parts of the other teeth started to fall out. The teeth were old and had to go. The first handful contained two small green filaments. My friends said, "That's really good, it's Dentyne, it will make brand new teeth; save them." One of the filaments dropped and I was concerned that I would not have enough. Then, more teeth came out in waves with more green filaments. I got more and more, in fact, there was an abundance of green filaments to make new structures.

The activity of exercising in this dream indicates doing something positive for me and my development. The friends represented my guides letting me know that it was perfectly all right that those teeth (structures in my life) be released. It was important for them to come out, as they were no longer needed. The fact that the root was long indicated some really deeply rooted condition of the past. The green filaments represented health, well being, prosperity, romance, and the ability to re-build myself even better than before.

This dream about green filaments and my teeth corresponded to planetary cycles and a message I had experienced while doing table tipping, another form of Guidance like the pendulum, in which a table is used. The teeth in this dream are reflected by the planet Saturn. Saturn represents all of the structures in our physical body, our spine, our teeth, and all of our bones. The dream was true to my process at that exact planetary cycle. The results were that everything was going to be okay, that was the exact message I received from my departed parents during a "table tipping" Guidance session. (See Chapter on Astrology, Numbers & Other Divination Arts, Allowing the Spirits to Come Through, for more information.)

Three different methods indicated the same Guidance regarding the message about letting go and rebuilding new structures. I was really glad to have received this Guidance as I had two serious accidents in less than two years and was in a great deal of intense pain. It was so very reassuring at a time when I really needed it. This dream gave me understanding, hope for the future and a sense of peace.

It is comforting to note that Guidance is reflective in its many forms, from dreams to colors to numbers to planets to symbology to tables to body parts. As we become more experienced about Guidance, we will notice the theme repeating in each tool that we use. In the beginning, I used to use several tools for one question. As I became more experienced, it was no longer necessary as I saw the interrelatedness of the symbology of the tools and the messages. I received the same messages from the various tools. Now I only need to use one tool or just my intuitive knowing.

Our dreams reveal the contents of our unconscious mind. In the dreamtime we can tune into our Superconscious, which knows all, to get more clarity and understanding about our life's process and direction. The symbols in our dreams, as we recognize what they represent, assist us in assessing ourselves and give greater understanding about what needs more attention and balance for Guidance, wholeness and healing.

Many people say they don't dream or they don't remember. Most of us dream and many times forget. I suggest you keep paper and pen or a hand held recorder right next to your bed where you can reach it, without opening your eyes. When you awaken, do not jump up or open your eyes or you can loose the information. Lie quietly; review the scene, the characters, the emotional climate and the action. Without opening your eyes, begin reporting and writing the information immediately. You can rewrite more legibly after your notes are safely recorded. If you are recording, transcribe immediately and you will remember more. If you are having a difficult time getting a dream, here is another tip. Write a letter to your Inner Self, God or Higher Power, whatever you want to pray to or access. Example:

Dear Inner Self/Divine Source,

Please tell me in a dream in a clear manner: (Choose one appropriate question.)

Where I am in my development process?

What choice do I need to make for my highest and best?

What kind of action or timeout do I need to take?

What is the best investment for my time and energy right now?

What is the solution to a specific (describe) problem or challenge?

What does this situation (describe) mean?

Close with thank you, date and sign it! Thank you, _________

Remember, unless the dream is clairvoyant, we are all the characters in our dream. The women represent the feminine part of us and the men, the masculine part. Think about your free associations with the people appearing in your dream. Do you like them? How do you feel about what happens? Describe your feelings and thoughts that are present during the dream. Notice if there are animals or other beings. Look up the messages that are recorded in the Guidance Groupings. Sometimes you will notice colors in your dreams. Look closely at the colors; are they muddied, muted or unattractive? If this is the case, read the challenging messages more closely. Are the colors pretty pastels; or strong, vibrant and beautiful? In this example, read the highest expression more closely.

In the beginning, your success with interpretation of your dreams may vary. It is difficult to see all of the characters in our dreams, as ourselves, particularly when they are negative or undesirable. These characters represent different aspects of our psyche that want and need to integrate to be truly successful in life. Don't be afraid or embarrassed, we have all had many qualities of our self to heal over many lifetimes. I have had dreams when I realized I was the victim and the perpetrator.

Our willingness to be open to receive the truth about ourselves is vital. Whatever it is, we can heal and change! That is what we are here to do.

Chapter 8
Nature's Reflections of Divine Order

By virtue of a Divine Intelligence creating the Universe, there is Divine Order in all of nature. Nature reflects all of our experience perfectly. Native peoples have known this for eons. They have honored it in their lives and in their ceremonies. Native peoples had animal spirits that they believed were specifically there to protect and guide them. They also studied the heavens to observe their cycles. It was their religion and they lived, as they believed. It was a matter of life or death for them.

"For centuries, the Red people have used the omens of nature to arrive at the decisions of entire Nations. All living creatures have their own Medicine messages to share with those who are willing to learn their language."[39]

It is my purpose to share the language, as I understand it. Different traditions may have different interpretations. I am suggesting a system that links several traditions. There is a synergy of energy and symbology. There is Divine Order and repeating patterns in everything and we can learn it.

Repeating Patterns

Four of nature's elements reflect the "duality" of Creation with a positive or negative charge. Human beings and creatures in Creation are masculine or feminine and that continues the theme of duality. Colors reflect the Light of Creation; Universal Harmonic Sound vibrates to create all matter and our individual Ultrasonic core current. These colors and sounds have a specific resonance with our different energy centers. Our bodies and their parts reflect the qualities of specific elements, sounds, emotions, messages, animals, colors, numbers, planets and luminaries which are the stars and moons.

The signs of the zodiac and the planets in our solar system reflect our energies. Numbers, symbols, and geometry give form, meaning and a basis for learning about and applying this information. Our palms, ears, face, and feet reflect our whole body. The state of the entire body can be read on each of these parts. Each body part or area has a correlation with each sign of the various star groupings.

[39]Jamie Sams, *Sacred Path Cards: The Discovery of Self through Native Teaching* (Harper Collins, 1990), 5.

Everything & Everyone Reflects Our Energies

There is unity in everything and everything reflects everything else. The Native Americans called it the "Uniworld, the Universal Family of Creation." We see it in ourselves, in other people, in nature, and even in machines. This is understood and experienced frequently by psychics.

For example, a client called to get some Guidance. While we were on the telephone I immediately started coughing, I could barely speak. I had been totally symptom-free prior to that phone call. I knew immediately that it was reflecting something going on with the client because it was so strong and unfamiliar. When I stopped coughing, I asked her if she has been having problems with her throat. She said that she had been coughing a lot for the last two weeks. She was in a relationship in which she had not worked through certain emotions and communications. They were stuck in her throat.

When she arrived, I was working on this book and the computer locked up. The computer had been working perfectly up until her arrival. Isn't it interesting to see the energy of blocked emotions and communications reflected in a machine? This is an example where my body and my computer responded and reflected her energy. This is a representation of what Carl Jung identified in his book *Synchronicities*—the observation that there is a corresponding timing and energy for all things.

Can you imagine how interesting it is in relationships when our partner is reflecting our energy and we think it's theirs? Many times we project on our loved ones that which we are responsible for. We can take greater responsibility for ourselves when we understand the wisdom of the situation.

The Native Americans believed that the air element was a great portender of wisdom. They felt that the wind spoke to them. Since air is involved with the breath and all vocal communications, it stands to reason. In this tradition, these people would go into to the forest or the mountains to see nature's reflection and meaning as to what they needed to balance or what changes in their life's direction they needed to make. The wind would speak to them by the direction it originated from. They also observed the cycles and used them in practical ways. The wise ones did not force things during a cycle of contraction. They would sit in the silence and wait for messages and the proper timing. They knew how to utilize the energy of these cycles as it manifested.

There are cycles of expansion and contraction; it is best to know what cycle we are in so that we do not have to feel frustrated when we're in a contraction cycle. When our work is slow, it may be that this is a time that we need more silence, contemplation, meditation, healing, and retreat time. When our energy is low, instead of deciding that it is not to our benefit, maybe we need to take time out to receive energy. As we move in to a more expanded cycle, we will feel more energy; there will be more jobs and money to be made. We can see it as perfect timing, Divine timing. It is much easier to flow with the current instead of swimming against it and wearing ourselves out. The wise person understands when the current isn't moving in the direction they desire and doesn't force it. The insightful one knows their cycle, honors it and makes the best use of it!

Elements and Polarity Charge

There are five basic and essential elements in Creation: earth, water, fire, air and ether. Most scientific resources do not include ether, because it is invisible, an unseen force. Each element, with the exception of ether, has a charge of positive or negative. We live in a world of duality or polarity, which is how electricity and sexual attraction are created. Electrons have a negative force field and protons have a positive force field. One is no better or worse than the other! Electrical charge is manifested by an accumulation of electrons to create a negative (receiving) charge. To create a positive (broadcasting) charge there is a loss of electrons.

The masculine has a positive charge and the elements associated with it are fire and air. The feminine carries a negative charge and is associated with earth and water. We generally are polarized more toward one or the other. That is one of the reasons we attract certain people and circumstances. When we have this understanding and know how to apply it, we can balance ourselves better.

Ether is neutral and has no charge; it is free of duality and polarity. It is a Higher expression of energy. It is more Cosmic or Universal and closer to the true "Essence" that Divinity is, in perfect balance and in perfect union. Neutral is whole and stable, not preferring masculine or feminine, yet honoring both. This is our Highest Expressions as human Beings.

The goal is to balance ourselves so we can become neutral and more equal in the natural charge of all of the elements. It is important to take time to be in the elements of nature. They are healing, balancing and recharge us in a more natural way. When in a nature environment, I discharge negativity into the earth and water, I recharge positively with the air and the sun. Natural elementals feed and nurture our being and all of our bodies; physically, mentally, Spiritually and emotionally. They are a resonance of the Divine, wholeness and balance, that carry us through all of our challenges and all of our expressions in a more natural and neutral way. Nature is sacred and heals us, it deserves to be cherished, honored and kept free of pollution. Our health and well being depend on it.

It is important to know whether our personal charge is positive, air and fire, or negative which is water and earth. It will give us a clue as to what comes natural and easy and what needs to be developed to become more whole and neutral. To establish our personal polarity we need to know what elements we have in abundance. We can determine this by astrological charting of our planets and luminaries at the place and time of our birth. It is determined by looking at the elemental makeup of the Sun, Moon and Ascendant, the rising sign. Another way is to look at all the planets and luminaries in our chart for too much or too little air and fire which is masculine (+) and water and earth which is feminine (-) energy.

For example, my sun is in Leo, which is masculine/fire. My moon is in Taurus, which is feminine/earth and my ascendant is in Gemini, which is masculine/air. This gives me a double masculine polarity even though I am in a feminine body. All masculine things come easily and naturally to me. I can learn mental concepts easily and physical prowess comes effortlessly. I have had to learn and develop the feminine qualities of unity, compassion, patience, and acceptance as they were unfamiliar to me in the past. I might have given them to others, yet neglected to give them to myself. I needed to learn to understand and express my emotional and Spiritual qualities. In this way, I have been balancing myself and coming into greater wholeness. It is my Soul's work. Our health and well being depend upon it and it is a continuing process. It is a lifetime focus and dedication. Our relationships require greater understanding and acceptance of the opposite polarity, so we don't have to have the battle of the sexes. We can all be more neutral and whole without challenging each other with a strong positive or negative charge.

If you have a triple masculine or feminine charge, you can exhibit both imbalances at different times. Like the pendulum, you can swing back and forth to the extremes. Sometimes you can be extremely passive, until things build up. Then, you demonstrate the opposite aggressive behavior in an extreme manner. This occurs frequently as the experience of the victim/victimizer roles and passive/aggressive behavior.

Knowing our polarity charge is important in order to balance ourselves better. Burnout happens when we are constantly broadcasting and projecting our energy outward. It is impossible to receive anything while we are broadcasting. My complaint was "When do I get to receive?" I didn't realize I was filling all of the space and there was no room to receive. It is a way to attempt to control people and situations. If we are always passive and receptive, we may not be noticed or taken into account. Our complaint might be, "Isn't anyone listening to me or isn't my point of view important?" We might not understand that we are not actively broadcasting. It is a way to not take more responsibility for ourselves. Balancing polarity is balancing our ability to broadcast and receive. It is balancing our masculine and feminine charge/qualities. In this way, we may draw on either depending on the situation or person.

Health is the Balance of all Elements

Health is a sense of vitality, wholeness and neutrality, where all energy currents and paths are open and functioning. Life force is moving through us unimpeded creating more energy for all the organ systems and every cell in our body. It is the balance of all charge or tension with all discharge or lack of tension in our body to create wholeness. Our thoughts and feelings need to be more neutral and not extreme to maintain this balance. The blood also needs to display a neutral pH to be healthy, not too acidic and a little more alkaline. To accomplish this, we need a more alkaline diet in a ratio of 80% alkaline to 20% acid. Acid foods are all red and white meats, caffeine, sugar, dairy, white rice and flours. Alkaline foods are the vegetables, especially the dark leafy greens.

If we choose to keep all aspects of ourselves open and neutral, without too much or too little positive or negative charge, not too acid or alkaline, we will be healthy and well balanced. Our life force will flow freely up and down our bodies with no impediments or blocks.

The elements show up quite literally in our dreams and experience. This gives us a clue as to what is going on in our experience. All we need to know is what they represent in our life. With that knowledge, we have the ability to rebalance ourselves.

The Elements

Ether—Union/Balance

Ether has no charge; it is whole and neutral. Ether represents at the Highest level, devotion to the Divine and the Unity of all things. It is essential to receive this element fully through the crown. It comprises our Ultrasonic core current. When ether is minimally present due to poor posture, injury or lack of focus, we find lack of devotion, grief and emptiness. If in our experience or in our dreams, we are crying and grieving and sad a lot, there is a desire for a closer connection to our Divine Mother/Father and our Divine Inner Self. This is the answer to all separation anxiety. No matter what loss we have suffered, that occurrence challenges us to re-experience Divine love, our own love, peace, harmony and fulfillment.

Ether is like the sound medium of Creation. In Physics, there exists the concept of Particle Theory in which sound vibrates to manifest matter. Another way to express it is that the energy of consciousness vibrates and steps down in frequency and separates or polarizes into the other elements with positive and negative charge. The more neutral we are, not too electric or magnetic; we demonstrate the wholeness of ether. It is the closest experience of Divinity we can embody in ourselves.

Air—Expression/Communication/Beliefs

Air has a masculine/positive polarity charge. In our experience and in dream language, air represents our thoughts, our desires and our ability to communicate. If there are gentle breezes in our dreams, our communications are sensitive and successful. When there are hurricanes, tornadoes or dust devils, we can see that we may be raising our voices in an unkind or forceful manner or we can see the power of withholding speaking our truth and the degree of destruction that it causes. We can determine from the symbology which it is.

In our life experience, it gives a general impression of how we air our thoughts and feelings. How do we communicate with others, especially our loved ones? Do we speak our truth honorably or do we blast others with it? Air is electric and an experience of broadcasting or sending energy out. It gives us the power of speech.

Fire—Passion/Power

Fire has a masculine/positive polarity charge. In our experience and in dream language, fire represents our passion for the things that we love as well as our arousal, inspiration and brilliance. It also represents anger, frustration and impatience. Our dream or life experience can indicate the warmth of passion like a sweet toasted marshmallow. Or it can reflect a conflagration (a major fire) of anger out of control, suffering or distress, tribulation, infection, fever. Our waking experience can reveal how much rage we have by how we respond to traffic, waiting in lines or dealing with our loved ones.

We can determine from the symbology, how enormous and intense the passion is, depending on how big it is and how much it is directed with force or kindness. Fire is electric and is an experience of broadcasting or sending energy out. It gives us the power of passion.

Water—Emotions/Sexuality

Water has a feminine/negative polarity charge. In dream language and our direct experience, water represents our emotional attachments, creativity and our sexuality. When there is a body of water in our dreams, we can tell by the color, purity and clarity, literally, if we are clear and at peace in still blue waters or emotionally confused in dark, churning or murky waters. Is the water placid, churning, steamy, fluid, or frozen?

In our life's experience, we may have swelling in a part of our body or feel very emotional. These clues give us an indication of how we need to nurture ourselves. We may be giving or nurturing others and not giving enough to ourselves. It can make us feel weak, diluted or powerless. Water is magnetic and an experience of receiving or an accumulation of inward energy. It gives us the power to nurture and sustain ourselves and others.

Earth—Foundation/Material World

Earth has a feminine/negative polarity charge. In our experience and in dream language, the earth represents our personal stability, worldly things, our foundation and our financial picture. In our experience and in our dreams, it reflects our ability to plant or germinate new seeds for security and prosperity. If the ground or our foundation is muddy or wobbly, it indicates our own insecurity, impracticality, or instability. An earthquake in our dream can reflect a sensation of fear that everything will be shaken up or fall apart. Everything is quite literal in the language of earth's symbology.

In our life experience, if we are not saving money, we can feel insecure. Especially if our life is going through upheavals, it is good to know the rent or mortgage is paid. Earth is also magnetic and a receiving or accumulation of inward energy. It bestows the power to create a good foundation of personal and financial security.

Body Wisdom

Even our body reflects the whole structure in individual parts like the hands, feet, ears and face. Here again, we see the Divine Plan repeating. The face, ears, palms and the soles of the feet tell the story of our entire physical body. The health of the body can be diagnosed and treated by some health professionals just by looking at those areas. This is information is used regularly by Chinese doctors of Acupuncture. Healing arts professionals, like massage therapists, polarity therapists, foot reflexologists, etc., pay close attention to these areas.

Palm readers can see talents, abilities and personality characteristics in our hands. Certain psychics read the personality and past in our face. The individual parts of the body reveal so much.

Our symptoms and conditions and where they occur can reflect our imbalances. For example, I had hypoglycemicia (low blood sugar) and arthritis (inflammation of the joints) early in my life. I used to get so angry, frustrated and irritated; I would literally burn up my blood glucose. My joints were on fire. I felt I had to be perfect and had become rigid in this belief. If I was not perfect, I would turn the anger in on myself. When I learned to discharge the backlog of anger and vent my anger in healthy ways, and accept myself as perfectly "imperfect," my conditions disappeared. Emotional baggage can create so much damage to the physical body and those around us. I believe that modern day "road rage" and tragic fatal shootings are the accumulation of a backlog of anger and suppressed irritation, frustration and rage.

The body never lies. Its' symptoms are important cues as to what needs to be healed. It is valuable to be very vigilant in perceiving this information. Our health depends upon it. Most people are not even aware of what is happening in their bodies. We are "too busy" as a society. There has been a prevailing attitude that is changing, to not take personal responsibility for our own health care. Many people wait until their health breaks down and the condition is serious before they pay attention. Then it becomes imperative and necessary to see a medical doctor. If they could have identified the imbalance earlier and focused on healing it, they may not have to seek medical intervention. Conditions don't have to get out of control. We can balance and take responsibility for our own imbalances initially, instead of relying on our doctor to fix it for us. There are underlying causes for all illnesses and our responsibility to our Self is to identify the need for healing and then to do something about it before it becomes critical. Even genetic illness can indicate imbalances in family patterns and karma.

In stretching, Yoga, massage and other conscious body experiences, we have the opportunity to notice which side of our body or body parts are more tight and contracted and unable to balance and be flexible. This gives us clues to personal imbalances depending on whether it is the right or left side of the body. Our emotions will give us hints as to what disease and disharmony we are most susceptible to. For example, if our strongest attribute is our intellect and we focus only on that in our life, we will be unbalanced with the element of air (+). It is too much energy out that may encourage migraine headaches, brain aneurisms, head injuries, neurological disorders or other head related conditions. You may have heard the expression, "he or she is too much into their head." If we entertain fearful or negative thoughts and ideas, are constantly mentally "on" consistently or chronically, we can develop tension symptoms or chronic conditions.

Most people use medicine to cover over the symptoms instead of understanding what the body is trying to communicate. Listen first, and then act to rebalance. If we need to, we can relieve the symptoms with our doctor's prescription and/or herbal remedies and our health will be better for it. Look at the messages in the Guidance Groupings so you can get a sense of what your symptoms are about. Our body will reflect symptoms to cue us on what healthful changes we need to make. Our Divination experiences will give us that same opportunity without having to manifest the physical symptom or ailment, if we are paying attention and balancing the appropriate elements. Healthful changes can be made before something happens on the physical level. The physical level is the densest, grossest level and therefore the most difficult to clear up. Unhealthful conditions can be cleared up more quickly on the emotional, mental and etheric levels. The idea is to make choices that do not promote dis-harmony or dis-ease on any of the various levels; Spiritually, mentally, physically or emotionally. Make choices that balance all areas and levels. We have been given free will to use in any manner we wish. Let's use it to heal, balance, be healthy and change our destiny!

The body is divided into two sides; each governed by a right or left cerebral hemisphere. The right brain controls the left side of the body, which is feminine and has a negative charge. *"The right brain is more sensitive to touch, to pressure, sensation, to painful stimuli, and even to how one is being touched, whether roughly or lovingly. In consequence, the right brain is more concerned with how others interact with us intimately and physically; it is the cuddly, huggable, touchy-feely half of the brain."* [40] The left brain controls the right side of the body, which is masculine and has a positive charge. The left brain is more rational, linear and logical in its process.

If we choose to become more aware and use Divination, we can determine what side of the body is experiencing disharmony. Odd sensations, i.e. pain, tightness, tingling, throbbing, discomfort, itching, coolness, warmth, etc. can reflect it. Or it can be reflected as lacking sensation, i.e. numbness. When we identify the sensation or numbness, the side of the body and the area, we will know which of the duality principles are being misused or need attention. The masculine principle consists of the body and mind and feminine is the heart and soul. We need all four parts in balance: physical, mental, emotional and Spiritual for a well balanced foundation. We have focused a lot on the mind/body connection in our modern day awareness, which are only two legs of the foundation. We need to focus on the heart/soul connection equally, as our ancient ancestors did. How to balance the "four corner" foundation principles of Spiritual, mental, physical, and emotional well being, will be clearer as we study ourselves.

Pain is the result of congestion of the tissues due to a blockage in the energy flow through the body, downward. Too much contraction from gravity, life experiences, muscular workouts, accidents, injuries, negative emotions, the weight of responsibility, etc.; presses down on us. It creates an energy dam in the affected areas, usually the neck, shoulders and back. Then we get to experience that "dam pain." Numbness is the experience of energy not being able to move upwards through the body. It is blocked from moving upward, perhaps from trauma or unexpressed feelings because life can sometimes be

---

[40] Robert Ornstein, *The Psychology of Consciousness* (W.H. Freeman and Co., 1972)

so painful. We unconsciously withdraw life force and awareness from the affected areas. We need to become aware and unblock these life energies to feel good in our bodies.

Energy Centers of the Body & the Corresponding Colors

Our body has seven major energy centers located down the midline of the body which correspond to all of the colors of the rainbow, including black and white. Black represents the absence of color and white represent all the colors. When white light is refracted, we see a rainbow of the colors of Creation.

The Ultrasonic core current which moves through the spinal column provides a sound resonance of energy for each energy center. It begins as the element of ether comes in through the crown of our heads as sound, to form the Ultrasonic core current that moves up and down our spine. Ether also travels on the breath, bringing in more life force and light. Breath and sound meet in the crown of the head. There is a repeating theme of light and sound for manifestation in Creation. There is a stepping down in energy vibration to form the various elements of air, fire, water and earth which are associated with each energy center.

In our DNA encoding, there is a consciousness of energy that is inbred and embodied in these seven major energy centers that responds to this Ultrasonic core current. As we breathe into the sinus cavities, pure light and sound come together in the crown of our head feeding this whirling vortex or energy center and the one above the crown. This union of energies continues down the Ultrasonic core in the middle of the body for five more vortices of energy that are referred to as chakras or centers. It provides us with vitality and life force.

The more balance and flow we create with breath and sound inside us, the greater the balance of energy in each of these centers. It requires releasing physical, mental, Spiritual and emotional tension. Each center can demonstrate either an overcharged or an undercharged state. The energy center becomes more vibrant as it whirls in the proper direction, either clockwise or counterclockwise. The vitality of these centers determines how healthy the corresponding organs and tissues are.

Crown Center—White and Purple

This is the area of the Highest part of us, our Spiritual Self, through which our Ultrasonic core current (sound) spirals into our body which can be referred to as our Soul essence. It is pure Love and it is our connection with Source. This center is located a couple of inches above the crown of our head. When I had experiences of seeing angels I noticed that they appeared as pastel rainbow colors of refracted white light, representing this level.

This center represents purity, clarity and wisdom. It is about being a shining light and a positive influence on others. It is an opportunity for connection with Super Consciousness and our Spiritual Self. If it doesn't function properly, we can be ungrateful or make the wrong choices in life. We can be misguided in our judgment and leadership. We can be oppressive, dominating and want power over others.

Perceptual Center or 3rd Eye—Indigo Blue

This is the center that represents Inner knowing and our perceptions beyond our five senses. It is the area associated with telepathy, intuition, deep insight, clairvoyance, clairaudience, and clairsentience. It is our access to multi-dimensional experience. It is located in the middle of the forehead between the eyebrows, about one inch inward. We have heard the expression, "I have seen the light!" It means that we have seen our truth or wisdom with a Higher part of our Selves. As we breathe in air, our "Inspiration" (notice the root of this word is Spirit) comes through our nose and sinus cavities and connects with the Ultrasonic core current or Soul essence. Spirit and Soul become one. We can visualize, as they connect, lighting up with Divine wisdom and love.

This center represents stillness, peace and serenity. It is about utilizing Inner Guidance, and possessing receptivity, grace, harmony, joy and compassion. It gives us the opportunity to experience unconditional love and unity. If it doesn't function properly, we can be out of touch with our Inner Self and our perceptions. We can feel separated, disconnected, confused or obsessed. We can be a martyr for love or demonstrate hopelessness, unloving or addictive behavior.

Throat or Communication Center—Aqua and Turquoise

This is the center that represents our expression of personal communications and Self in the world. It is located in the neck area at the vocal chords. It is our ability to speak our truth and express devotion to something greater.

Sound vibration is produced in the vocal cords by the breath from our inspiration moving through the vocal chords. We can direct our awareness to the Higher centers, by focusing our attention upward. When we do this successfully, we are speaking a Higher truth or projecting our Creative Soul expression.

This center represents speaking truth and communicating with compassion. It is about being vocally creative. It gives us the opportunity to experience ecstasy, harmony and beauty. We can feel in the flow and possess determination and practicality while enjoying comfort and pleasure. If it doesn't function properly, we can feel blocked in our ability to communicate and express our feelings and beliefs. We can feel fearful about voicing our truth and values. We can be a people-pleaser, hedonistic, full of sadness and grief or need to change our direction in life.

Heart or Love Center—Emerald Green and Pastel Shades of Green, Pink and Blue

This is the center of our emotional connection with others in the love and relationship experience. It is located at the area of the sternum in the center of the chest. It is associated with the Soul. We hear the expression; "this music has heart and soul." It indicates it is touching us on those deeper levels. Our feelings are important! We cannot continue to push them down, divert our attention, block them or rationalize them away. They don't go away. They get stuck in our emotional bodies and ultimately affect our physical bodies. Our feelings and thoughts need to be able to circulate freely and then be released without getting stuck; just like the circulation of blood and air flowing through us, is essential to life!

This center represents experiencing healing and loving ways in our life. It is about being healthy, growing and flourishing. It gives us the opportunity to make observations, share ideas, initiate and begin new things and manifest prosperity, money and success. We can feel more feminine, compassionate, patient and magnetic. We can experience the love of home and family as well as feeling nurtured, protected and secure. If it doesn't function properly, we can feel immature, gullible, superficial or selfish. We can be too active, busy or have a negative attitude. We can be envious, participate in ego games or be out of touch with our hearts. We can feel alienated, insecure or smothered. We can lack boundaries, demonstrate passive aggressive behavior or try to deny or feelings. Heart disease is our number one health challenge as a result of a dysfunctional way of being due to lack of balance in this area.

Solar Plexus/Naval or Power Center—Yellow

This is the center of our experience of personal power and digestion. It is located at the apex where the ribs join together and the abdomen begins, at the sternum and below to the navel. In some traditions, it is only the area of the naval. When we feel a sense of disempowerment, our ego feels challenged, scared and powerless. It is not uncommon to have digestive problems. When we experience a Higher connection, we feel a greater sense of Self-empowerment. We are more courageous when the Higher Self is at the helm.

This center represents empowerment, joy, luck, courage and Higher Intellect. It is about having great integrity, confidence, many talents and a gifted intellect. It gives us the opportunity to experience benevolence, generosity, to be protective and have abundant energy. We can feel more masculine, sporty and electric. We can provide great service, process many details and file them appropriately. If it doesn't function properly, we can feel dis-empowered, drained, deteriorated or cowardly. We can feel dominating, fiery, angry or greedy. We can need to be the center of attention, an addicted gambler, or we can be lazy, impetuous and indolent. We can feel inadequate about our training and education. We can be a doormat for control types, demonstrate anal retentive behavior or worry, fret and overwork ourselves. We can also nag and be critical with unrealistic standards of perfection.

Creative and Sexual Center—Orange and Red

This is the center of our creative and sexual experience. It is located a couple of inches below our navel. Our potential to create life and sexual organs are located here. When expressing sexuality is not appropriate, we can use this energy to be extremely creative and artistic. This center connects us physically or sexually with others and demonstrates our attachment to loved ones in our lives. We tend to store many of our feelings in this area as excess weight, bloat or a "spare tire." We can observe in others and ourselves how fit and shapely this area is, to determine if unexpressed emotions reside here.

Sexual energy has great power. In many religious traditions, it has been the source of denial. Sexual energy and Spiritual energy go together if we want them to. It can be a loving, enriching and healthy experience. Or, it can be misused to gain or loose power in negative ritual or in other inappropriate circumstances.

This center represents sexuality for bonding, procreation and regeneration. In addition, it is creativity for expression and transformation. It is about being political, holding power in a responsible manner for the good of the whole instead of personal gain. It gives us the opportunity to develop executive ability and leadership in worldly affairs. We can enjoy physical power, action, sports, speed and thrills. If it doesn't function properly, we can feel blocked in our sexuality, creativity and physical power. We can be manipulative, controlling and participate in ego games with jealousy, possessiveness, guilt and insecurity. We can be a victim or a victimizer or both. We can be sexually abused, permissive or demonstrate emotional or sexual dysfunction. We can be egocentric, pushy, selfish, angry, frustrated, headstrong, confrontational, selfish, dictatorial or in survival mode.

Elimination and Foundation Center—Black

This is the center for elimination of all that is no longer needed in our lives. It is located at the base of the spine. To be healthy, it is our responsibility to let go of everything that is no longer serving us in our life i.e., people, possessions, outworn conditions, emotions or situations. We also need to effectively eliminate the unusable remains of the digestive process. That process sometimes gets backed up or blocked. It has meaning in our live as well. It can indicate that we are in a constipated or contracted cycle and need to reflect on what needs to be eliminated or reformatted in our lives.

This center also represents our foundation. It consists of the base of the spine, the sacrum and the pelvic girdle on which the entire spine rests. We need a strong and well balanced foundation. The main energy channel of the Ultrasonic core current and the all energy centers depend on this foundation. We need the best possible alignment of the crown, sacrum and pelvic girdle to be fully healthy, vibrant and vital. A good foundation is like the roots of trees. The branches of the tree can lift outward and higher with deeper, well-branched roots without being knocked down by wind due to the expansion of the foundation. We can expand more Spiritually if we have a good, grounded physical base to support it.

This center represents material stability and being grounded. It is about being patient, ambitious and accomplishing great things. It gives us the opportunity to experience the manifestation of physical and financial success with managerial ability. We can be a good problem solver. We can feel courageous, stable and secure. If it doesn't function properly, we can feel blocked, thwarted, depressed, contracted, inhibited and pessimistic. We can feel fearful and insecure about our finances and future. We can be severely critical, judgmental, rigid, stern or morose. We can feel ungrounded, without a good foundation or be in survival mode. We can have serious, dogmatic thoughts and karmic lessons that may be challenging, dangerous, dark or crushing. We can be evil or feel dirty. It is acting without Higher Guidance in order to survive.

Colors

Colors reflect the light of Creation, according to their specific wavelength. The primary colors of the spectrum are red, yellow and blue. If we combine any of these three colors, we can produce any of the other colors. Black is the complete absorption of light rays, so as to appear to be an absence of light. It represents our first energy center, which has the greatest density like the energy of the earth. White produces the primary colors when it is refracted. It is the perfect integration of all of the colors of the rainbow. It is associated with our seventh energy center, which is the most Spiritual, pure love energy, light and unity.

If the color is bright and true, it represents a "Higher" expression. If the color is dark, murky, mottled or brownish, it is usually the "lower" expression. The pastel colors have a softer tonality than the stronger, darker colors. Each color resonates with a specific energy center in your body and specific body parts or regions. Some colors are combinations of others. For example, the color salmon has a pink (heart center), a yellow (power center) and an orange (sexual and creative center.) We can wear semi-precious stones made into jewelry or laid in a pattern during healing and meditation for certain areas to amplify or to quiet the energy center. Colors are associated with certain emotions and the qualities of specific planets and astrological signs.

Use color therapy in your home décor, with your personal clothing and in your business environment to assist in balancing and creating what you want. Choose colors that reflect the qualities you want to embody. If you wish to energize, obtain bright and radiant colors to emphasize. If you want to calm, use pastels or you can use neutrals to neutralize. You can actually feel the effect. Most decorators are very knowledgeable about the qualities and characteristics of color. You can be too!

If our health is being challenged in any of our energy centers, we can choose the appropriate color to assist us. By using the Guidance Groupings in Chapter 11, we can determine what is out of balance or not healthy with the lowest, then read the highest expression to determine what we need to give more focus to. Use the appropriate color to assist in balancing and healing. Let's provide ourselves with the right color vibration. The following explanations delineate the meaning and vibration of each color.

White

White and purple represent the seventh energy center, which is the crown center, located a couple of inches above the crown of the head as well as Universal and Cosmic energy. If there are problems with the head, the brain, tumors, etc., in this area, the following can give us some insight.

Highest—demonstrates the most pure love and light energy. White produces the primary colors when it is refracted. It indicates being fully integrated and is positive, whole energy. It also represents the light of the sun which is referred to as masculine.

Lowest—indicates wrong choices, soiled, spoiled, impure and incorrect. Not being fully integrated or allowing our true radiance to shine.

Purple

Purple represents the seventh energy center, which is the crown center, located a couple of inches above the crown of the head as well as Universal and Cosmic energy. If there are problems with the head, the brain, tumors, etc., in this area, the following can give us some insight.

Highest—demonstrates royalty, imperial, high ranking positions or rank at birth (we are Divine Children) ornate, elaborate. Knowing and applying the Superconscious, Oneness, "Selfullness," "Soulfullness," illumination, integrity and our Highest and Best.

Lowest—indicates the misuse of rule or leadership, misguided leadership, personality and ego selfishness, and dictatorship. Our Spirituality and these characteristics need serious attention.

Indigo Blue

Indigo Blue represents the sixth energy center, which is the perceptual center or 3rd Eye. It also represents the planet Neptune and the sign of Pisces. If there are challenges with the pituitary or the pineal glands or the feet, we may obtain insight from the following.

Highest—demonstrates Spiritual seeing, accessing Inner Self and perception, unity, intuition, serenity and surrender. It represents wholeness, multi-dimensional perception, receptivity, grace and compassion.

Lowest—indicates being out of touch with our Inner Self and Self perceptions, feeling unloved or unloving, separation, confusion, disconnection, martyrdom, addiction and obsession. It indicates unhealthy color of the skin, bruised, murky, indecent, sad and gloomy and melancholy.

Aqua or Turquoise

Turquoise or Aqua represents the fifth energy center, which is the communication center. It symbolizes the planet Venus, the sign of Taurus and the emotions of devotion and grief. If we have issues with our throat, vocal chords, our thyroid or parathyroid, we may need this information.

Highest—demonstrates communication and speaking our truth, vocal and emotional creative Self-expression. We may be experiencing devotion to a Higher power, ecstasy, harmony, beauty and feel in the flow.

Lowest—indicates blocks to Self-expression, speech or truth. We can be fearful of voicing our truth or values, without devotion, or may be experiencing sadness, loss and grief.

Emerald Green

Green and milky white represent the fourth energy center, which is the heart center, located at the sternum. There are other pastel colors that represent love in this heart center:

pastel green, pink and blue. Their interpretation would include a lighter expression than the richer colored green with regard to the domain of loving.

Green and silver signify the planet Mercury, the sign of Gemini, from the shoulders to the heart. It also represents the thymus gland, lungs, arms and hands. If we have questions about unfulfilled desires, Self-acceptance, beliefs, personal expression, and communication as indicated by these body parts, we may find this information valuable.

Highest—demonstrates communicating our feelings, going, growing, being healthy, healing, loving, having prosperity, money, news, messages, ideas, data integration, being nutrient rich, successful.

Lowest—indicates not being aware of our feelings, being immature, easily deceived, simple, naive, envious, sickly, diseased, too busy, gullible, superficial, thinking negatively or selfishly.

Milky White

The color milky white represents the moon in the sign of Cancer, at the heart and nipple line, the breasts, down to the solar plexus. If there are health threats with these areas, please read the following.

Highest—demonstrates attuning to our feelings, home, being nurtured and nurturing, loved, protected, comforted, secure, magnetic and camouflaged.

Lowest—indicates feeling alienated, abusing our body, insecure, hiding, possessing no boundaries or unhealthy ones, over-nurturing others, smothering, feeling abused or abusing others.

Yellow

Yellow represents the third energy center, which is the power center. It represents the Sun in the sign of Leo and is located at the solar plexus. It includes the heart and spleen. If there are concerns about anger, power and fear, you may be interested in this information.

Highest—Demonstrates empowerment, personal power, joy, luck, talent, benevolence, courage, being a shining light, protective, generous, masculine, electric, intellectual and confident. It represents the day.

Lowest—Indicates dis-empowerment, caution, being drained or aged, yellowing as in deterioration, being scared, a coward, being like a predator, dominating, angry or greedy.

Orange

Orange and Red represent the second energy center. It is located a couple of inches below the navel. It is our sexual and creative center. It includes the sexual reproductive organs and glands. The healthiest expression of these colors is of contentment and healthy passion. A lower expression is concerns about regeneration, emotions of attachment like jealousy, possessiveness, control, and victimization issues. It also represents our creativity, our sexuality and our sexual organs. If we have any challenges with these, we will want to read this. Orange is symbolic of the planet Pluto and the sign of Scorpio. It is associated with feelings of attachment and sexual power. If there are problems with sexuality and the ego, you will find this information helpful.

Highest—Demonstrates enjoyment of social activities, creative projects, sexual experiences, and emotional empowerment. It is concerned with political situations and our creativity; It exhibits qualities of penetrating insight, transformation, regeneration and death/rebirth.

Lowest—Indicates misuse of power in social, creative, political, sexual and emotional situations. It exhibits manipulation, control games, jealousy, guilt, victim/victimizer behavior, destruction without transformation and unhealthy secrets.

Red

Red represents the second energy center and is adjacent to the first energy center. It corresponds to the planet Mars in the sign of Aries. Red is the color of emotions involved with anger, frustration, irritation and impatience. It deals with passion, raw sexual energy and physical power. It draws attention and sends out these signals.

Highest—Demonstrates the ability to initiate, energy, activity, action, executive ability, sports, passion, speed, thrills, natural sexuality, wildness and drive.

Lowest—Indicates an emergency, the need to stop, release, let go or speed up. We can be in the "red" financially or be angry, sore or inflamed. It is too much fire which can promote arthritis and any other infection or "itis." It designates being overly sexually permissive, blocked creativity, emotional and sexual dysfunction, selfishness and emotional survival.

Black

Black represents more earthly energy; it is the first energy center, the foundation and elimination center. It is located at the base of the spine. Black is the seeming absence of color by absorption of light. It is associated with the planet Saturn and the sign of Capricorn. The healthiest expression is to transform fear into courage and success. It includes the base of the spine, the bones, teeth, knees and the Sigmoid colon. If you have any challenges with these areas, read this.

Highest—Demonstrates manifestation, release, letting go, stability, a good foundation, and physical and financial success. It signifies patience, the void, space, and the night. It is the feminine and possesses managerial ability.

Lowest—Indicates being challenged, dirty, dark, dangerous, evil or acting without a Higher Power, being critical, pessimistic, moody, and severe. It denotes karma or lessons of life and being inhibited, blocked, rigid, inflexible, judgmental, ungrounded, in survival, too stern or depressed.

Gemstones

Just as color reflects the light of creation, so does the color of each gemstone. The same principles that apply to color apply to gemstones. Once again, if the color is bright and true, it is a Higher expression and has more value. If the color is dark, murky, mottled, or brownish, it is a lower expression and has less value. Just as the colors are attributed to each energy center of the seven in and above our body, the gemstones resonate, by color, with each of those same energy centers.

There was a fad where "power beads" became a fashion statement. People wore semi-precious stones and were linking the meaning and the value of the stone with what they wanted to project in their lives. This wisdom is being used commercially to sell semi-precious gems and to assist people. If it were not fashionable, very few people would be relating semi-precious stones for a special purpose.

Synthetic stones, those made by man, do not have the same energy and resonance as those that exist in nature. They are not natural and have a different vibration. If you are looking for specific results, rather than just cosmetic appearance, go for natural precious and semi-precious stones. These natural stones assist us in coming back into balance with our true nature. They are natural, with a natural vibration and represent the way Source created nature!

When working with crystals, semi-precious and precious stones in healing, it is useful to apply them to the energy center that they are designed by color and frequency to represent. (See the Guidance Groupings.) Unless you are given a strong intuition about the placement of the stone, it will have the best effect being closer to the energy center that it was designed to enhance.

I want to give you examples of what each color gemstone would signify. For example:

White (Clear) and Purple Stones

Clear Quartz crystal is used the most frequently by so many. There are different kinds of clear Quartz, like the tabular variety, which forms in flat layers. Another kind is the recorder crystals; they are believed to have history and great wisdom encoded within them. If we wish to have more clarity, purity and wisdom, keep these stones around, especially if we are feeling unclear, impure or are making the wrong choices in life. Additional qualities: they assist us in being a shining light, a leader and a positive influence on others. Other stones of this category are: Herkimer diamond, Selenite, clear Topaz.

Amethyst, Charoite and Sugilite contain the color purple and if the color is deep and true, it would represent royalty, inspiration, and Superconscious. If we wish to feel more royal or Spiritual, we would wear these stones, especially if we are feeling misguided in judgment or leadership. Additional qualities: they assist in realizing the Superconscious and the Spiritual Self, expressing our Highest and Best, feeling Oneness and being impeccable by honoring the integrity of Self.

Indigo Blue Stones

If the color is dark blue, like Lapis Lazuli or Sapphire, it would be the vibration of Higher perception. These stones allow us to feel a sense of unity with everything. We can manifest peace, joy, unconditional love and serenity more easily. If we wish to quiet the mind to access the Inner dimensions and experience wholeness, we would use the dark blue stones. We can also enhance our Inner Guidance, receptivity, grace, compassion, joy and unconditional love. If we are experiencing addiction, confusion, obsession, separation or disconnection, we would enjoy wearing these as well: Sodalite, Azurite, Opal, blue Tourmaline, Celestite, Iolite and Tanzanite.

Aqua and Turquoise Stones

When the color is blue-green like Turquoise or Chrysophrase, it indicates our Self-expression and communication. These stones assist us in speaking our truth and communicating with compassion. They expand our ability to experience ecstasy, harmony and beauty. We can feel more in the flow and generous with others. If we desire more devotion in our life, we would wear these stones. When we feel blocked or have fear in expressing ourselves or our beliefs, these stones are suggested. If we are healing sadness and grief in our life, these stones would be very valuable as well: blue Topaz, Gem Silica, Chysacholla, Aquamarine, and Alexandrite.

Turquoise and blue Topaz stones have additional qualities such as promoting great humor, ethics, Spiritual law, wisdom and a philosophical nature. They enhance the qualities of a dynamic instructor and support generosity, honesty, love of liberty and freedom. If we are too overzealous, righteous, dogmatic or fanatic, these stones can help balance us. If we jump to conclusions, hurt others by expressing truth in a harsh manner or put our foot in our mouths, these stones are for us!

Aquamarine also has additional characteristics that support being humanitarian, advocating Universal law, brotherhood and friendship. These stones bring enlightenment, equality and ingenuity into the world by enhancing avant-garde thinking. They enhance talent with electronics, innovation and invention and promote determination, originality and excellent memory. If we are radical, unpredictable, erratic or eccentric to the extreme, we need these stones. If we are argumentative, hypocritical, rebellious, anxious, nervous or apprehensive, aquamarine can assist us.

Emerald Green & Pastel Stones of Green, Pink & Blue

The color green presents the heart center, healing, loving, prosperity, and money. Stones like Emerald and Aventurine assist us in being more healthy; growing and flourishing. Also, it is easier to initiate new things to create more prosperity, money and success. We can integrate new ideas, make observations and honor our feelings more. If our desire nature is out of balance, or if we want good health, and abundance, the green stones would be very helpful. If you are learning to accept yourself, or others, these additional stones are very healing: Malachite and green Tourmaline, Agate and Jade. Green stones assist us in acceptance of self and others and in sharing our beliefs and love from our hearts.

There are other colors associated with this grouping, they include pink, light blue, and light yellow greens and can be used for the same purposes. These stones include pink Tourmaline, Rose Quartz, Rhodochrosite and Kunzite. Some light blue stones are Blue Lace Agate and Chalcedony. The yellow-green category is Peridot; it combines the qualities of the colors green with that of yellow. All of these stones and especially the pink are particularly good for enhancing your ability to love and your "lovability".

There seem to be so many more stones and colors associated with the heart center. Could that indicate that we need more assistance in this area? Since heart disease kills more people than any other disease, I believe this is true. We need to learn to love ourselves in a more comprehensive manner so we can love others better.

Milky White Stones

Mother of Pearl, Moonstone, Pearl and Mabe are the color milky white, like mother's milk. They are related to qualities that are comforting, nurturing and softening. They assist us in feeling the love of home and family. We can feel more protected and secure like a pearl embedded in an oyster. We can cherish and be cherishing, more easily. These stones are the most feminine of all; representing the heart and soul of the family and domesticity. They have a wonderful quality that soothes us. Reach for them to feel nurtured and comforted. When you are feeling hurt, need mothering, or are alienated or insecure use them to feel more contentment.

Yellow Stones

The next category is the yellow stones like yellow Diamond and Topaz. These stones represent intuitive intelligence, joy, empowerment, mental ability and masculinity. They can assist us in feeling greater integrity, confidence, courage and more talented. These can be used to enhance the qualities of benevolence, generosity and the ability to be protective and be a way shower for others. Yellow Citrine, Aragonite and Tiger's Eye can also be very helpful in creating more kindness and courage, especially if we are healing the emotional expression of anger. If we are feeling scared, cowardly, dis-empowered or deteriorated, using these stones is helpful. Yellow stones promote personal power and intuitive intelligence.

Brown Stones

The color brown characterizes being earthy, sensual and tactile. This category also includes stones that are both red and green which comprise the color brown, like Bloodstone. These stones give us the energy of dedication, discernment and the ability to work with many details. We can demonstrate meticulous behavior and provide great service. They are helpful if we are processing and filing information and data. These stones assist us if we are feeling inferior or inadequate about our training or education. It may be that we are being too critical with unrealistic standards of perfection. If we worry, overwork or have anxiety about our performance or are anal retentive in or behavior or attitude we can use brown Smokey Quartz to assist us. Brown stones give us more courage, ground us and enhance material stability.

Black & White Stones

There are few stones that actually have black and white in them. Some white quartz has a vein of black in them. They would be in this category. There is also another category of stones that have the absorption of light or have light reflecting through them, these stones are opals. There are black opals and white opals. They both display a beautiful array of color. Opals are magical in there ability to enhance diplomacy, harmony and appreciation. Both kinds can assist in balance, communication, relationships, the arts, justice and psychology. If we are feeling unbalanced, polarized or addicted, these stones are helpful. When we are feeling superficial or over-rationalizing our situation, these stones can bring balance with the heart and mind.

Orange Stones

Not feeling sexy? Do we want to amplify our creative energy? The orange stones like carnelian and amber are for us. In addition, these stones assist in transformation, regeneration and deep probing insight. It is the energy of being socially and politically correct. If we wish to heal the loss of emotional attachment, deal with manipulation, insecurity, jealousy and guilt, use the orange stones. When we feel like a victim or victimized, are out of balance with our desires, destructive, or secretive to the detriment of intimacy, orange Citrine and Jade may also support us. If we want to expand our sense of contentment, we can use orange stones. They can also assist with healing sexuality and procreative ability.

Red Stones

The red stones are utilized for action, sports, passion, etc. Much like a man who buys red roses for a woman to express his fervent ardor, and love; Ruby and Garnet are for resonating passion and physical power. They also promote executive ability and evolved leadership in worldly matters. They assist in enjoying sexual activity and in expressing our natural, uninhibited qualities. It is easier to initiate any activity and oversee it to completion with the help of these stones. If we have too much ego, anger, sexual passion or are physically rough, overly sexual permissive, selfish, frustrated or impatient, we may want to rebalance with bloodstone, red Jasper, Coral or Onyx. When we are pushy, confrontational, headstrong, helpless or weak, dictatorial or in survival mode, we can use them too.

Black Stones

For grounding, physical and financial success, and femininity, we can use the black stones. They promote healthy ambition and the courage to accomplish great things. They assist with problem solving and intuition. We can utilize them to build a stronger foundation of economic security with great stability. They encourage patience and the ability to let go when that is appropriate. Some of these stones would include black Tourmaline and Onyx, and Hematite. If our challenge is fear, Obsidian and black Jade will also help ground and integrate us within our own foundation. They will assist us in releasing rigidity and blocked energy. We can be less rigid, critical, inhibited, and stern or contracted when we apply these stones. If we are too negative, depressed, blocked or morose these stones can help us.

Application of Stones

We can use stones regularly to help us balance our cycles and energies. It is a wise choice and practice to employ these stones. They are useful and produce results. I have experimented and found in my own experience, benefits for each of the color groupings. Knowing the colors allows us to understand the healing effect more clearly, just as knowing the colors of each of the energy centers of the body will assist us in knowing what we need to balance and what stone we need. They are all related. There is Divine Order that resonates with colors, gemstones and energy centers.

Animals & Beings

In American culture we use expressions that describe certain people or behaviors by comparing them to animals. We sometimes refer to a man as "he's catting around", meaning he's out late at night on the prowl. When we say "he's a dog", we are referring either to his being territorial or smelling around the neighbor's "flower gardens!" There is the description "faithful as a dog" for the ever-trusty individual. We call people "predators", we say "they swim like a fish or drink like a fish", "he struts like a peacock". We talk about clumsiness as a "bull in a china shop". Human behavior can be described as "he roars like a lion" or "he's as low as a snake in the grass."

We use words that describe animal behavior for people like "quit your squawking or they're cackling like hens" "she stings like a scorpion" usually attributed to a woman. Being a "social butterfly" suggests flitting around from person to person at a social gathering. A person can be described as "laughing like a hyena" or "she's as gentle as a lamb". Someone's movement may be described as "cat-like finesse" another person that is agile, can be "monkey-like". They can demonstrate either the higher qualities or the lower ones. There are so many combinations of qualities; it's like playing with the genetic codes of DNA, amazing combinations!

Pay close attention to animal behavior wherever you are. Animals can sense changing weather patterns and earthquakes. The have amazing sensory skills. They can reflect guidance in our life if we are consciously open to seeing it. Many people can exhibit many different traits at different times of various species. Some animals demonstrate the qualities of several categories. All of these emotional and behavioral characteristics can be clues in our dreams and nature experiences about what we need to learn about and heal in ourselves.

I have classified the animals and beings according to the signs of the zodiac and their behavior traits in order to provide organization and association with the astrological information in the next chapter. I am also identifying the positive and challenging emotions that each group represents as an opportunity to restore balance, if you receive a message regarding emotions. If the animal or being is in a positive situation, it speaks of our highest and best expression. We can feel affirmed that we are demonstrating our best by reading the highest and best message. If we notice a problem with the beings or animals in our dreams or in our lives, it is the challenging emotion. If that is the case, we need to heal and focus on the challenges and growth opportunities of the messages more. We may be experiencing the exact opposite of the positive qualities. Different cultures may revere different aspects of the same animal. It is good to notice your personal preferences.

> *"Every fellow Creature-being or life-form is a teacher and a potential friend. Each teacher in nature holds a deep abiding love for Great Mystery and will impart messages to those who seek the mysteries of the Void."*[41]

We can see Divinity and truth in the reflection of birds, insects and animals when we tune in and ask for Guidance. Certain characteristics and traits are unique to certain animals. By studying the habitat, the habits, the mental traits, the emotions and the physical body, it is possible to understand the symbology that each creature represents.

Animals appear to us in nature and in our dreamtime. They reflect important wisdom and guidance in our lives. There are certain behaviors that are attributed to various species that they are known by. These characteristic behaviors can teach us many things.

I was taking a small group out for a nature experience, a short "Medicine walk." We all set our intention as to what area of our lives we wished to receive a message about. I asked for some clarity about a surgical operation that I was about to have concerning my fertility. We were not a hundred yards into the hike, when I had an intuitive message to go to some bushes on the side of the trail. I parted the bushes to display two chartreuse green Chrysophilos flies, mating. My message was a positive green light for fertility for me. I went into my operation with complete confidence and trust that all would turn out well and it did.

> *"Once we understand which type of lesson is coming our way on our Medicine Walk, we can then proceed by noticing which Allies call to us. When something catches our eye, it has called our attention and is speaking to us through the Language of Love."*[42]

---

[41]Sams, 6.
[42]Sams, 7.

I had been living next door to a Hawaiian family who had a miniature rooster. We learned to co-exist as long as that little rooster was on the other side of the house. Recently, wild roosters have been drawn to the same house. Last night I was awakened at 3 am and again at 4:30, 5 and 6 by roosters. At first I was angry because I don't like to lose precious sleep. I was ready to wring the roosters' necks. Then, I realized there was a message for me. I thought about what rooster energy is about. It is masculine and assertive in coming forward, calling and commanding. When I finally got the message, I received a phone call from a male friend I really wanted to hear from, asking me out to dinner. The rooster was simply telling me to expect that call.

This is another example of animals answering my prayers for guidance. One beautiful tropical day we were going into Kaaawa Valley on a hike and it began raining hard. The ridge trail was narrow, tenuous, muddy and slippery. I was not sure if hiking into the valley in the rain was such a good idea, so I asked for Divine Guidance. We were perched up on a narrow ridge looking into the valley. When I was through with my prayer, after accessing Spirit, I looked up and saw 25 green parrots flying out of the valley make a U-turn directly in front of us and head back into the valley. I saw this as a definite "green light" from the Universe. We enjoyed an immensely powerful nature experience that day in trust and safety knowing that we were being guided all of the way

If we had not asked for Guidance, we would have turned back because of the rain. It looked too dangerous. Or, we could have proceeded in uncertainty, which could have resulted in an accident. It is so rewarding and reassuring to have Guidance!

I feel blessed to have received the green lights from the Universe when I asked. I feel blessed to have received the red lights too; they have saved me from injury and perhaps even death. My prayer is always that I am guided in each moment. I feel this is what has saved my life and is making it richer.

I am sure people get messages all of the time. Some act on them and some ignore them. Many people don't even know they can ask for assistance. Others forget they can ask for Guidance. Those who were taught about animals may find this to be a natural experience.

Animals & Beings Categorized by Signs & Emotions

Universe: Unity or Separation with Creation

The beings and animals in this category encourage and are revered as representations of Spiritual teachers, guides, balance, leadership, unity, purity, clarity or wisdom. They represent the Crown center and they have the energy of the Cosmos and the Universe. They are universal and are characterized by the element of ether. The beings are depicted by Angels, Enlightened Beings, Masters and Spirit guides. All men and women who are consciously aware, Spiritually focused (enlightened), well balanced in their masculine and feminine and realizing their fullest unique expression; would be at the highest end of the classification spectrum. The qualities are universal love, enlightenment, neutrality, perception beyond the five senses and multidimensionality.

When in an unbalanced state, these teachers and leaders can be misguided in judgment or leadership, and create separation rather than unity. They can be spoiled, lack gratitude and a connection with others. They can make the wrong choices. They can experience problems with the crown of the head and the tissues in that area.

Jaguars, unicorns and eagles are included in this category. The jaguar was the animal that represented the highest expression of consciousness to the Mayan culture. It was ruler of all forest animals, of the night and day, lunar and solar and feminine and masculine; in perfect balance and perfect unity. In Native American culture it is symbolic of integrity and impeccability. The unicorn has been written about in fantasy and myths for its unique consciousness. The horn coming from the middle of the forehead is symbolic of wisdom and the beautiful white coat, purity. The eagle is symbolic of power, focus and amazing vision.

Pisces: Serenity or Hopelessness with High Self

The beings and animals in this category encourage devotion, peace, serenity, grace, harmony and compassion, and represent the Perceptual center or Third Eye. They have the energy of Neptune and the sign of Pisces. They are characterized by the element of water. The beings are represented by psychics, mystics, priests, ministers, nurses and artists. The qualities are perception beyond the five senses, unconditional love and multidimensionality.

When in an unbalanced state, they can experience separation, disconnection, confusion or addiction and hopelessness. They may feel obsessive or like a martyr if they are out of touch with their Inner Self. They may have problems with the pituitary or pineal glands, the area just between the eye brows or the feet.

Most of the animals in this group are located in the ocean or fresh water. There is great serenity in the aquatic world. All fish and ocean vertebrates (with a spinal column), represent the perceptual center. Native Americans revere the salmon for the wisdom of coming full circle. Their behavior of swimming upstream, returning to its place of creation, signifies reconnecting with Great Spirit in the grand circle of life. Best known for their telepathy, intelligence, longevity on the planet and intuition are the cetaceans, the whales and dolphins. Whales have been known to recall their last song during the mating season. When they come back to the same place the following season, they pick up exactly where they left off! They symbolize the knowing of ancient history and other information from the Universe encoded in sound language or frequencies. That is how many psychics and mystics attune to information through the sound currents from the Universe moving through their ultrasonic core current, although they seem to come up with it out of nowhere. Autistic children, who have never spoken before, have been known to begin speaking after a dolphin encounter. Native Americans honor the dolphin and the breath of life it represents. Although living in water, it must surface to breathe, speaking of our connection through the breath with the Divine. In the Hindu culture, the swan is seen as perfect peace, serenity and Spirituality. In Native American culture, it is a symbol of grace and receptivity to Great Spirit's plan. If we observe the peacock we can't help noticing the perfectly shaped eyes on each of their plumes. The Egyptian culture used the eye of Horus and the ibis, a bird, to symbolize the wisdom of the third eye or perceptual center. The octopus surrounds itself in dark ink to confuse and evade predators while maintaining its peace and serenity. The blue heron is known for discovering self in the deep waters of consciousness. The raven is reputed to be the carrier of magic and the ability to change consciousness. Owls are known for being wise, psychic and clairvoyant as they can see in the dark and past the deception of ulterior motive according to some traditions.

Taurus: Devotion or Grief with Self Expression

These beings and the animals in this category encourage devotion to expressing Self, speaking our truth, communicating with compassion and represent the Communication Center. They have the energy of Venus and the sign of Taurus. They are characterized by the element of earth and being efficient in earthly or physical matters. The beings are represented by singers, art dealers, investors, distributors of goods and beauty professionals. The qualities are devotion, determination, ecstasy, harmony and beauty.

When in an unbalanced state, they can be blocked in their ability to communicate, fear expressing themselves or experience deep sadness and grief. They may be people pleasers, possessive or hedonistic. They may experience problems with their neck, parathyroid and thyroid gland or their throat.

The animals associated with this group are the larger animals that sometimes are slow and lumbering like bulls, buffalo, cows, bears and moose. They represent being steady, reaching goals and being well grounded. They are socially devoted to being communal and hanging out in herds. They enjoy eating and moving leisurely. Buffalo signify prayer, abundance and the use of everything in a sacred way. Bears love the sweetness of honey which represents the love of speaking our truth and hibernate, demonstrating the need for rest and regeneration. Pigs enjoy the comfort and sensuality of food and a great mud bath. The moose takes pleasure in expressing itself by bellowing for the benefit of the females, teaching us self-esteem. All talking birds like parrots and cockatiels resonate with this group. One of the larger ground species of birds, the turkey, enjoys expressing itself with "gobble, gobble, gobble."

Gemini: Acceptance or Unfulfilled Desire with Self

The beings and animals in this category encourage expression of love, beliefs, integration of ideas, observations and productivity, and represent the Heart or Love Center. They have the energy of Mercury and the sign of Gemini. They are characterized by the element of air. The beings are represented by writers, teachers, speakers, communicators, students, social butterflies and siblings. The qualities are quick minds, effective strategies, excellent hand eye co-ordination and great conversation. It is important that they learn acceptance of themselves and others in order to generate prosperity, money and success.

When in an unbalanced state, some may be so busy and active spending time doing and thinking that they forget to take time to be and feel. Their hearts or emotional life may suffer from the lack of self acceptance, stillness and tranquility; resulting in restlessness. They can be gullible, foolish, immature, superficial and selfish or have unfulfilled dreams. They create too many diversions. They may have problems with their shoulders, arms, hands, thymus gland or lungs.

Most flying insects, especially bees, exemplify the busyness and industry of this category. Dragonflies reflect communication and change. They are constantly on the move. Butterflies are frequently changing direction like they know their mind and then change it. All flying birds in this selection may represent Mercury, the winged messenger or Angel messengers. They bring messages from the heavens to us. Ravens represent the magic of receiving a message. Hawks teach us to look and observe. Roosters call us to work by heralding the dawn with their crowing. Animals that travel in a pack and howl in the moonlight like hyenas, coyotes and wolves, are in this group. Hyenas laugh seemingly superficially. Coyotes act foolishly and are tricksters at heart. Wolves are thought by some natives to bring new ideas and are teachers and communicators. Weasels have the powers of observation. Opossums use the strategy of playing dead to escape, and symbolize diversion.

Cancer: Contentment or Attachment with Emotions

The beings and animals in this category encourage emotions, femininity, domesticity, the love of home and family, feeling nurtured and secure, and being comforted and cherished. They also represent the Heart or Love Center. They have the energy of the Moon and the sign of Cancer. They are characterized by the element of water. The beings are represented by mothers, mermaids, domestic help, cooks, chefs, food servers, wet nurses, nannies and day care workers. The qualities are contentment, being nurturing, comforting, and cherishing. Mothers are responsible for the heart and soul of the family. They teach their children the language of emotions and listening to their Inner guidance. They assume the protection of the offspring when the father is not available. They transform the house into a home by making it comfortable and inviting. They serve wonderful, nutritious and tasty food. They are more receptive and respect masculinity when they are in balance.

When in an unbalanced state, their hearts or emotional life may suffer if they lack boundaries or allow hurt in the name of love. They may feel alienated, insecure and smothering. They can demonstrate passive aggressive behavior, extreme sensitivity, upset, intolerance, and distress. They can implode with negative feelings. They can be too attached to love ones and forget themselves. They can have problems with the chest, the breasts or the backside of that area and level.

Sea life that is more community and family oriented like sea turtles and those in protective shells like crabs, oysters, clams and lobsters are in this category. They live in their homes at all times. They also represent being crabby, clamming up or giving a good pinch! Turtles represent motherhood. Other animals in this category include cows and goats that are utilized for milk production. Loyal animals that serve and protect the home and family, like dogs, are in this group. The fox has great ability to protect their family. With great speed, it can vanish and disappear, leading invaders away from their den.

Leo: Kindness or Anger with Personal Power

The beings and animals in this category encourage empowerment, joy, luck, courage, Higher intellect and personal power with kindness. They represent the Power Center. They have the energy of the Sun and the sign of Leo. They are characterized by the element of fire. The beings are represented by fathers, professors, coaches, trainers and athletes. Their qualities are personal power and intuitive intelligence. They possess integrity, confidence, many talents and a gifted intellect. They can be Spiritual and inspirational. They polarize masculine, are sporty and electric, cherish femininity, and provide and protect others, when they are in balance. They encourage Self-empowerment in others.

In an unbalanced state, some may be dis-empowered or dis-empowering, drained, deteriorated or blaming. Some may be dominating, fiery, prideful, angry or greedy. They can express egocentric ideas, need to be the center of attention or be too cowardly and cautious in behavior. They may be showy, lazy, impetuous, indolent or irresponsible gamblers. In the extreme, they are angry predators enjoying power over others. They can have problems with the solar plexus area, the heart or spleen and the liver or cardiovascular system.

The animals in this group include all lions, tigers, panthers and cats. They hunt to provide their prides with nourishment. They are extremely powerful, athletic, have great confidence and are kind to their families. It is interesting that the name of their family group is a "pride." Pride may be defined as arrogance or Self-respect, there is a fine line. Hummingbirds are revered in some cultures as a representation of a great Spiritual energy or the joy and pure bliss of an open heart. Falcons are a sporting and hunting energy. The peacocks' trait of showing their plumage is indicative of the showy nature of this group. The raccoon is known for its protective and generous way of providing for those in need. Raccoon energy is about assisting others without dis-empowering them.

Virgo: Courage or Fear with Service

The beings and animals in this category encourage service and material utilization. They represent two centers, the Sexual and Creative and the Foundation and Elimination Centers. They have the energy of Mercury and the sign of Virgo. The beings are represented by maidens, virgins, animal lovers and innocents like children, who are naturally earthy, sensual and tactile. This group is also represented by veterinarians, massage therapists, most personnel, clerks, purchasing and procurement agents and accountants. The qualities are dedication, discernment, meticulous behavior, and great service and detail orientation. They like to process information and file it accordingly. They are usually educated, well trained and engage the mind as a servant of the Spirit or others.

When out of balance, some may feel inadequate and inferior about their training or education. They feel like they are not prepared enough. They can be anal retentive in behavior or attitude. They might worry, fret, overwork or have anxiety about performance. They can nag or be critical with unrealistic standards of perfection and work production. They may have problems with the abdominal area, the bowels or the colon.

The animals in this group live on land. They include the deer for their gentleness and caring which can touch those who are in need of healing. The squirrel teaches us to plan, account and save for the winter or a rainy day. Mice and rats know more detail by touching things up close and personal with their whiskers. The land turtle symbolizes being grounded and slowing down to take care of the details of our material world. Ants remind us of a good work ethic and to take care of the details. The otter, which lives on land, is adventurous and curious to know things and shares the wisdom of sisterhood. Some may have heard the expression, "scared like a rabbit." Burrowing animals like rabbits and prairie dogs run back to their dens when they feel fearful to retreat, rest, relax and replenish their life force. There are times when we need to regroup.

Libra: Acceptance or Unfulfilled Desire with Relationship

The beings and animals in this category encourage expression of peace, diplomacy, harmony in relationships and appreciation of balance and fairness. They represent both the Power Center and the Creative and Sexual Center. They have the energy of Venus and the sign of Libra. They are characterized by the element of air. The beings are represented by partners, diplomats, ambassadors, representatives, senators, arbitrators, mediators, umpires and referees. Notice that referees wear black and white shirts to symbolize fairness, equality and justice. The qualities are a high regard for fairness, relationship, psychology and admiration of the arts. They want to be meticulously articulate in their expression and in communication. They want acceptance with others and prefer being a partner or committed to someone or something.

When in an unbalanced state, some may be biased, polarized toward one side or superficial in their lives or relationships. They may be living beyond their means for appearance sake. They can value their heads over their hearts causing overly rational behavior. They may go from partner to partner or develop addictions due to their unfilled desires in relationship or trying to find sweetness in life. They can create or be enemies and rivals. They can have problems with the area just below the waistline, the kidneys or pancreas.

All creatures that mate for life and all black and white animals like birds, skunks and zebras are included in this selection. They bring the message of relationship; being in relationship with another and your self, in balance. The black and white represent honoring the masculine and feminine in balance. Love birds are included in this category. Skunks teach us to respect others and ourselves in our relationships.

Scorpio: Contentment or Emotional Attachment with Sex & Social Power

The beings and animals in this category encourage transformation, regeneration and sexual creativity, and represent the Sexual and Creative Center. They have the energy of Pluto and the sign of Scorpio. They are characterized by the element of water. The beings are represented by healers, shamans, magicians, doctors, psychoanalysts, politicians, strippers, exotic dancers and prostitutes. The qualities are deep and penetrating insight and the ability to analyze, probe and investigate the nature of things. It is important that they learn how to transform the nature of their sexuality and relationship with power and develop contentment with their creative Self. The highest expression is to be socially and politically correct and constructive with one's energy. For politicians, it is to hold office for the people and not for personal gain.

When in an unbalanced state, some may be too attached to sex, power, position, outcome or people. Their emotional life may suffer from not developing their creativity or by attempting to gain power over another. They might be manipulative or controlling. They may use ego games of jealousy, possessiveness, guilt or insecurity to maintain power over others. They can be pathetic victims or victimizers with a sting. Some might be destructive, withholding and secretive to get their way. Their sexual desire can be out of balance. They may have problems with the pelvic area or sexual organs; the uterus, ovaries, vagina, penis, testes, prostate gland, etc.

All creatures that transform from one form to another like the phoenix, frogs, dragonflies and butterflies are included in this category. The phoenix is said to rise from the ashes, be reborn and live again. Frogs are revered by some cultures for fertility and abundance and in others, for singing to create rain for cleansing and purifying the land and our hearts. Dragonflies, butterflies and moths all go through a chrysalis or cocoon stage before rebirth as a winged insect. Animals that have a good sting or bite like scorpions, snakes, alligators, centipedes and tarantulas are in this category. Scorpions sting when threatened. Snakes transform by shedding old skins. Alligators teach us to go deeper with our experience of integration that just surface level and were venerated by the Egyptians. Centipedes seem to signify that which we are afraid of that may bite us in the night. Tarantulas give us that hairy-scary feeling of disempowerment. Other reptiles also include dragons and lizards. Dragons are powerful symbols of supremacy and authority in many cultures, especially with the Chinese. Lizards are known for their psychic powers, the ability to dream the future while sunning on a rock. Animals of the night, like bats and animals of death, like vultures are included, too. Bats are symbolic of rebirth; leaving our ego and old patterns behind and being reborn into a new life. Vultures devour what is no longer needed. The trait of the opossum of excreting the musk of the death scent is represented also. The lynx is celebrated for being a knower of secrets and the nature of the great mysteries of life.

Aries: Kindness or Anger with Ego, Sexual Passion & Physical Power

The beings and animals in this category encourage sexual passion, physical power, drive, execution, creative executive ability and leadership in business matters, and represent the Sexual and Creative Center. They have the energy of Mars and the sign of Aries. They are characterized by the element of fire. The beings are represented by business executives, dancers, soldiers, warriors, athletes and sports enthusiasts. The qualities are enjoyment of action, speed, thrills, competition and passion. They are easily promoted, can initiate activity and oversee to completion. They enjoy sexual activity and a natural uninhibited expression. It is important that they learn to be kind in the pursuit and drive for what they want.

When in an unbalanced state, some may be too ego-oriented, frustrated, pushy, forceful, aggressive, confrontational or headstrong. They might be selfish, angry, impatient or dictatorial. They can demonstrate the exact opposite by being helpless, weak or in denial. They may be sexually permissive, demonstrating emotional and sexual dysfunction with blocked creativity. They might manifest a crisis, emergency or an accident. The desire nature can be out of balance. They may also have problems with the pelvic area or sexual organs; the uterus, ovaries, vagina, penis, testes, prostate gland, etc.

All creatures engaged in the act of mating, demonstrating aggressive traits or agility are in this category. The rabbits' traits of sexual activity and speed would be a part of this selection. The grouse is reported to symbolize the kundalini sexual spiral of energy. The badger, the fighting cock and the shark attack and fight for what they want with a vicious, angry and aggressive energy. Some have heard the idiom, about being "badgered." Wild boars, rams and rhinos are known for their aggressive and confrontational manner as well as their ability to use their heads as weapons. While the rhino is likely to be aggressive when protecting her offspring, wild boars tear up everything in their path. They bring the wisdom of confronting yourself, instead of others, about shortcomings. Apes, monkeys and gorillas symbolize agility and dexterity.

Sagittarius: Kindness or Anger with Humor & Philosophical Power

The beings and animals in this category encourage the expression of humor, honesty, wisdom, philosophy, ethics and Spiritual law, and represent the area of the hips and thighs. They have the energy of Jupiter and the sign of Sagittarius. They are characterized by the element of fire. The beings are represented by comedians, clowns, philosophers, lawyers, in-laws, travelers, foreigners and zealots. They are big energetically, outgoing, love liberty or foreign ways. They can be inspirational instructors regarding studying, traveling and foreign cultures. Their qualities are generosity, honesty and straightforwardness. It is important that they learn kindness with their honesty, humor and philosophy.

When in an unbalanced state, some may be too overzealous, righteous, dogmatic or fanatic. They may be judgmental, limited in experience or jump to conclusions. They can be loud and discharge energy with frivolous activity or take on too much. They can suffer greatly by trying to find their truth outside of themselves. They may have problems with their hips and thighs.

All creatures that have powerful legs for moving forward or jumping like centaurs, horses, unicorns, rhinos, kangaroos and elephants are in this group. Horses can get hoof and mouth diseases as can the beings listed above, by opening their mouths and inserting their foot. They can also teach us the wisdom that all paths and philosophies have validity. Unicorns teach us to use the magic of our wisdom to move forward. Rhinos carry a lot of body weight and can run fast. This can be symbolic of the weight of responsibility for creating a philosophy in life that moves us forward in an ethical manner. Kangaroos are known for their ability to leap a great distance which can represent taking a leap of faith or jumping to conclusions. Elephants have great strength to clear land and roads. The elephant god, Ganesh is revered by the Hindus as a remover of obstacles and a source of wisdom.

Capricorn: Courage or Fear and Insecurity with Foundation

The beings and animals in this category encourage ambition, accomplishment, problem solving and the manifestation of physical and financial security with managerial ability, and represent the Foundation and Elimination Center. They have the energy of Saturn and the sign of Capricorn. They are characterized by the element of earth. The beings are represented by authorities, corporate officers, governors, judges, inspectors, management, conservatives, conservationists and organizers. The qualities are intuitive minds, stability, organization, patience and perseverance. They have the ability to manifest and produce structure for creation. It is important that they learn to let go when it is appropriate.

When in an unbalanced state, some may be judgmental, pessimistic, depressed or blocked. This condition can be reflected by physical, mental, emotional or Spiritual constipation. They might be severely critical, rigid, inhibited, and stern. The muscles may be tight or contracted. Their hearts or emotional life can suffer from too much seriousness or melancholy resulting in depression and negativity. They might have a survival mentality or ungrounded methods. They may have problems with their knees, spine, skeletal structure, bones and teeth.

Most sure-footed mountain and cargo animals are represented in this category, especially goats, deer, antelopes, camels and lamas; they exemplify the ability to carry the burden of responsibility with nimbleness and courage. They can go the distance, some carry material goods for trade. Their legs are long, yet the knees can be vulnerable. They symbolize karmic lessons and retribution; make one false step and the consequences may be falling into a ravine and getting hurt. The giraffe reflects the ability of these beings to stick their necks out with intuitive problem solving skills for solutions. The prairie dog shares the wisdom of taking time for inactivity and silent retreat to garner solutions through dreams and visions away from the chaos of the world. The crow signifies the laws of sacredness and makes its caw sound to remind us to pay attention. It is known in Native American tradition to be a shape-shifter, suspending physical law. Animals that are black, like black panthers, symbolize the night, femininity with authority and facing the unknown without fear. The black panther symbolizes embracing the void or the unknown, without fear. The porcupine reminds us that fear is powerful and can hurt as quills are released in fear. Also, that trust, innocence and child-like play can keep us from too much seriousness. Spiders denote the ability to manifest or create with their weaving ability. Ants represent the patience required for a group project. They will carry materials for miles to their nests. Beavers create dams with many escape routes, which teaches the wisdom of building, boundaries and alternatives. The armadillo wears its armor to protect and set boundaries or rolls up in a ball when in fear.

Aquarius: Acceptance or Unfulfilled Desires with Humanitarianism

The beings and animals in this category encourage humanitarianism, brotherhood, freedom and friendship, and represent the ankles. They have the energy of Uranus and the sign of Aquarius. They are characterized by the element of air. The beings are represented by humanitarians, brotherhood organizations, friends, social groups, inventors, electronic engineers, computer technicians and bohemians. They bring qualities of enlightenment, equality and ingenuity into our world with avant-garde thinking. They have talent with electronics, innovation and invention. They are determined and independent, original and possess excellent memory. It is important that they learn to create change in a constructive manner, rather than a radical or rebellious manner.

When in an unbalanced state, some might be unpredictable, erratic or eccentric to the extreme. They can be off center and desire change in a revolutionary way. They may rebel and live outside the status quo, pushing the boundaries. They might argue, create opposition or be hypocritical. This condition can be reflected by anxiety, nervousness or apprehensiveness. They may demonstrate shaky movement or exaggerate troubles. They might have problems with their ankles.

Divine Reason & Rhyme

The animals included in this category are: elk, elephants, dogs, crows and raccoons. The elk symbolizes stamina with the antlers as lofty ideas. It is important to be able to go the distance with great ideas and not be thwarted. The elephant is known for its excellent memory. Many of us remember the adage, "elephants never forget." Dogs are acclaimed as "man's best friend and signify the importance of being loyal and a good friend to the trustworthy. Crows are notorious for their powerful voice to speak out against injustice and to create balance when there is inequality. They want change to create a better world for humanity. We can also "eat crow" when we don't follow through on walking our talk. The raccoon is painted as the "little bandit," like Zorro, giving caring and generosity to those in need and righting injustices. It is the protector of the needs of the community.

Associations with Animals & Beings

Please remember that your personal correlation when reading the message of the animal or being is important and takes precedence over other associations. Take note of the emotions that are indicated in order to be more balanced and to restore integrity. Also, the same animal may be representative of different groupings according to its perceived traits.

Chapter 9

Astrology, Numbers & Other Divination Methods

Reading the Energy of Symbology

All things in Creation have meaning and reflect specific energies whether we are aware of it or not. It is our responsibility to learn their relevance. The more clearly we understand what these symbols represent, the more effective our ability to understand and act on Guidance.

Astrology

What is the value of Astrology applied in our life? Andrew Carnegie once said, "Millionaires do not use astrologers, billionaires do!" If we understand that it is a Divine Reflection of the energies and cycles, we too can use it to our benefit. Great leaders of religions and countries use this information to their benefit. There is great strength in understanding and using the energies and cycles. Knowledge is powerful. This is an introduction to astrology, a science and an art.

Just as we observe in nature, there are seasons and cycles for planting and some for harvesting. We have documented that early astrologers would examine and record their observations about the position of the stars, the signs of the zodiac, the sun and the moon. For them, it was like a Divine message written in the sky. It was what brought the Three Wise Men to the birth of Jesus in Bethlehem. We hear of people born "under a lucky star" and others are said to have been "star-crossed". This is modern day language; referring to the sagacity and insight that our Universe holds as a Divine Creation.

The study of Astrology is extremely comprehensive. For one person's birth chart, there are 12 houses, 12 signs, and more than 12 points, planetary and luminary (sun and moon) positions to be crossed referenced and inter-related by their geometric configurations in degrees. These relationships are known as conjunctions (0*), sextiles (60*), squares (90*), trines (120*), and oppositions (180*). Then, we can learn about these aspects or angles of relationship between the planets and what they represent. This is just for a birth chart. When we get into forecasting, we position the transiting planets around the birth chart and we have another set of 12 X 12 X 12. When we compare the charts of two people for love or business, we have two different charts to be accounted for. We will not be going into that kind of depth in this book, it is too much information. I just want to acquaint you with the basics of planets/luminaries and the signs of the zodiac.

Astrology is the most specific tool of Guidance I have utilized in my practice. The timing and descriptions of cycles are extremely accurate. It is not for everyone, in that it takes a tremendous amount of dedication and devotion to learn and become proficient with. We can become skilled at understanding the basics of the energies that are represented by each planet and sign. Most people already know their birth sign. The planet that "rules" or represents each astrological "sign" has the same kind of characteristics and interpretations as that sign. We will be identifying those in this chapter. We can learn all twelve if we like!

The basis for our comprehension of how astrology works is that we are born on earth at a specific time, at a certain point in longitude and latitude. Our birth time and location can be calculated to determine local time, then Greenwich Mean Time and finally Universal time. Universal time creates a map of the sky as to where the planets and luminaries are and the sign of the zodiac. This map reflects our patterns, challenges, talents and abilities and gives us the opportunity to manifest our best, if we are aware of it. The planets are located in our own solar system: Mercury, Venus, Mars, Jupiter, Saturn, Uranus, Neptune and Pluto. The luminaries are the Sun and Moon. The zodiac signs are Aries, Taurus, Gemini, Cancer, Leo, Virgo, Libra, Scorpio, Sagittarius, Capricorn, Aquarius and Pisces.

These heavenly bodies simply reflect the energy that was present when we initiated our life on earth. It describes us. We are born to the perfect family experience that provides the exact patterns that we need to heal and grow in this life. We came to this world to transform ourselves, although we can choose to repeat the same painful, self-limiting patterns. These patterns can keep us from claiming true Self-empowerment unless we make some serious realizations of what we need to change about ourselves and then take action. They indicate our potential for evolution and creative expression. It is our free will choice; we can change our lives. We have the power to change those behaviors, decisions, attitudes, beliefs and emotions that have kept us from success in relationships and life. The first step is to know ourselves through our birth chart.

Astrology is a Spiritual tool to understand ourselves better and what we need to learn; to evolve, grow and to express love better. It is also a mental, physical and emotional guide. It gives us a greater understanding of others, as we are not all the same. There is a tendency to think that everyone is like us. It simply isn't true. The human condition may be similar, but not everyone thinks like us or emotes like us or has the same physicality. Astrology assists us in realizing and recognizing personal variations. This in turn gives us relationship sensitivity and freedom from judging others, who do not think, act or feel like us. There are higher and lower expressions of this diversity. Each one of us is on our own evolutionary path in our own time. It may not be the time and evolution others want for us. If we honor others and their path, it allows us to love and accept all, which is a Spiritual principal. We can truly celebrate our diversity if we all comprehend that Divine Source intended for there to be diversity in the Universe.

Astrology is the most practical tool that I have experienced with regard to accurate and correct timing. We know when the energy is conducive to initiation, when the energy is appearing blocked or stopped and we can use that to modulate our lives. We don't want to open a new business or invest when the energy is challenging and obstructed. We can, as we have free will, it just takes more energy and the results are not as successful. When we launch new business, projects or relationships, timing is everything.

There are cycles of expansion and contraction. If we know what cycle we are in and what cycle is coming up, we can plan in a very practical way. We can save money during the cycles of expansion, where money is plentiful, to use during the times of contraction. We can know how long a challenging cycle will last. This is crucial, since some people think that things will not get better. Then it is possible to do something unwise and foolish; such as taking our life, quitting a relationship, or giving up just before a new cycle is to begin.

If we do not learn the lesson of the cycle, it can be very painful, psychologically depressing and we can feel very hopeless, like life is not worth living. If we learn the lesson of each pattern and cycle, we can empower ourselves and become a dynamic expression of our Highest and best understanding.

Astrological Signs, Ruling Planets & Houses

In the last chapter, the signs of the zodiac, the higher and lower emotion related to each sign, and the beings and animals were all introduced. Planets and luminaries can be associated with the signs of the Zodiac & the houses of our chart, making our Divination practice even simpler. We call it rulership. All three categories indicate similar meanings:

Aries—Mars—1
Taurus—Venus—2
Gemini—Mercury—3
Cancer—Moon—4
Leo—Sun—5
Virgo—Mercury—6
Libra—Venus—7
Scorpio —Mars, Pluto—8

Sagittarius—Jupiter—9
Capricorn—Saturn—10
Aquarius—Uranus—11
Pisces—Neptune—12

We see Divine Plan, reflections, cycles and tendencies as we observe the planets and the luminaries in our galaxy, the Milky Way. It is most likely similar in other galaxies, as there is unity and repeating patterns in the Universe. A luminary is any heavenly body emanating or reflecting light. At this time we will be describing the planets in our Solar system and the luminaries, which are the sun and earth's moon.

There is one important message I want to communicate. The planets and stars do not dictate our lives. They do not rule us; they simply reflect our experience, tendencies and our cycles. We reflect them and they reflect us. We are one. We can be truly at choice in our life if we are fully aware, understand the messages in the reflections of these heavenly bodies and exercise our free will.

In 1982, I had a series of five car accidents in a period of about two years. Most all were minor except one that left me bedridden. Before that time, I had many injuries from minor accidents, but no car accidents. My logical mind could not understand what was happening. I had always had pretty good luck with other things. As I lay in bed, I contemplated my life. Since I was flat on my back, with no place to go, I had the perfect opportunity to face myself. Why were all of these car accidents happening? My curriculum in college was pre-med. and totally scientific, certainly not esoteric. My left brain, linear mind just could not figure it out.

My mother, on the other hand, was very psychic and practiced Astrology as a hobby. She suggested that I study my own chart. Up until this point in my life, I considered Astrology to be unrealistic and impractical. Regardless, I decided to study the planets and the stars to determine what was going on since I was bed-ridden for the next ten months. I couldn't do anything else anyway. I felt I needed to do something productive with my mind. I couldn't just lie there in the stillness! (Sound familiar?)

I studied everyday. As a result of my study, I found that I had a tendency to have more serious accidents during certain cycles as shown in my personal natal or birth chart. It was being challenged during this period. This more serious accident predisposition was different from what I considered my normal cuts, scrapes, stitches and sprains.

Astrology changed my life. No longer was I unaware of my circumstances. I studied 17 hours a day. I compared interpretations in numerous natal chart and predictive Astrology books. Not trusting what these experts said, I observed and recorded the cycles like a scientist. I did it to be certain there was value in the art and science of Astrology.

By analyzing the planetary configurations, I was able to understand what energies needed to be balanced within myself. I learned about how my personality makeup contributed to my accidents. My lesson was to harmonize my emotional energy and to slow down and balance my outer activity with Inner Spiritual awareness.

From studying and reading about my planetary aspects and positions, I realized that I was receiving a message to let go of my ego and to learn to trust that I am a child of Divinity and would always be cared for. This was new to me. I never trusted anyone to be there. I had to rely on myself. I always thought that my life was all on my shoulders and there was no one there for me, but me. Those accidents were the best thing that ever happened to me in the way of a message to learn to trust in Divine Source. These experiences have transformed my life.

Magical things happened when I learned to trust in my Divine Parents. While lying in bed disabled, I had no obvious income. I didn't have any idea how I was going to pay the rent. Just in time, a truck backed into my car, causing just enough damage to pay my rent. The vehicle was hardly damaged. This is an example of an unusual "blessing." I was unable to figure out how to get the money. It was then, I realized I was truly being cared for and was not alone. The check was sent within a week, which is unheard of in the insurance world. This was a true miracle to me.

The time I spent injured and in bed was downtime for me. I couldn't go out and expand my activities in the world outside. I was limited to the inside, literally. I had contracted muscles from my injuries. My spine was sprained. I spent time with my Self. It was important and necessary for me to stop and take a look to evaluate and reformulate who I was and where I was going. I needed contemplation and reflection. I needed a cycle of contraction to do this as I would not have done it on my own. If I had done this of my own free will during this time, I might not have had to have the injuries to force me to stay still.

It is important to understand that there are expansion and contraction cycles. In my experience, I find that during contraction cycles, if I stay positive, create a new foundation and realign myself, I can expand Higher and better. There is an expression, "as above, so below". If we buy into the appearance of things staying contracted, uncomfortable, painful, we will create ourselves as a "victim." If we choose to understand that it's simply a realignment process to expand our base and develop our foundation, we will expand commensurately with the work we have invested during our contraction cycle.

When we have such great pain that saps our energy, exhausts us and we feel like we are breaking down emotionally and physically, we know we are experiencing a contraction cycle. It is humbling and forces us to be still to listen to our Inner wisdom. Use your healing time creatively. During my healing time I used hypnosis, subconscious reprogramming, prayer, dream work and visualization, as well as listening for new Guidance to come through. If we do not, our enthusiasm for life will decline. It will not be worth living. If we realize that the expansion cycle will follow with opportunities, we can make it through the pain. Many people take their own lives during their difficult cycles thinking that it is never going to change and that they don't have the power to change it. By knowing our cycles, we will understand what needs transforming, we will know when the pain cycle will end and the blessings begin.

Even though I have experienced a lot of pain and suffering, I have created an opportunity for myself, each time, no matter how bleak things looked. By attuning to the cycles and the reflection of the wisdom they contained, I have had the opportunity to experience miracles in my healing process. It has not been suffering in vain, which is seriously depressing, thwarting and life threatening. We were not created to suffer in vain. In the Bible, Jesus did not suffer in vain; he demonstrated the miracle of transforming suffering, pain and separation into a Higher purpose of freedom for everyone who chooses the same.

The expression, "timing is everything.' is true in many ways. When we initiate business, projects, relationships, etc.; there are cycles that are more conducive to success. We can do things whenever our free will chooses. I prefer to launch my "ship" when the tide is going out. In that way, I can utilize the energies already present. It is easier, more productive and less stressful to ride the energy like a wave instead of swimming against the current. I know I can do it when the tide is coming in, yet that choice does not indicate a wise use of time and resources. It can build stress and disharmony and ultimately cause disease.

I now understand this principle better. Those of us who understand the physical laws of physics can appreciate this. There is a principle in physics about contraction and expansion; for every action, there is an equal and opposite reaction for a balanced and stable system. Even though there is great suffering and pain on this earth, there is incredible pleasure and joy. For those who don't know physics, an example would be the intense and unbearable pain when the muscles in a mother's body contract before she opens and expands to give birth in joy and ecstasy. Each time you go through a difficult contraction, you too can give birth to a miracle if you have the right attitude and behavior. This is true empowerment.

It is written, "An evil generation seeks a sign". We are told that astrology and other Divination methods are "tools of the devil." Who is the devil anyway? Could the devil possibly be those doing evil or those attempting to control and manipulate our actions?

How could "Divination" methods be tools of the devil? Divination refers to the Divine. The Divine is our Source, our Creator, and our Mother/Father. Divinity wants us to follow the signs, to be empowered in the unfolding of Divine Plan.

We are told that we are supposed to believe in Divine Source without any external evidence or signs through faith. Most evidence of astrology and astrological signs was eliminated from the bible except for a few, like the Three Wise Men that followed the star to Bethlehem. There is a discrepancy here. If Christianity declares signs are evil, why would three "wise" men follow them? How could a sign like a "star" (astrological) possibly result in showing the holy birthplace of Jesus in the story of the Nativity? Are there those who do not wish for us to be truly empowered? Are there those in power who are able to control others with the wisdom we all need, whilst we are told it is wrong?

We see the separation of the physical/natural from the Spiritual/supernatural in most modern religions. How are we supposed to pray for and listen to Divine wisdom and plan for our self if we have no tangible way of seeing and understanding it through signs and the messages of creation?

We were created in a physical, tangible environment as Spiritual and physical beings. Why would Divine Source not give us Spiritual and physical messages and signs that we can understand? If a Divine Source is the Creator of all of nature, why would Divine Guidance not be reflected in it? It is not evil to seek the Guidance of Divine wisdom in our life in the Divine reflection of creation and nature. We are missing out on the empowerment of the insight that it reflects if we choose not to pay attention.

I believe that this essential part of our education has been missing. We have not been trained to see signs and understand their messages. We were not trained to listen to the voice of our Inner Self. I believe that we are more easily controlled and victimized when we don't listen to and see the messages and signs of our own Divine Guidance. We don't have to be powerless from not knowing. We don't have to give our power away to others if we know. There does not have to be a total mystery about life if we learn Divination principles.

In Fatima, witnesses reported the phenomena of the sun dancing in the sky during the apparition of the Virgin Mary. This is a great sign that the feminine principles of heart and soul need to be re-established on this earth with the masculine principals (symbolized by the sun.) I too, have seen the sun dancing in the sky during a celebration of the feminine at a Goddess retreat. It was a spectacular experience of wholeness in a Supernatural expression.

The planets are Divine Reflections and have certain characteristics. Each one reflects a higher and lower expression. It is up to us to maximize the Highest Expression and to transform the lower expression.

Planets, Luminaries & Elements

Mercury

Mercury has two elemental expressions, air and earth.

Highest expression:

Air—communications, messages, intellect or belief systems.

Earth—detailed, meticulous, health oriented, discerning or hard working.

Challenging expression:

Air—mental confusion, inhibited intellect, immaturity, naiveté, gullibility or too busy.

Earth—critical, picky, dense, gross, coarse in communication or feels inferior. If Mercury reflects any kind of cycle of inhibition, it affects our thinking and it can be a bad brain day!

Venus

Venus also has two elemental expressions, air and earth.

Highest expression:

Air—relationship oriented, balanced, likes justice, psychological talent, an agreeable communicator, diplomacy or artistic appreciation.

Earth—sensual, likes things that feel good, smell good, taste good and look good, likes to possess the finer things of life, art, beauty, earthy desires, or creates harmony in life and communication.

Challenging expression:

Air—into the head rather than feelings, rationalizing, superficial, unbalanced, or other-oriented with loss of self.

Earth—hedonistic, addictive, pleasing others rather than Self, blocked communication, or hoarding instead of sharing. If Venus reflects too much desire for the sweetness of life, everything good can be used in an undisciplined way! Time for indulgence out of control!

Mars

Mars has two elemental expressions, fire and water.

Highest expression:

Fire—leader, initiator, executive, action oriented or strong drive.

Water—natural sexuality, healthy passion or creating life.

Challenging expression:

Fire—argumentative, bossy, selfish, competitive, forceful, selfish or angry.

Water—power hungry, forceful or dysfunctional with sexual relations. If Mars reflects too much passion, we can burn out our loved ones!

Jupiter

Jupiter has one elemental expression, fire.

Highest expression: direct, inspiring, philosophical, adventurous, or humorous.

Challenging expression: undiplomatic, confrontational with truth, looking for truth on outside, over zealous, righteous, talking too much or excessive. If Jupiter reflects too much philosophical dialog, notice if someone leaves the room while we're still talking!

Saturn

Saturn has one elemental expression, earth.

Highest expression: major managerial skills, great manifestation skills, maturity, patience or financial security.

Challenging expression: too much structure and scheduling, critical, rigid, stern, overworking, blocked or inhibited. If Saturn reflects too much restriction, we can tie up our partner to lighten things up or go on retreat and wait it out!

Uranus

Uranus has one elemental expression, air.

Highest expression: humanitarian, evokes evolution, enlightenment, freedom, brotherhood or friendship.

Challenging expression: radical, excessively eccentric, unpredictable, rebellious, out of time and out of place or too much nervous tension. If Uranus reflects nervous tension, we can see our energy bouncing off the walls! We may have to shake our booty to release it.

Neptune

Neptune has one elemental expression, water.

Highest expression: Spiritual, psychic, artistic, serene, demonstrates wholeness, multidimensionality, into unity or unconditional love.

Challenging expression: separation, disconnection, psychological confusion, obsession, addiction, unreliable or spacey. If Neptune reflects a "spaced out" condition, we may have already forgotten the details!

Pluto

Pluto has one elemental expression, water.

Highest expression: transformation, regeneration, analyzing, probing, penetrating insight, sexually creative, empowering or being socially and politically correct.

Challenging expression: vindictive, mean, manipulating and controlling, participation in ego games, jealousy, guilt, possessiveness or insecurity. If Pluto reflects cycles of drama with control games, we may be the "entertainment" director until we learn to stop playing those games!

Sun

The sun has one elemental expression, fire.

Highest expression: illuminated, empowered, strength in wisdom and truth, Spiritual, extremely energetic, courageous, provider, protector, generosity, joy or luck. *Challenging expression:* egotistical, elitist, dominating, controlling, aggressive, hot tempered, greedy, cowardly, blaming, lazy, impetuous or needing to be the center of attention. If the Sun reflects a cycle of too much energy, we're can burn out the competition and everyone else in range!

Moon

The moon has one elemental expression, water.

Highest expression: intuitive, reflective, nurturing, emotional, flowing, unconditional love, to love home and family, to be comforting and cherishing, domestic or sensitive.

Challenging expression: lunacy, insecurity, alienation, extremely passive, emotions out of control or inhibited, implode with negative feelings, passive aggressive with anger, lacking boundaries, allowing hurt in the name of love or to hide feelings. If the Moon reflects a cycle of too much emotional stress, take care of yourself in the comfort and safety of your own room and bring out the "security blanket".

Numerology

Just as heavenly bodies reflect wisdom, so does our number system. This section is devoted to the meaning of different numbers. With our birth date alone we can determine our overall expression. From our birth date and the number of the current year, we can determine the overall cycle of the year ahead. I was guided to move to Hawaii during a number one year. It was a year of new beginnings and that is exactly what the number one is about. It is about starting new things, initiation.

We can determine what the energy of our name is about. When people say our name, there is a sound being broadcast back to us each time they say it. It is good to know if that energy reflects what we want to have broadcast. I recognized in the early 80's that my name was not quite right. I consulted another psychic and she validated the feeling that I had regarding my middle name, Ann. I did not like the feeling or the vibration of the energy of the name Ann for me. My mother had wanted to name me Sundae, yet "Sundae" was not a recognized Saint's name. In order to be baptized in the Catholic Church, she needed to choose another name for me and never told me about it. Years later, I had the intuition that I was to be named Sundae. I called my mother up; I said "Mom, I'm changing my name to Sundae." She said, "I wanted to name you that, how did you know that?" and proceeded to tell me the story.

We can also understand more about our Self-expression. When I calculated my surname, I did not like the vibration for what I wanted to accomplish in the world. I changed that name to a name that gave me the kind of energy I wanted to support the kind of work that I was doing. It was an amazing experience to change my name. I noticed how life and people around me responded to me differently than when I used the names of the past.

You can support your heart's desire, and your soul's expression through the science of numbers and the interpretation. You can change many of your characteristics by changing your name. It in turn, changes your vibration. Remember, like planets and just about everything else, each number has a higher and a challenging expression.

Notice the symbol of each number and how much it is like its meaning. Take the number one; it begins from a point above and in one straight line, ends at a point below. Compare it with the number two. Notice how the two has curves, and realize in relationship and diplomacy how important it is to say things in a softer way, whereas the number one says it sharply and directly, straight to the point. If you look at the number three, it holds a lot of energy, there are two "cups" and can be filled with energy like the jovial number three. There are three specific points in the symbol that represent the beneficial trine energy. You can look at any number symbol and ascertain the meaning directly from the shape.

Each number has a sound and vibration. It gives the number a special meaning and resonance. Some of the numbers are widely utilized in everyday conversation. Their meanings are quite literal and practical, while other numbers require study, insight and contemplation. Numbers have many meanings beyond the counting function.

There are two categories of numbers, regular and master. The regular numbers include all numbers, except for repeating digits. The regular numbers are always added together to make up one digit. They are more earthly and indicative of a person's experience and existence on our planet. There is a specific reflection of energy in each number format.

The "master" or double-digit numbers are different in that they are more universal, mystical and visionary. They are never reduced to a single digit. The master numbers include 11, 22, 33, 44, 55, etc. They have a Higher vibration. Many times the birth dates of people who might be considered "old souls" can have a master number when added together. They seem to have more clarity, naturally and tend to be leaders and masters of certain disciplines.

The master numbers are the Highest expression of that number in a Divine format with a clarity, expression and manifestation of Divinity. The first nine numbers are more humanly oriented; the master numbers are more Divinely ordained.

One

One is oneness, unity, union, wholeness, integration, and initiation. It is courage, ambition and leadership. Think of the word one. When we begin to count we usually begin at one. It is a point of initiation; it designates a new beginning. An example would be January; it is the first month which begins the whole year. One also represents the "whole"; as in a whole pie, there are no parts, no separation, nothing is missing, it is all together. In this format it also represents all parts or units coming together to form one unit of wholeness. An example would be to consider that we have four bodies. We have a mental body, an emotional body, a Spiritual body and a physical body. Together they form one being. If one or more of those bodies becomes disconnected or unhealthy, we are not whole. We are not integrated. We can attract someone to complete us or we can balance our self to become more complete. The highest form of the number one energy is to create equilibrium and wholeness so we are complete or are available to unite with another well integrated being.

Union is another demonstration of the number one. When two people take a vow of marriage, they form a bond. They become one family. Choices are no longer made that do not consider the union, or they risk the possibility of losing that union. Our great country is one indivisible nation, a union with diversity of race, creed, color, sex and points of view. It is possible to create unity with diversity. We all share one planet in the same solar system, in the same galaxy as all the other people on our earth.

When we accept a conscious, focused relationship with a Divine Mother/Father, we can experience Oneness. We become one with our Divine family. There is incredible power in Oneness.

Challenging expression: alone, egotistical, alienated, frustrated, pushy, tyrannical, antagonistic or unable to initiate.

Two

Two is balance, polarity, two different energies, positive and negative; in balance. Two is also cooperation, diplomacy and consideration. The number two is commonly referred to as a couple or a pair. The meaning of the number two is represented when two people begin to spend more time together; they are thought of as a couple or a pair. It can be two similar units, like two young girls that play together and are seemingly inseparable or two different kinds of units like a man and a woman or a male animal and female animal. Different sexes create a polarity pair, two of the opposite sex coming together.

Opposites do attract. It is the attraction of their electromagnetic charge. It is possible for a male to carry more feminine polarity and the women, more masculine. This results in different combinations of pairs. The man may choose to be the house husband and the women the provider. It may create either homosexual or heterosexual relationships. We have many types of relationships; i.e. inter-cultural, inter-species and sexes intermingle. They are attracting just the right polarity for them and their soul's unfoldment. It is most important not to judge or put down inter-racial couples or homosexual relationships. They are right for their personal experience, their soul's unfoldment and development.

Balance is another expression of the number two. Just like a hanging scale and a teeter-totter, the heavier side goes down further and the lighter side lifts up. When the two weights are equal they are said to be balanced. Sometimes it takes the form of personal growth or counseling to balance one's masculine and feminine qualities. Then one is more prepared to become a couple and there is more understanding, experience and compassion with regard to the opposite sex or polarity.

Challenging expression: addicted, unbalanced, disharmonious, divorced, uncooperative, unfair, undiplomatic or disregard for relationship.

Three

Three is artistic expression, imagination, talent, kindness, a trine, a trinity or a triangle. One of the most powerful angles in geometry is the triangle. It represents two lines of force shooting upward and connecting at the top creating an apex of energy. It has three different sides. It brings a sense of being lifted upward, of inspiration, power, optimism and joy. In the great Roman triumvirate, there were three powerful leaders united in rulership over most of the known world. Sometimes it is difficult to do it all alone or on our own. In certain religions there is a representation of Divine Source as a trinity, in Catholicism; a Father, Son and Holy Spirit or in Hinduism; Brahma, Vishnu and Shiva.

When we observe the way the number three is written, it is a curvy symbol with two major curves and is more lighthearted and not as serious in its expression, yet extremely powerful and creative energy. It is the energy of artistic expression, sociability and friendliness, talent and imagination.

Challenging expression: disempowered, extravagant, exaggerated, vanity, prideful, negative, pessimistic or righteous, without humor or philosophy, untalented, uncreative or without imagination.

Four

Four is the base, foundation, structure, the ability to handle survival issues. It is being economical, exact, conservative and functional. Four is the number that represents a firm and enduring foundation. Most well designed buildings are more stable and possess more space with four corners. It is more sensible and serves a better purpose to use space wisely when building. It is a more precise and meticulous way of organizing space. Number four is a very realistic number and indicates great organization, service and practicality.

Our earthly tangible components are comprised of the balance of 4 elements (air, fire, earth and water; ether being intangible). In many native traditions, the four directions are acknowledged and revered as sacred. Each prayer would include the honoring of the four directions and elements at the beginning of each ceremony. In this way, native people seem to have more harmony with nature and the elements and are able to handle very difficult survival situations. The four corners of yoga represent the physical, mental, Spiritual and emotional.

Challenging expression: inadequate or inferior, uneconomical, inaccurate, without a base, to worry, fret or feel anxiety about survival, impractical, seeking elusive perfection.

Five

Five is communication, information, fast moving data and concepts, adaptability, experiential, mentally adept, and adventurous. It is clever, versatile, and changeable. Five is the number of communication. It represents the sharing of experience and news, the latest and most up to "datest" information and trends. The energy moves fast. The mental processes are very agile and curious. There is great ability to collect information and utilize it new ways. There is love of diversity and dislike for the routine. There is a great need to collect more data and come up with new teaching methods and philosophies. Five also represents sociability and sharing.

One of the most misunderstood geometrical forms is the pentagram, the five-pointed star. In polarity therapy, an energy balancing therapy, the shoulders and hips form four points and the top of the star points to the ether element at the throat. Ether is the fifth element and it is related to creation. When praying or practicing positive affirmations, we are utilizing the ether element and the voice to transmit sound vibration in order to manifest in our lives. It is a positive and constructive use of the magical pentagram. At a certain point in history, all magic and witchcraft were thought to be evil and bad. That is why the pentagram was feared. Any time power over others or hurtful destruction is employed, it is a misuse of energy. When the intention is changed for the highest and best, the five-pointed star is a positive utilization of the energy and element of ether.

Challenging expression: lack of communication or information, inability to adapt or experience, immature, gullible, superficial, too active or busy, unsociable, irresponsible, inconsistency, procrastination or selfish.

Six

Six is exuberance, ecstasy, harmony, beauty, and domesticity. It is sympathy, understanding and conscientiousness and justice, balance and healing. The number six conveys the feeling of catching a wave and riding it effortlessly, moving in the flow. It is round like a wave and includes a circle at the end. It is a feeling of being completely in peace, accord and equilibrium. It is the expression of going with the flow not fighting it. It is a wave of ecstatic energy that moves us to great things.

When we observe the Hebrew Star of David, we see a six-pointed star. The six-pointed star represents a time where responsibility guardianship, protection and justice were coming into the community to create more unity. In polarity energy therapy, we have two triangles; one that points upward connecting us Spiritually and one that points downward toward the physical. They come together and form the six-pointed star to create great balance and harmony in the physical body. We can not have good health and well being with this area out of relationship.

When thinking of home and family, think of the number six. It is like going home again. Everything is familiar, comfortable, fills our heart and enhances our Spirit. The number six feels good when in its highest expression.

Challenging expression: unbalanced, unjust, apathetic, agonizing, discordant, domestic tyranny, cynicism, unattractive, struggling, out of the flow, uproar, unfamiliar or uncomfortable.

Seven

Seven is about stillness, studying, contemplating. It is refinement, mental analysis and technical. The number seven refers to trust, great introspection, looking for the truth deep inside one's Self. It probes, researching thoroughly either scientifically or Spiritually, and evolves great truths and wisdom from contemplation. It is a sense of enjoying being alone and the silence; yet not being lonely. It is the pleasure of spending time working on projects and new thought.

The adventure for number seven is feeding and reconstituting the meditational fire in more refined ways. There is a need for silence. New theories are developed and contribute to the ability to catalyze others as well as self.

Challenging expression: sarcasm, skepticism, unimproved, distrusting, too much movement to concentrate, ignoring transformation, thoughtless, assumptive, without truth or wisdom, lonely, bored, victim or victimizer.

Eight

Eight is manifestation, coming into physical form, material success, accomplishment, order and the strong structure of economic stability. It is authority, administrators and supervisors. The power to manifest comes through with the number eight. It is a powerful demonstration of energy into material form. It has executive ability, leadership and practicality to produce form and material success. The number eight can represent a challenge to which great accomplishment can be realized when utilizing Self-reliance, problem solving and the power to succeed. It is the wise management of material goods that creates material freedom; like good investments and a balanced portfolio.

It is also an expression of creating order. It was in the last millennium that family order was arranged into a patriarchal structure. In the past, it was a matrilineal family tradition. Consequentially, the patriarchal order utilizes the father's family name instead of the mother's.

The number eight on its side represents infinity and the cycle of death and rebirth. Eight also represents challenging and/or positive opportunities having to do with the energy that an individual extends into the world. If one is conscientious and discerning with their behavior and puts out positive considerate action, it will be returned. Likewise, any intolerance, scheming, poor judgment, mis-spent energy will return similar results.

Challenging expression: intolerance, impatience, impracticality, survival, unsuccessful, without accomplishment, poor structure, economic instability, inability to manifest, blocked, ungrounded, critical or rigid.

Nine

Nine is about humanitarianism, completion, a returning to the beginning, bringing it all together, finishing and completing. The number nine energy represents having an elevated earthly expression of kindness and charity and compassion for humankind. It is a true humanitarian attitude and behavior that reflects giving service to others as one has grown and developed in one's life. It is the practice of the principle of brotherhood, Higher Law, Universal Love and understanding. It is a very generous or romantic manner.

It also reflects one's preparedness to move on to another level. It is the completion of one's life lessons that equips an earthly soul for a transformation and ascension into a higher dimension.

Nine is an expression with more emotional, intuitive and artistic focus. The physical and mental attributes have already been achieved as the soul refines to higher levels of Spiritual and emotional balance and attainment. The number nine is also like the harvest after great striving, weeding and planting with one's consciousness there are many gifts or fruits to be enjoyed in terms of creativity.

Challenging expression: uncaring, uncivilized, rebellious, unkind, dissipation, immoral, hyper-emotional, incomplete, unfinished, unsympathetic, inhumane, self-serving or not prepared.

Ten

Ten is transformation and surrender to a Higher Power. In some traditions, the number ten is not reduced to a single digit, one. It indicates the kind of transformation that is necessary to take us to a new level. It is the experience of the butterfly emerging from the cocoon in a different form, more beautiful and free than ever. This can only happen when one surrenders to a Creator, Higher Power, a Divine Mother/Father or whatever we choose to call it. It is impossible to make it on our own, in truth; we are part of a glorious creation that is inter-related.

Challenging expression: unchanged, unaltered, in need of a makeover, unyielding, holding out, lack of submission or unrelated.

Eleven

Eleven is a knowingness of the Divine plan without having to think about it. The number eleven epitomizes Divine Guidance. It represents the mystics and the dreamers who have the gifts of clairaudience or clairvoyance. It is that intuitive ability to attract and interpret symbols and revelations. It is a higher vibration and a master number. The first master number represents Spirituality, idealism, poetry and art. It manifests naturally and without effort.

There are times when number elevens are not practical or down to earth enough to be materially successful. It doesn't really matter because it is not important to them anyway.

People who have the number eleven as part of their every make-up are naturally clear and give a good example as a role model without even thinking about it. It just seems natural and effortless. There is simplicity and an angelic quality about them. They have no ulterior motives other than simple truth and love.

Challenging expression: unknowing, unguided, not seeing or hearing on a higher level, obtuse, lacking intuition, interpretation, Spirituality, poetry or art.

Twelve

Twelve is an expression of natural order. There were twelve tribes that arose from Israel. There are twelve signs in our zodiac. Of the four earthly elements: air fire, earth and water that make up every sign, each have a total of three manifestations which together form twelve elemental expressions. There are some who say that the twelve apostles at the famous "last supper" painting represented this. There are twelve houses in astrological charting; 360 degrees in a circle break easily into twelve, 30 degree sections. We have 12 months in a year. Twelve is an expression of Universal Law and natural cycles which bring more predictability into our lives.

Challenging expression: unnatural order, chaos, anarchy, confusion, unpredictability or erratic energy.

Thirteen

Thirteen is the power of the feminine in a mystical format related to the moon. The feminine represents the power of intuition, the unconditional love of a mother, nurturing, comforting and cherishing. The first calendars were based on lunar cycles; the old lunar calendar had 13 months. If we multiply 13 times 28 days, the result is 364.

The cycles of the moon were celebrated and utilized so much more in the past. When we realize the incredible power the moon has to influence the tides of our great oceans, we can recognize the importance of this number. Since our bodies are made up of about 72-76% water, we can imagine how the moon reflects our emotions and attitudes.

The number thirteen has been diminished in its importance and labeled and downgraded to the realm of the superstitious. This has been the same with the feminine aspect and Divination Arts. Older calendars were based on the cycles of the moon. There were 13 moons with exactly 28 days for every year. It is interesting to see that when the Julian calendar began, it took the focus off the moon and put it on the sun (the masculine symbol). It had 12 months varying from 28-31 days. Thus began a more patriarchal expression in our world. We notice the phases of the moon on our calendars yet most have little understanding of the importance of these cycles. Some of us have forgotten to honor the feminine principles reflected by this number.

Challenging expression: superstitious, lacking intuition and unconditional love, to alienate, abuse, to demonstrate intolerance, distress, to be smothering or unsupportive.

Twenty-two

Twenty-two indicates a master builder, an architect of Divine plan. Unlike the eleven, the twenty-two is more realistic with Divine plan. This energy has the power to utilize visionary and mystical revelations and apply it practically with incredible results. The purpose is to benefit humankind. Many saints who have reincarnated to be "way-showers" and "light bearers," have this energy vibration. They don't need to be here to grow and develop; they choose to be here because they already have attained the kind of development that they are promoting in service to mankind.

They usually work for family, community and countries. They work with the masses and do not separate themselves from them because they are recognizing the Spiritual unity of all. Some are not aware of or are not awakened to their purpose initially, and realize it later. Some work inconspicuously and others are well known.

Challenging expression: being destructive, using mysticism to further evil or harm for selfish benefit, promoting darkness, wickedness, malevolence and immorality on a larger scale.

Tarot

The tarot deck has been used for centuries for Divination. Each card has specific meaning and symbology. A deck is comprised of 22 cards representing the major "arcana," which means "secrets" and 14 minor arcana with four different suits or elements to create 56 cards, for a total of 78 cards. The meanings of the pictorial symbols, elements and numbers are read as well.

There is variety in different decks. Some use other total numbers of major or minor arcana. Some systems use only 13 minor arcana and no major. This would be true of the Destiny cards.

All minor arcana are comprised of numbers and face cards very similar to our modern playing cards. For example, hearts represent water, diamonds represent earth, clubs represent air, and spades represent fire. Much like astrology, these elements assist us in understanding the elemental balance of things. The tarot also has a Sun and a Moon card. In addition, the tarot has picture symbols in the major arcana that can represent different astrological aspects in one card. There are no geometrical calculations or aspects that need to be remembered. This method is much easier for beginners.

When you need quick answers and insight, use a tarot deck. It is a great tool to connect with other people and share wisdom. When I do party entertainment, I have three to five minutes with each person. I need to be able to give people immediate, quick perception about their lives in the shortest amount of time. This Guidance can be a remedy for their current situation; it needs to have value and practicality to be of use. The tarot gets to the essence of things very quickly and provides good details. The more we learn symbology; we can understand that the tarot combines pictures, numbers and elemental information to provide greater comprehension of our life's process.

Other Divination Arts

Symbology is the study of different objects: stones, bones, signs, playing cards, dice, a handwriting sample, tea leaves or coffee grinds to ascertain information about a person's life. There is meaning associated with the objects that can be read by those familiar with the method.

Stones/Bones

These natural objects are thrown and the resulting pattern is interpreted to give meaning to the query. Any kind of stone or bone can be used. Significance is given to the item by where it is derived from, the qualities of that place elementally and the shape of the item. The stones can come from a volcano: fire, a distinctive mountain: earth, an extraordinary river: water, a particular ocean or a special lake. It may come from a very holy or sacred place: Spiritual. The bone may come from a human, a chicken, a goat, a horse, an antelope, etc. and represents the special qualities of that animal. For example, a flying bird may represent air.

I Ching

This is an ancient Chinese system, somewhat more complex and uses a system of symbolic Ingrams to interpret information for the inquirer. Each Ingram is comprised of six combinations of two different symbols. Six pennies can be used to create the pattern for the Ingrams. Each one has a head and a tail side. The meanings a very symbolic and make use of more ancient Chinese philosophy. Some people can relate and interpret it and others do not find it practical and down-to-earth enough.

Runes

No one seems to truly know the origins of this system of Divination or oracle. The Viking, the Celtic, Anglo-Saxon England, the Gaelic and Germanic people passed on this method. When the Germanic alphabet with 24 letters was created, they referred to each letter as a rune. Similar to the I Ching and yet more simple, the oracle of the runes uses 24 glyphs on small rectangular clay or stone pieces and one blank one that represent specific symbolic messages to inform the inquiring person about the answers to their questions. The querent can choose blindly from bag of runes, drawing one, three or more runes. Three is the most common.

Tea Cups and Coffee Grinds

The multinational Gypsies and the Turks developed and utilized this system. First the leaves or ground beans are brewed. When the beverage is drunk, the person turns over their cup in a ritual fashion like inverting the cup and turning it 3 times in a clockwise direction in the saucer. Rituals vary from tribe to tribe. The resulting patterns are read. Both the dark and the empty spaces create symbols or pictures which have meaning.

Astro Dice

Three dice with four sides are imprinted; one with the number of the houses 1-12, another with 12 astrological signs of our zodiac and the last with 12 planets and luminaries. These dice are thrown and the faces of the dice are read in an astrological manner.

Palm and Face Reading

There is a repeating pattern of the entire body and one's experience in the palm and in the face. Different lines indicate emotional, physical, mental and Spiritual information including the personality and the quality of life by where it appears on the hand or face. Lines change over time with the choices we make in life.

Handwriting Analysis

One's handwriting tells so much about a person and their character. It is interesting to note that character can mean the nature of someone or can mean the actual letter, by definition. That is what our handwriting does by how we use the space on the paper, the firmness of our grip and our attention to form. We can discern our mental and emotional states based on the clarity, spacing, slant and shape of the characters or strokes. Generally, the more rounded the letters, the more emotionally based they are. The closer the letters are, the more mental. The more forward slant is looking to the future; the back slant is more rooted in the past. A slightly forward slant or more upright, the more presently based we are. The height and depth of the letters can determine the Spiritual and physical nature. The higher the stroke, the more Spirituality we express. The lower the stroke from the base line, the more physicality we convey.

Medicine Cards

This system uses different animals; mammals, sea creatures and birds depicted on cards, to create a representation of the four elements and different characteristics based on animal habitat, appearance and characteristics.

Feeling the Energy Move Through

This classification utilizes the energy of the person doing the reading and the energy of the person it is being done for. The more centered, competent and confidant a person is at describing their sensory impressions, the better the reading.

Dousing

It is utilizing a divining rod to search for a source of water, minerals or answers to questions. The direction of the rod is the key element to observe. It can also respond to and measure how far the human energy field is emanating outward, when directed toward someone.

Pendulum

I described this system in detail in Chapter 7, page 93. It is a very simple way to obtain quick answers to yes and no questions in our life simply by observing the swing of the object.

Flipping a Coin

Nearly everyone, at one time or another, has flipped a coin for an answer to who will begin first; as in an athletic game. This method is about the simplest technique to receive a yes or no response short of Divine intervention and messages called out from the beyond!

Psychometry

All one must do in this approach, is to hold an object of someone's, close their eyes and focus, to get impressions of the person. The person need not be present for this divination technique to work. The energy of the person remains on the object and can be read.

Body Symptoms

Each symptom of the body is symbolic of what is out of balance in the person's life. For example, if the heart, circulatory system or bodily fluids are compromised, it has to do with one's emotional life. When it's the brain or nervous system, it is about our mental state. If it is about elimination, the spine or the bone structure it is referring to our physicality. When we are unable to sleep, eat or have no passion for life, it can be about loosing our self, our Spirit or Spirituality. When reading the symptoms, it is important to tune into how the indicator reflects that person's life experience.

Phrenology

This is the study of the shape and protuberances of the skull, based on the now discredited belief that they reveal character and mental capacity.[43] I never knew this one existed until a friend shared it with me. I can only speculate that there are repeating themes throughout the body and the skull may be representative of that.

Gazing with the Perceptual Center

This technique uses one's ability to alter their consciousness into an alpha state by side tracking their normal linear visual perception and allowing higher perceptions to come through while staring intently at an object or in the direction of the perceptual center.

---

[43]Excerpted from *The American Heritage® Dictionary of the English Language, Third Edition* © 1996 by Houghton Mifflin Company. Electronic version licensed from INSO Corporation; further reproduction and distribution in accordance with the Copyright Law of the United States. All rights reserved.

Perceptual Center (3rd Eye)

This practice is used when we lift our open eyes upward and inward in the direction of the perceptual center and allow Guidance to come through. It can be used with all of the Guidance techniques.

Scrying

Using a special mirror, one can gaze into it with our perceptual eye and see events and important messages. Scrutinizing the mirror, careful attention is given to what images appear.

Crystal Ball Gazing

Using our perceptual eye, looking intently into a crystal ball, we can see the reflection of the images of wisdom, messages and events.

Spiritualism, Allowing Spirits to Come Through

Automatic Writing

Relaxing and allowing our self to open as an instrument of Divinity, writing everything that pops into consciousness. It seems to stream forth effortlessly and when we are complete, it seems to have emanated from a different consciousness.

Channeling

Relaxing, going into a trance state and allowing disembodied spirits to speak through our body. The most difficult part for some is to get out of the way with the personality self. It is important to ask for the kind of spirit guide we wish to have come through. We want the more enlightened kind. Many times our accent or other vocal characteristics will change. Some people go to channels to receive messages from loved ones that have passed on.

Table Tipping

A small group sits on the floor around a small table. Each person puts their hands on the edge and they begin rocking the table effortlessly. They determine the yes/no movements of the table and ask questions observing which way the table shifts. Intuition is used by each member of the group to hear more and clarify answers.

Chapter 10
Guidelines for Guidance

Messages

Messages are our medicine to our souls. Messages keep us more in tune with a Higher Power, our Higher Self, our relations, nature and all of creation. Any message that gives clues or direct information that allows us to heal our emotions, our body, mind or Spirit is medicine to us. The key is to apply the message in our life. It is not enough to get a message and then not act on it. Divination techniques give us the means by which we can learn more. Creation provides us with the opportunity to see messages reflected back to us. These reflections are important to perceive, contemplate, and understand in our life process and evolution.

> *"In Native American Tradition, Medicine is anything that will aid the seeker in feeling more connected and in harmony with nature and all life-forms. Anything that is healing to the body, mind, and/or spirit is Medicine. To find a special Medicine that would give answers for a personal challenge or problem, our Ancestors would often walk in the forests or on the mesas to observe the portents or signs that would assist them in healing and seeking wisdom. The Medicine Walk was a way to reestablish the link to the Allies, or Medicine Helpers. A medicine Walk is still possible in today's busy world if the seeker knows how to read nature's signs."*[44]

It is up to us to learn to read nature's signs. First we determine the meaning of the various reflections of nature, and then we integrate the meaning of every part into a whole meaning. Look for colors, sex, elements, numbers, names, animal allies, body parts and location, direction changes and metaphors. Break everything down in parts. As we study, contemplate and meditate on all of the related information in the Guidance Groupings, we are able to see a more complete picture. An issue or a theme will emerge even better, as we write about it. Journaling or writing about our process will stimulate our intuition and give us an opportunity to hear our Higher Self come through automatic writing.

[44] Sams, 5.

It is important to notice if there is a polarity charge associated with our situation. (See page 107.) What elements are involved? Look for masculine or feminine values that need to be developed or softened. Polarity charge tells us what is more dominant and out of balance. The key is to create equilibrium within the masculine and feminine and with the four elements of air, fire, water and earth. Then we become more neutral like the element of ether. Health and a happy life are derived from that balance.

We need to know what emotions are involved in order to heal them. This information is vital to our health and well being. The emotional and mental bodies need healing and clearing continually or they can manifest disharmony and disease in the physical body. Stress is the number one killer. It is no accident that heart disease and cancer are the leading diseases. They are stress-related. We need to relieve emotional and mental tension. This is the area we most neglect in our busy lives and most find it difficult to do without assistance from a therapist who knows how to release the emotions and can assist us with letting go of negative, limiting beliefs. It can be done most effectively through reprogramming the subconscious mind, bodywork, regression, journaling, yoga, breathing techniques, healthy venting, etc. Learn how to do it for yourself or find someone to assist you!

Colors and gemstones are significant. Notice if you are attracted to a certain color or are avoiding a color. It is essential to know the colors to determine what gemstones to use to assist in balancing. I needed to wear blues and greens for several years to cool and heal the fire element in me. After this period I was able to wear the fire colors again and feel balanced. I am very attracted to the application of gemstones. I use them with my clients and in my every day life. I will many times create an entire layout for all the energy centers and encourage meditation while the balancing is occurring. This is very effective when a client has a considerable emotional release during our session. It assists them in rebalancing. I love to wear gemstones, as they are beautiful, comforting and healing. I like to wear clothes with the colors I am working with. I enjoy decorating my home with those colors. I have even been told in dreams to use certain colors for decorating. When I moved from an exquisite ocean view with lots of blues, I was told in a dream to use those colors in my new house which had a view of the mountains and a beautiful stream with lots of greens. I like to choose what is best for me based on my emotions or mental state or I use my intuition to decide what will be the greatest equalizer for the occasion.

There are corresponding numbers for each category. A number may be a recurring theme in your life. There was a time when 11:11 would continually appear when I would glance up at the clock. This occurred many times as the year 2000 approached. It is also helpful for you to know your own birth force number. To determine that number, simply add up your birth date. For example, 7-27-1951 is my birth date. I add 7+27+1+9+5+1= 50.

Then add that number unless it is a repeating digit (22, 33, etc.) When I add 5+0=5, I discover what my birth force is. Looking at the message for the number 5, I recognize that I am here to express and communicate messages and ideas about health and healing. I integrate and synthesize important data so love and healing can be manifested more in my own life and for those who wish to create it too.

Notice that there are also body parts and energy centers that are involved with each message. Our body will perfectly reflect the message that we need. We may notice injuries, symptoms, sensations, numbness and/or problems with those areas that are related to our message. I received many injuries to my lower back that represented building more creativity and passion in my life and career. I was also injured in the base of my spine which represents my foundation. I was dealing with the emotion of fear and I was challenged financially as well as physically. I recognized that I was going in new directions when my neck was injured. Injuries can be the body's way to inform us what is out of balance, what needs to be healed and rebuilt or a new direction we need to take. The body doesn't lie; it simply reflects "what condition our condition is in!" In my practice, I have a session dedicated to a dialogue with the physical body in the alpha state of relaxation. It is amazing how the body tells the story of our patterns and what we need to do to correct them. The energy centers need to be operating at their best for optimum health. In order to heal a specific part of us, we need to focus on the growth opportunities and the Highest and best expression that is indicated for that area, in the Guidance Groupings.

There is a corresponding planet and/or luminary, like the sun or moon that is a reflection of our message. Study what the numbers, the planets and luminaries have to offer us with their natural wisdom. And finally, there is an animal or zodiac configuration that corresponds to our message that repeats and integrates all of this information.

Listen to music with the kind of instruments designated in the Guidance Groupings and it will assist in providing a sound healing. We may also sing or hum the musical note suggested as we go about our daily activities.

When we study the Guidance Groups and see the message, we can discern which expression we are projecting. We can determine whether it is our Highest and best expression or if it presents a challenge or growth opportunity. Sometimes, we may be expressing some of both. We can know precisely what we need to focus on. It is evident what needs to be healed from that specific message. Identify it and commit to your Higher Self to work on it.

As I have stated before, nature, the cosmos and the Universe are reflections of what we need to know to heal and balance ourselves, naturally. They guide us in knowing what our path needs to be in order to fulfill and honor Divine Will. According to Divine will, we have a perfect expression for each one of us that we need to discover and experience. Be more aware in each moment about what you see, hear and feel and relate it to all of the categories that I have suggested in the Guidance Groupings and in these chapters. This can assist us all in getting on track with the highest and best expression that the Higher Power has for each and every one of us.

Ask For Divine Time, Not My Time

The ego wants all its desires fulfilled immediately, just like the infant crying for its needs to be met. It is a survival mechanism and not an enlightened way of being. There is a time and a season for everything. We may not understand why and we just need to trust. That means we need to trust even when the income is not flowing, that special mate is not in our lives, our loved ones have passed away, etc.

Our Divine Parents have a plan for each and every one of us, no matter how lowly or lofty we interpret it to be. There is a purpose and a soul mission for us if we pay attention. There is a precise time for the manifestation of our Highest and best. No matter how hard we try, we will be unsuccessful trying to jump-start or hurry our outcome. We can attempt to change the timing on things, yet we will not receive the same results.

It is much wiser to accept and affirm Divine time. Our egos are far too limited to see the benefits of Divine time. All we have to do is pray, focus, pay attention and be patient for our Highest and best. That is the most difficult part, having to wait. Do not expect a specific outcome; allow Divinity to manifest the Highest in our lives. Know that there is a reason and a season for everything. Our Divine Parents know best!

Trust

I have been blessed to hear and to learn to trust my Inner Guidance. I feel so fortunate with the outcomes I've experienced. Trusting and acting upon Guidance is such an integral part of the process. I feel like I have been blessed with so much trust innately, even when things looked really bleak. I learned not to act or react solely upon the appearances of what I saw. I learned that it was a means to an opportunity rather than to misfortune, if I were open to see it.

Isn't it amusing that what appears to be a mistake can turn out to be so right? It is really important to see the miracle of the Guidance and not interpret misfortune. I always trusted that something good would come out of each situation, even when there was great pain associated with it. I listened to my Guidance and something good, is what I got. This is the inspiration of what the outcome can be, no matter what the appearance or experience of the situation is.

Don't Force or Try to Control It

It is impossible to force Guidance to come through. We cannot control or manipulate it in any way. It has its own timing and manner of expression. All we can do is to pray, relax, be patient, focus and notice everything.

It we get a message and try to force the outcome, it will fail. Forcing pushes away the very thing or outcome we desire. It literally repels it. Everything has its moment and time of manifestation. We will know when it is harvest time. The gifts and fruits of the harvest are right in front of us for our enjoyment. They are attractive, available and ripe. We are the guest who is ready to receive at whatever time it appears.

Pray for the Highest and Best

We limit ourselves immensely when we try to visualize a specific outcome. Many "Positive Thinking" type classes suggest visualizing specifically what we want. I did that in the past and was able to create and obtain many things.

The method I prefer now is to pray and ask my Heavenly Parents for my Highest and best in certain categories without specific outcomes. What I receive is much more than I could have ever imagined. It is much more fulfilling and significant in my life. For example, I was guided to write this book. In the past, I never would of thought of it. I might have thought it too awesome an undertaking and that I might not be capable of it. Praying and asking for my Highest and best has been and is immensely satisfying and important in my life now.

Use It or Loose It

We are Divinely gifted with our ability to hear, see or feel our Guidance. If we listen and act on the wisdom of it, our life will become more alive, magical and heavenly. The more we utilize it, the more strongly it will manifest in our experience.

If we do not use our Guidance and/or discount it, we will feel disconnected and without direction. We may try to use our mental powers and/or our intellectual skills to attempt to figure it out. It is very likely that we will experience blocks, limitations and frustration. It feels like hell instead of the heaven we can create by following Guidance.

Born with It

We are all born with this gift of intuitive Guidance. Some are more gifted than others are. We can all develop it more. We are living on a planet that is a living reflection of Guidance. We are living in a Universe that is totally connected and resonates with the Divine. Only our mind can discount and invalidate it.

Please recall from reading earlier chapters, I grew up thinking I was only able to be scientific and linear. My masculine self was over-developed. At one point, I was an agnostic and very skeptical. I changed and balanced my life more powerfully than I could ever imagine, by developing my feminine self and learning about my Inner Guidance and acting on it.

Denial and Dis-Use

If we deny Guidance, it is like denying a Higher Power's wisdom and will. Remember that it was thought to be the "original sin" in the story of the Garden of Eden. Acting without Divine Guidance had the repercussion of life becoming a hardship. It was then that they had to work the land to be fed. It was after that mistake that child bearing was said to become a painful experience. We don't want to make that error, we can avoid it. Denial brings sorrow. We can find our own answers, even when authorities or others are saying something different.

Some authorities say it is not important to understand our body symptoms, our Inner voice or our planet's reflections. Some even say that it is evil to seek a sign. I totally disagree with that philosophy. The more we understand what our body, our Inner Guidance and what the Universe is reflecting, the better prepared we are to balance it or be affirmed by it. We can be more Self-empowered and really be in alignment with Divine Will.

Listen to Your Self, Even When Others Try to Deter

When we are blessed with Guidance information, hold dearly to it. No matter what others say to us or what appearances look like, endure and persist with the Guidance we have received.

After my first year in Hawaii, my earthly sources of income changed dramatically. My entertainment company in Los Angeles was not booking due to the economy and lack of sales. I was doing readings for a 900 psychic line and it folded. All of the people around me had the same message; the best route in Hawaii was to get into the hotel and tourist industry. I spent 5-6 months, with very little income, praying for Guidance. This time I was guided to create and offer the Mind Heart Harmony Program. I was intuitively given a precise ordering of sessions of healing work that I had learned from many people, plus my own to create an effective means by which to change unwanted limiting behaviors. I had not even considered creating a program to assist others in reprogramming their subconscious mind to heal painful emotional and mental patterns. I had been doing it exclusively for my own healing. This program and my service to it created the income I needed and I got to stay in alignment with Divine Will. In addition, many people have acknowledged that they have benefited greatly from the healing work they derived from their Mind Heart Harmony Program.

Asking for Others

When asking for others, it is wise to describe the energy, feeling or possible choices. We may say what we would do in their case. Yet it is important to encourage their free will choices and ask them to feel and choose according to their heart. If they are not in touch with their Inner Guidance, it is important that you don't choose for them, it takes away their free will. For example, if someone asks about a relationship that is not working and should they leave, I will suggest ways to heal themselves and the relationship. Then, I will encourage them to look into their own hearts to see if they would be best served by leaving it. It is my understanding that choosing or affirming negative messages for others have karmic retribution. When potential harm is indicated, it is important to share that information as a possibility and advise the person to use caution, not as an irrevocable fact to implant in their minds. Unless Guidance gives a specific and clear outcome for that person, encourage their Highest free will choice.

Don't Expect Others to Follow Your Guidance

Everyone has their own agenda and deeply ingrained patterns, unless they have done some important healing work. Not everyone is interested in Divine Will or the Highest plan for them. Remember that a lot of people are still coming from survival, scarcity and distrust of their selves and others. Many are looking for the fast buck or there is crisis in their lives and they want a quick fix solution.

One of my clients asked me about an investment that had been paying off considerably well for him. He wanted to know if he should make another rather sizable investment. In looking at his cycles, I told him it was not a favorable cycle for him to invest. I saw that there was a chance that the whole program he was investing in would expire in the month of August. He decided to put in more money, regardless of my counsel. Sure enough, the investment fell apart in August and he lost lots of money. He sheepishly returned to share his experience. He told me he wished he had listened. He made his own free will choice. I gave him the information and he decided not to follow it. It was his choice; he gets to take responsibility for this choice. Please do not be invested in the choices of others. Stay as neutral as possible, especially when counseling about relationships!

Gratitude

I am so thankful that I can hear, see and feel and act on Divine Guidance. I attempt to remember to thank Mother/Father God every morning upon waking and every night before sleep. They are my true Parents. If I didn't have their Guidance, my life would be hell or I would have died from a stress related disease. I would have no purpose or soul mission. I would not have the satisfying and fulfilling experience that I currently enjoy, if it wasn't for their Guidance and Direction.

I believe that gratitude is one of the most important aspects of the process of Guidance. It is our opportunity to send the energy back to our Divine Parents. Let's face it; our earthly parents want to be appreciated and to receive gratitude for the love and guidance they have provided. As above, so below and vice versa! Thank your Divine Parents profusely; they have truly given you Guidance, life and purpose. Listen to Their Will and Plan for you and be a mystical artist in your life, co-creating with your Divine Parents!

Chapter 11

Guidance Groupings

"Each person lives a Vision Quest on a daily basis. The key is to be aware of it. To seek the signs and omens that allow humans to make proper decisions, then act on those signs is a part of the Quest for life."[45]

There is Divine Order in the Universe, it is reflected in nature. The most incredible part is that everything reflects all things and that is the beauty and complexity of Creation. How awesome to have a Divine Reflection everywhere we look. It does call for a new way of perceiving with the right brain and symbology. I have cross-referenced the charge, elements, emotions, colors, gemstones, messages, numbers, energy centers, body parts, planets, luminaries, zodiac signs, animals and other beings and musical notes & instruments.

These groupings will empower and enable us to see the connectedness in Creation and receive wisdom and understanding in relation to our self and our process. As we study these groupings and the different categories, one clue can give us a specific message. We may get only a color or a number or an animal. It may be all we need to get the "aha" that we want. These Guidance Groupings will give us an effective method in which to get insight or messages and what it means to us. We can focus on living the higher message, balancing our polarity and emotion, applying the colors and gemstones we need to heal and listening to the perfect kind of music. We can pay more attention to the energy centers and body parts that are represented. In this way, we can prevent the disharmony that creates dis-ease. We can establish and take more responsibility for better relationships. These messages can clarify what we are going through and what to focus on for our Highest Expression of our growth and evolution.

I really would have loved to have had Guidance Groupings like these earlier in my life. This information represents a synergy and an integration of so much that I have learned through my own process of seeking and applying Guidance. I trust it will make a significant positive impact on your life and evolution with your own Guidance. We can truly access and manifest our own source of wisdom. We can express our Highest and best as we grow, heal, and meet our challenges and growth opportunities. We can be better, more Self actualized Divine children!

---

[45]Sams, 60.

GROUP 1, UNIVERSAL

Polarity Charge: Neutral—Spiritual Oneness, Light & Space.
Element: Ether
Emotional Representation:
Highest—Unity, Devotion & Balance.
Lowest—separation, being misguided, & dictatorial.

Healing Colors:
Highest: A. Bright/Deep, Attractive: White, Gold, Purple & Violet.
Message—Highest & Best Expression:
Royal, Spiritual, Superconscious, Highest & Best, Oneness, Impeccability, Illumination, Integrity, Purity, Light, Positive & Wisdom.
Lower: B. Muted/Muddy, Undesirable: (colors above)
Message—Challenges & Growth Opportunities:
Misguided leadership, autocratic, despotic, spirituality needs attention, soiled, spoiled, wrong choices or impure.
Healing Gemstones: Amethyst, Sugilite, Charoite, Goldstone, Quartz Crystal, Herkimer Diamond, Selenite, Silver & Topaz.

The Message: A. Highest & Best Expression:
To Demonstrate Royal Or Regal Behavior. Realizing Super Consciousness & the Spiritual Self. Expressing Our Highest and Best In Our Experience. Feeling a Oneness With All Of Creation. Manifesting Higher Self-Illumination. Being Impeccable and Honoring Higher Self-Integrity and Others. To Possess Clarity, Being a Shining Light or a Positive Influence On Others And Us.
The Message: B. Challenges & Growth Opportunities:
To be misguided in judgment or leadership. Demonstrating autocratic behavior. Needing to be right, oppression, domination or dictatorship over others to feel earthly power. To lack gratitude or a connection with others.
Numbers: 11, 22, 33, 44, 55, 66, 77, 88, 99-- all master numbers (same digits)
Energy Center: 7th—Crown Center
Body Parts: Crown of the Head & the area just above the Head.
Planet or Luminary: the entire Cosmos
Zodiac Zone: Universe
Beings & Animals: Angels, Our Spirit Guides, Enlightened Beings, Mythic Jaguars & Unicorns and Eagles.
Balancing Musical Note: B **Sound:** Eeee **Instrument:** Electronic Synthesizer.

GROUP 2, PISCES

Polarity Charge: Neutral & Feminine (-)
Elements: Ether & Water
Emotional Representation:
Highest—Serenity, Devotion, Unconditional Love & Compassion.
Lowest—hopelessness, confusion, obsession & addiction.

Healing Colors:
Highest: A Bright/Deep, Attractive: Indigo Blue, Cobalt & Purple Blue.
Message—Highest & Best Expression:
Unity, Intuition, Stillness, Serenity, Surrender, Wholeness, Multi-Dimension Awareness, Inner Self-Guidance, Receptivity, Grace, Compassion & Unconditional Love.
Lower: B. Muted/Muddy, Undesirable: (colors above)
Message—Challenges & Growth Opportunities:
Out of touch with inner self and perceptions, separation, confusion, disconnection, martyr for love, addicted, obsessed or unloving.
Healing Gemstones: Lapis Lazuli, Sodalite, Blue Sapphire, Azurite, Opal, Blue Tourmaline, Celestite, Iolite & Tanzanite.

The Message: A. Highest & Best Expression:
To Feel a Sense Of Unity With Everything. To Be Still, Surrender To a Higher Power and Manifest Peace and Serenity. To Demonstrate Wholeness and Multi-Dimensional Awareness. To Utilize Inner Self Guidance, Receptivity, Grace, Compassion and Unconditional Love.
The Message: B. Challenges & Growth Opportunities:
To be out of touch with Inner Self and our perceptions. To feel separated, disconnected, confused and obsessed. To be a martyr for love or to demonstrate unloving and addictive behavior.

Numbers: 10, 12
Energy Center: 6th—Perceptual Center or Third Eye.
Body Parts: Feet, Pituitary Gland, Pineal Gland.
Planet or Luminary: Neptune
Zodiac Zone: Pisces
Beings & Animals: Psychics, Mystics, Priests, Ministers, Nurses, Artists, Dolphins, Whales, Vertebrae Ocean Life, All fish, Octopus, Blue Herons, Swans, Peacocks & Ibis.
Balancing Musical Note: A **Sound:** Oooo **Instruments:** Tibetan Bells & Crystals Bowls.

GROUP 3, TAURUS

Polarity Charge: Neutral & Feminine (-)
Elements: Ether & Earth
Emotional Representation:
Highest—Expression of Self, Devotion, Harmony, & Beauty.
Lowest—grief, sadness, fear of communicating & hedonism.

Healing Colors:
Highest: A. Bright/Deep, Attractive: Turquoise, Aqua Green & Aqua Blue.
Message—Highest & Best Expression:
Communication and Speaking Our Truth, Vocal Creative Expression, Ecstasy, Harmony, Beauty in the Flow, Sharing, Collecting Art & Objects of Beauty.
Lower: B. Muted/Muddy, Undesirable: (colors above)
Message—Challenges & Growth Opportunities:
Blocked communication or self-expression, fear of voicing truth and values, hoarding, hedonistic, loss, sadness or people-pleasing.
Healing Gemstone: Turquoise, Chrysophrase, London Blue Topaz, Gem Silica, Tanzanite, Chysacholla, Aqua-Marine & Alexandrite.

The Message: A. Highest & Best Expression:
To Speak Our Truth and Communicate With Compassion. To Be Vocally Creative In Our Expression. To Experience Ecstasy, Harmony and Beauty. To Feel In The Flow and Generous With Others. Collecting Art and Objects of Beauty. To Possess Determination, Power, Practicality and Love Beauty, Exquisite Things, Comfort and Healthy Pleasure.
The Message: B. Challenges & Growth Opportunities:
To feel blocked in our ability to communicate and express our feelings and beliefs. To have fear of voicing our truth and values. Being a "people-pleaser." To be hedonistic in our appetites or hoard worldly goods. To experience sadness, loss and grief. To be possessive to ensure emotional or mental security.
Numbers: 6, 2
Energy Center: 5th—Communication Center
Body Parts: Throat, Neck, Thyroid Gland & Parathyroid.
Planet or Luminary: Venus
Zodiac Zone: Taurus
Beings & Animals: Singers, Art Dealers, Investors, Distributors of Fine Goods, Beauty Professionals, Bulls, Buffalos, Cows, Talking Birds, Bears, Moose & Turkeys.
Balancing Musical Note: G **Sound:** Iiii **Instruments:** Human Voice & Woodwinds.

GROUP 4, GEMINI

Polarity Charge: Masculine (+)
Element: Air
Emotional Representation:
Highest—Acceptance, Expression of Love and Beliefs & Healing Communication.
Lowest—unfulfilled desire, restless, longing for what we don't have, superficial & negative.

Healing Colors:

Highest: A. Bright/Deep, Attractive: Green, Pink, Light Blue & Silver.
Message—Highest & Best Expression:
Go, Grow, Healthy, Healing, Forgiving, Loving, Prosperity, Money, Observation, News, Message, Ideas, Data, Integration & Success.
Lower: B. Muted/Muddy, Undesirable: (colors above)
Message—Challenges & Growth Opportunities:
Immaturity, being simple, naiveté, envious, sickly, diseased, too busy, gullible, superficial, playing ego games, holding grudges, creating diversions, negative thinking or selfishness.
Healing Gemstones: Emerald, Jade, Malachite, Aventurine, Pink & Green Tourmaline, Blue Lace & Green Agate, Rose Quartz, Rhodochrosite, Kunzite, Jasper, Variscite, Peridot Chalcedony & Apatite.

The Message: A. Highest & Best Expression:
To Experience Healing and Loving Ways In Our Life. To Be Healthy, Growing and Flourishing. To Initiate and Begin New Things. To Manifest Prosperity, Money and Success. To Make Observations and Integrate Ideas, Data and News.
The Message: B. Challenges & Growth Opportunities:
To be immature, gullible, superficial or selfish. To be too active and busy all of the time. To think negatively or get off track with diversions. To be simple or naive. To be envious or participate in ego games. To be out of balance with the heart or sickly. To be in need of stillness and tranquility.
Number: 5
Energy Center: 4th—Heart Center
Body Parts: Lungs, Shoulders, Arms & Hands, Thymus Gland & Sternum.
Planet or Luminary: Mercury **Zodiac Zone:** Gemini
Beings & Animals: Writers, Speakers, Teachers, Communicators, Announcers, Students, Siblings, Social Butterflies, Flying birds, Hawks, Ravens, Flying Insects, Bees, Wolves, Coyotes, Hyena, Weasels, Opossums, Rabbits & Roosters.
Balancing Musical Note: F **Sound:** Haaa **Instruments:** Harp & Flute.

GROUP 5, CANCER

Polarity Charge: Feminine (-)
Element: Water
Emotional Representation:
Highest—Emotional & Domestic Contentment.
Lowest—attachment, being smothering & insecure.

Healing Color:

Highest: A. Bright/deep, Attractive: Milky White.
Message—Highest & Best Expression:
Loving Home, Nurturing, Comforting, Protected, Secure & Camouflaged.
Lower: B. Muted/Muddy, Undesirable: (color above)
Message—Challenges & Growth Opportunities:
Being alienated, insecure, shy, abusing our body, no boundaries with being too nurturing, smothering, allowing abuse or hiding.
Healing Gemstones: Pearl, Mother of Pearl, Mabe, Moonstone & Calcite.

The Message: A. Highest & Best Expression:
To Love Home and Family. To Feel Nurtured, Protected and Secure. To Be Nurturing, Content, Comforting and Cherishing With Self and Others. To Respect and Honor Masculinity. To Be Responsible for The Heart and Soul Of The Family. To Protect Children, Be Domestic and Sensitive.
The Message: B. Challenges & Growth Opportunities:
To feel alienated, insecure or smothering others. To be abused and to demonstrate passive-aggressive anger. To implode with negative feelings. To lack boundaries and allow abuse in the name of love. To hide or camouflage our feelings. To possess extreme sensitivity, intolerance or disconnection from family.

Numbers: 2, 6, 13
Energy Center: 4th—Heart Center
Body Part: Sternum, Chest at Nipple Line & Breasts.
Planet or Luminary: Moon **Zodiac Zone:** Cancer
Beings & Animals: Mothers, Nurses, Domestic Help, Cooks, Chefs, Food Servers, Wet Nurses, Nannies, Water Beings, Mermaids, Mermen, Sea Nymphs, Sea Turtles, Cows, Dogs, Ocean Invertebrates, Shellfish & Foxes.
Balancing Musical Note: F **Sound:** Haaa **Instruments:** Harp & Flute.

GROUP 6, LEO

Polarity Charge: Masculine (+)
Element: Fire
Emotional Representation:
Highest—Personal Power, Emotional Passion, Kindness & Intuitive Intelligence.
Lowest—anger, egocentric, drained & burned out.

Healing Colors:
Highest: A. Bright/deep, Attractive: Yellow, Yellow Green & Yellow Brown.
Message—Highest & Best Expression:
Joy, Empowerment, Talent, Benevolence, Courage, Protective, Generous, Masculine, Electric, Intuitive Intellect & Confidence. Also, the Power of the Trine or of the Day.
Lower: B. Muted/Muddy, Undesirable: (colors above)
Message—Challenges & Growth Opportunities:
Overly cautious, scared, cowardly, dominating personality, deteriorating health, energy-drained, angry or greedy, predator behavior, being disempowered or disempowering others.
Healing Gemstones: Yellow Diamond, Yellow Citrine, Yellow Topaz, Yellow Calcite, Arazonite, Peridot & Tiger's Eye.

The Message: A. Highest & Best Expression:
To Experience Empowerment, Joy, Luck, Courage or Higher Intellect. To Have Great Integrity, Confidence, Many Talents or a Gifted Intellect. To Demonstrate Benevolence, Generosity, To Be Protective of Others and Have Abundant Energy. To Be Masculine, Sporty and Electric, Like The Light of Day. To Be Spiritual, Inspirational or Philosophical.
The Message: B. Challenges & Growth Opportunities:
To feel dis-empowered, drained, deteriorated, blaming or cowardly. To be dominating, fiery, angry or greedy. To exhibit predator-like stalking behavior. To express egocentric ideas or be overly cautious in behavior. Needing to be too dramatic or the center of attention, always. To be lazy, impetuous or indolent. To be addicted to gambling.
Numbers: 9, 3, 1
Energy Center: 3rd—Power Center
Body Parts: Solar Plexus, Heart, Spleen, Liver & Cardiovascular System.
Planet or Luminary: Sun
Zodiac Zone: Leo
Beings & Animals: Regal People, Professors, Fathers, Coaches, Trainers, Facilitators, Athletes, Lions, Tigers, Panthers, All Cats, Falcons, Raccoons, Humming Birds & Peacocks.
Balancing Musical Note: E **Sound:** Hooo **Instruments:** Guitar & Piano

GROUP 7, VIRGO

Polarity Charge: Feminine (-)
Element: Earth
Emotional Representation:
Highest— Courage, Letting Go, Service, Groundedness & Conservationist.
Lowest—fear, insecurity, feeling inferior, picky & worrisome.

Healing Colors:

Highest: A. Bright/deep, Attractive: Brown, Brown Yellow, Brown Green & Brown Red.
Message—Highest & Best Expression: Discerning, Meticulous with Detail, Design Oriented, Material Planning and Saving & a Dedicated Worker.
Lower: B. Muted/Muddy, Undesirable: (colors above)
Message—Challenges & Growth Opportunities:
Inferiority complex, too picky, too much worry, too perfectionistic or to be used by others.
Healing Gemstones: Bloodstone & Brown Smokey Quartz.

The Message: A. Highest & Best Expression:
To Demonstrate Meticulous Behavior and Provide Great Service. To Be Dedicated, Discerning or To Work With Many Details. To Process Information and File It Accordingly. To Be Earthy, Sensual and Tactile. To Be Educated and Well Trained. To Engage The Mind as The Servant To Our Spirit. Acting With a High Level of Discernment.
The Message: B. Challenges & Growth Opportunities:
To feel inferior or inadequate about training and education. To be a doormat for control types. To be anal retentive in behavior or attitude. To worry, overwork, fret or have anxiety about performance. To nag or be critical with unrealistic standards of perfection.

Numbers: 4, 8
Energy Centers: 3rd—Power Center, 2nd—Sexual and Creative Center & 1st—Foundation and Elimination Center.
Body Parts: Upper and Lower Abdomen, Colon & Bowels.
Planet or Luminary: Mercury
Zodiac Zone: Virgo
Beings & Animals: Veterinarians, Massage Therapists, Office Personnel, Clerks, Purchasing and Service Agents, Accountants, Children, Workers, Maidens, Virgins, Deer, Squirrels, Mice, Rats, Rabbits, Land Turtles, Otters, Burrowing Animals & Ants.
Balancing Musical Notes: E, C & D **Sounds:** Hooo, Huuu & Aaaa **Instruments:** Guitar, Piano, Drums, Percussion Instruments, Saxophone, Bass & Electric Guitar.

GROUP 8, LIBRA

Polarity Charge: Masculine (+)
Element: Air
Emotional Representation:
Highest—Acceptance, Expression & Communication in Relationship.
Lowest—desire, vanity, addiction to relationship & unbalanced.

Healing Colors:
Highest: A. Bright/deep, Attractive: Black & White, Opalescence.
Message—Highest & Best Expression:
Being Balanced or a Couple, In Relationship, Promotion or Advertising, Appreciation of Arts, Supporting Justice, Diplomacy, Harmony & Communication. A Moment of Glory.
Lower: B. Muted/Muddy, Undesirable: (colors above)
Message—Challenges & Growth Opportunities:
Polarized, separated, unbalanced or indecisive, looking for the sweetness in life, addictive, or rationalizing emotions, vain, superficial or ego-oriented.
Healing Gemstones: Opal & White Quartz with Black Veins.

The Message: A. Highest & Best Expression:
To Display Diplomacy, Harmony and Appreciation. To Feel Balanced In Behavior and Communication. To Have Respect and High Regard for Relationships, The Arts, Justice and Psychology. To Prefer Being a Partner. To Be Melodiously Articulate, With Finesse.
The Message: B. Challenges & Growth Opportunities:
To feel unbalanced, polarized or addicted. To live beyond our means for appearance sake. To be addicted to sweetness. To be superficial or over-rationalizing. To be indecisive. To value our head more than our heart. To create enemies and rivals.

Numbers: 2, 6
Energy Centers: 2nd—Sexual and Creative Center & 3rd—Power Center
Body Parts: Kidneys, Pancreas & Area at Waistline.
Planet or Luminary: Venus
Zodiac Zone: Libra
Beings & Animals: Partners, Diplomats, Ambassadors, Representatives, Senators, Arbitrators, Mediators, Umpires, Referees, Enemies, Rivals, Birds that mate for life, Doves, Love birds, Humming birds, Skunks, Zebras & Black and White Animals.
Balancing Musical Notes: E, D **Sounds:** Hooo, Aaaa **Instruments:** Piano, Guitar, Saxophone, Bass & Electric Guitar.

GROUP 9, SCORPIO

Polarity Charge: Feminine (-)
Element: Water
Emotional Representation:
Highest—Contentment, Balanced Sexual & Political Power & Kindness.
Lowest—emotional attachment to someone or something, jealously, possessiveness & anger.

Healing Colors:
Highest: A. Bright/deep, Attractive: Orange, Orange Yellow, Orange Red & Orange Rust.
Message—Highest & Best Expression:
Transformation to Higher Expression, Regeneration, Analyze, Probe, Investigate, Penetrating Insight, Financial Acumen & Sexual Creativity.
Lower: B. Muted/Muddy, Undesirable: (colors above)
Message—Challenges & Growth Opportunities:
Manipulation, control games, jealousy, guilt, or being a victim and/or a victimizer, manifesting destruction or secrets. Regeneration and healing are essential.
Healing Gemstones: Orange Citrine, Orange Jade, Amber & Carnelian.
The Message: A. Highest & Best Expression:
To Experience Transformation (Death/Rebirth), Regeneration, To Study, Analyze, Probe and Investigate The Nature of Things. To Possess Deep and Penetrating Insight. To Demonstrate Sexual Creativity. To Be Social and Politically Correct. To Hold Office or Power for The Greater Good, Sharing Resources.
The Message: B. Challenges & Growth Opportunities:
To utilize manipulation or control for power. To participate in ego games using jealousy, possessiveness, guilt or insecurity. To be a victim or a victimizer. To be destructive, withholding or secret to get our way. To be out of balance with our sexual energy. To misuse political and financial power. To be secretive to the detriment of intimacy.
Number: 7
Energy Centers: 2nd—Sexual & Creative Center
Body Parts: Sexual Organs, Ovaries, Testes, Prostate Gland & Pelvic Area.
Planet or Luminary: Pluto
Zodiac Zone: Scorpio
Beings & Animals: Healers, Shamans, Magicians, Doctors, Politicians, Exotic Dancers, Prostitutes, Scorpions, Snakes, Bats, Frogs, Lizards, Dragons, Alligators, Phoenixes, Vultures, Lynxes, Opossums, Centipedes, Tarantulas, Dragonflies, Mosquitoes & Jellyfishes.
Balancing Musical Note: D **Sound:** Aaaa **Instruments:** Saxophone & Bass Electric Guitar.

GROUP 10, ARIES

Polarity Charge: Masculine (+)
Element: Fire
Emotional Representation:
Highest—Kindness, Balanced Sexual Passion & Physical Power.
Lowest—anger, selfishness, frustration & headstrong.

Healing Colors:
Highest: A. Bright/deep, Attractive: Red, Red Orange & Red Brown.
Message—Highest & Best Expression:
Social, Creative, Sexual, Emotional, Passion, Speed, Thrills, Natural, Wild, Energy, Activity, Action, Executive Ability, Sports, Initiation, Completion, Promotion & Leadership.
Lower: B. Muted/Muddy, Undesirable: (colors above)
Message—Challenges & Growth Opportunities:
Sexually permissive, blocked creativity, emotional and sexual dysfunction, selfish, stop, emergency, angry, ego, frustrated, in debt, inflamed, survival, pushy, confrontation, too competitive, dictator, headstrong, helpless, in denial or weak. Healing is imperative.
Healing Gemstones: Bloodstone, Ruby, Garnets, Red Coral, Red Onyx & Red Jasper.

The Message: A. Highest & Best Expression:
To Demonstrate Executive Ability and Evolved Leadership In Worldly Matters. To Enjoy Action, Sports, Passions, Safe Speed and Thrills. To Enjoy Sexual Activity and a Natural, Uninhibited Expression. To Be Promoted, or Initiate Action and Oversee To Completion.
The Message: B. Challenges & Growth Opportunities:
To be sexually permissive, demonstrating emotional or sexual dysfunction with blocked creativity. To be in our ego, frustrated, pushy, confrontational or headstrong. To be selfish, angry, impatient, dictatorial or in survival mode. To feel helpless, weak or in denial. To manifest a crisis, emergency or an accident. To stop action or to force action.
Number: 1
Energy Center: 2nd—Sexual & Creative Center.
Body Parts: Head, Sexual Organs, Ovaries, Testes, Prostate Gland & Pelvic Area.
Planet or Luminary: Mars
Zodiac Sign: Aries
Beings & Animals: Business Executives, Officers, Soldiers, Warriors, Dancers, Athletes, Sports Enthusiasts, Grouse, Badgers, Animals Mating, Apes, Monkeys, Gorillas, Roosters, Rams, Rhinos, Wild boars, Sharks & Fighting Cocks.
Balancing Musical Note: D **Sound:** Aaaa **Instruments:** Saxophone, Bass & Electric Guitar.

GROUP 11, SAGITTARIUS

Polarity Charge: Masculine (+)
Element: Fire
Emotional Representation:
Highest—Kindness, Humor & Philosophical Power.
Lowest—fanatical, extreme, righteous & judgmental.

Healing Colors:

Highest A. Bright/deep, Attractive: Turquoise, Light Blue.
Message—Highest & Best Expression:
Joviality, Humor, Enjoyment, Fun, Excitement, Enthusiasm, Philosophy, Contemplating, Studying, Traveling, Foreign Cultures, Publishing, Higher Education & Wisdom.
Lower: B. Muted/Muddy, Undesirable: (colors above)
Message—Challenges & Growth Opportunities:
Dower, pessimistic, frivolous activity, not self-aware or seeking truth outside of one's Self.
Healing Gemstones: Turquoise & Blue topaz

The Message: A. Highest & Best Expression:
To Love Ethics and Spiritual Law. To Possess Great Humor, Zest, Joy, Exuberance and Wisdom and a Philosophical Nature. To Be a Dynamic Instructor and an Inspiration To Others Regarding Studying, Traveling and Foreign Cultures. To Be Generous, Honest and Straightforward, Loving Liberty and Freedom. To Be Big "Energetically" and Outgoing.
The Message: B. Challenges & Growth Opportunities:
To be overzealous, righteous, dogmatic or a religious fanatic. To seek truth outside of one's Self. To be negative, pessimistic or limited in experience. To discharge energy with frivolous activity. To jump to conclusions. To hurt others with harsh truth or to put foot in mouth. To be long-winded or enamored with hearing our self talk, deterring conversation.

Numbers: 3, 9
Energy Center: none
Body Parts: Hips & Thighs
Planet or Luminary: Jupiter
Zodiac Zone: Sagittarius
Beings & Animals: Comedians, Clowns, Lawyers, Foreigners, Philosophers, In-laws, Travelers, Zealots, Centaur, Unicorns, Rhinos, Horses, Elephants & Kangaroos.
Balancing Musical Notes: C, D **Sounds:** Huuu & Aaaa **Instruments:** Drums, Percussions Saxophone & Bass Electric Guitar.

GROUP 12, CAPRICORN

Polarity Charge: Feminine (-)
Element: Earth
Emotional Representation:
Highest—Material Stability, Groundedness & Courage.
Lowest—fear, insecurity, depression & negativity.

Healing Colors:
Highest: A. Bright/deep, Attractive: Black & Shiny Gray
Message—Highest & Best Expression:
Manifestation, Release, Letting Go, Stability, Foundation, Physical and Financial Success, Managerial Ability & Patience. Also, the Void, Space, Night & Feminine.
Lower: B. Muted/Muddy, Undesirable: (colors above)
Message—Challenges & Growth Opportunities:
Challenged, dirty, dark, dangerous, evil, overworking, critical, pessimistic, moody, severe, rigid, inhibited, ungrounded, depressed, blocked, stern, inflexible or judgmental.
Healing Gemstones: Hematite, Obsidian, Onyx, Smokey Quartz, Bl. Tourmaline & Jade.

The Message: A. Highest & Best Expression:
To Be Ambitious and Accomplish Great Things. To Be a Great Problem Solver With Excellent Intuition. Manifestation of Physical and Financial Success and Managerial Ability. To Have a Strong Foundation of Economic Security and Great Stability. To Demonstrate Patience and The Ability To Let Go When It's Appropriate. Also, The Void, Space, and The Night.
The Message: B. Challenges & Growth Opportunities:
To be severely critical, rigid, inhibited, stern or inflexible. To be judgmental, pessimistic, depressed or blocked. To feel ungrounded, without a foundation or in survival mode. To have serious, dogmatic thoughts or karmic lessons that may be challenging, dangerous, dark or crushing. To feel dirty, evil or acting without Higher Guidance.
Numbers: 4, 8
Energy Center: 1st—Foundation & Elimination Center
Body Parts: Base of Spine, Skeletal Structure, Bones, Teeth & Knees.
Planet or Luminary: Saturn **Zodiac Zone:** Capricorn
Beings & Animals: Authorities, Corporate Officers, Governors, Judges, Inspectors, Management, Conservatives, Organizers, Goats, Deer, Antelopes, Giraffes, Camels, Llamas, Crows, Black Panthers, Spiders, Porcupines, Beavers & Prairie Dogs.
Balancing Musical Note: C **Sound:** Huuu **Instruments:** Drums & Percussion Instruments.

GROUP 13, AQUARIUS

Polarity Charge: Masculine
Element: Air
Emotional Representation:
Highest—Humanitarian Expression, Free Communication & Brotherhood.
Lowest—unfulfilled desires, rebelliousness & radical.

Healing Color:
Highest: A. Bright/deep, Attractive: Very Light, White Blue
Message—Highest & Best Expression:
Enlightening, Humanitarian, Universal Laws, Inventive, Friend, Ingenious, Forward & Thinking
Lower: B. Muted/Muddy, Undesirable: (color above)
Message—Challenges & Growth Opportunities:
Eccentric, off-center, erratic, unpredictable, radical, selfish & change
Healing Gemstone: Aquamarine

The Message: A. Highest & Best Expression:
To Be a Humanitarian, Advocating Universal Law, Freedom, Brotherhood and Friendship. To Bring Enlightenment (Spiritual Energy), Equality and Ingenuity Into The World With Avant-Garde Thinking. To Have Talent With Electronics, Innovation, and Invention. To Be Determined, Original and Possess An Excellent Memory.
The Message: B. Challenges & Growth Opportunities:
To be radical, unpredictable, erratic and eccentric to the extreme. To rebel and live outside the status quo, pushing all boundaries. To argue, create opposition or be hypocritical. To be fundamentalist, extremist, desiring change in a more revolutionary manner. To possess a tendency to exaggerate problems. To be anxious, nervous and apprehensive. To demonstrate shaky movement.
Numbers: 11, 9
Energy Center: none
Body Parts: Ankles & Lower Leg
Planet or Luminary: Uranus
Zodiac Zone: Aquarius
Beings & Animals: Friends, Social Groups, Inventors, Electronic Engineers, Bohemians, Humanitarian, Fundamentalists, Extremists, Computer Techies, Crows, Elks and Dogs.
Balancing Musical Notes: F, E & D **Sounds:** Haaa, Hooo & Aaaa **Instruments:** Harp, Flute, Guitar, Piano, Saxophone, Bass & Electric Guitar.

Guidance Affirmations: Song & Chant

Pump Up the Higher Self

Rap Song by Sundae Merrick 2-21-00

Divine Reason and Rhyme, use it all the time.
You need to know, what is so, Divine Reason and Rhyme!
Look in the mirror, at your own reflection.
With Divine Guidance, make the right selection.

Anger and aggression was a reaction.
Now we want peace, love and compassion.
Let off some steam, let go of the theme, of poor self-esteem!
You can be a victim, if you want to be, understand with certainty,
You want to know, you have a choice, give Guidance a voice!

Pump up the Self, Pump up the Self, Pump up the Higher Self!
Put your ego on the shelf, be your Higher Self.

Dream a dream of a Divine King and Queen,
Divine family, reigning supreme.
My Divine Father tells me the reason.
For every act, there is a season.
My Divine Mother tells me the rhyme.
Pray for Guidance, all the time!

Where Self isn't, there's no "you."
If you don't know Self, you haven't got a clue.
If you want to be, Divine family, listen to me!
Parents and teachers, give us a chance.
We want to learn the "Inner Self" dance.

Pump up the Self, Pump up the Self, Pump up the Higher Self!
Put your ego on the shelf, be your Higher Self.

I always pray for my Highest and best.
I allow the Divine, to do the rest.
I have angels here for me.
Don't have to say "oh poor me!"

The truth shall set me, oh so free.
I speak it now consistently!
To heal myself, I act on this rhyme.
I am with my Self, all the time!

Pump up the Self, Pump up the Self, Pump up the Higher Self!
Put your ego on the shelf, be your Higher Self.

Divine Mind

Affirmation Chant by Sundae Merrick 7-11-03

Divine Mind Is My Mind.
Divine Mind Is So Fine.
Divine Mind Is So Kind.
Divine Mind Is So Refined.

Divine Mind Is The Grand Design.
My Life Can Be Divinely Defined.
With Divine Mind, Perfect Answers I Find.
With Divine Mind, I Can Unwind.
Life Can Be So Sweetly Sublime.
My Path, My Mission, Never Left Behind.

Bibliography

Video: "Signs from God"

Webster's New World Dictionary, 2nd Edition
(Cleveland: William Collins Publishers, 1979

Michael Loewe and Carmen Bacher, ed.
Oracles and Divination
(New York: Random House, 1981)

H. Spencer Lewis,
The Mystical Life of Jesus
(San Jose: Supreme Grand Lodge of Amore, 1953)

Lee McCann, Nostrodamus,
The Man Who Saw Through Time
(New York: Farrat, Staus, Girouz, 1941)

Jeanne Avery,
The Rising Sign: Wer Astrological Mark
(Garden City: Doubleday, 1982)

Jamie Sams,
Sacred Path Cards: Discovery of Self through Native Teachings
(Harper Collins Publishers, 1990)

Robert Ornstein,
The Psychology of Consciousness
(W.H. Freeman & Co., 1972)

Frances Sakoian & Louis S. Acker,
The Astrologer's Handbook
(Harper & Row Publishers, 1973)

Robert Hand,
Planets in Transit
(Para Research Gloucester Massachusetts, 1976)

Arne Lein
What's Your Card?
(Meta-Card, Third Printing 1982)

Jamie Sams & David Carson
Medicine Cards (revised expanded edition)

Florence Campbell
Your Days Are Numbered
(The Gateway, Tenth Edition 1966)

The American Heritage Dictionary of the English Language,
(Third Edition, 1996 Houghton, Mifflin Co. Electronic Version licensed from INSO Corporation)

About the Author

Sundae Merrick has a Bachelor of Arts in Education, majoring in Biological Sciences and a minor Physical Education. She has studied the major religions of the world, Universal laws, and Spirituality. She is a non-denominational Doctor of Divinity; she likes to call it Dr. of Go-"in"-ity, supporting the theme of finding our own answers inside our self. She has traveled to over 30 countries to experience and learn about many cultures, healing techniques, philosophies & Sacred Power Sites. She is an Educator, Facilitator, Minister, Intuitive Counselor, Astrologer, Entertainer and Yoga/Relaxation/Meditation, Dance & Healing Arts Instructor living in beautiful Hawaii.

She has created healing educational courses to support others who wish to access the power of love, healing and wisdom in their own lives. Her courses include Divination, Accessing our Higher Guidance; Mind Heart Harmony, Freeing Ourselves from the Past; Heavenly Wholeness & Sacred Mating. Sundae also facilitates Healing Nature Walks & Retreats and gives Polarity Therapy energy balancing sessions. Her Company, Shakti Entertainment, provides positive, uplifting singing and dancing telegrams and psychic astrological and tarot readings.

Sundae has had a weekly TV Series in Hawaii, called "Get Healthy, before you die!" It provides Health & Holistic Education, Yoga, Breathing and Meditation Techniques, in beautiful nature settings. She wants you to experience greater fulfillment in your life, with more love, peace, self-esteem, career success, creativity, and wealth and relationship harmony.

Quote: "When we learn to heal our emotions and negative self-concepts, we create harmony, develop wholeness and trust. When we strengthen our relationship with Divine Guidance, our lives reflect more Inner peace, no matter what the circumstances are."

Contact Information:

Sundae Merrick
Telephone: (808) 262-4404 or (888) 811-7161
Email: sundae@gethealthybeforeyoudie.com or aaashakti@msn.com
Website: gethealthybeforeyoudie.com

Professional Seminars & Retreats Include:

Divination, Accessing our Higher Guidance
Mind Heart Harmony, Freeing Ourselves from the Past
Heavenly Wholeness, Balancing all Aspects of Ourselves
Sacred Mating, Creating Blessed Relationships
Relaxation for Success, Let go of Ego and Open to Innate Talent
The Beauty Way, Embracing the Feminine
Taoist Energy in Nature, Communing with Heaven, Earth and Trees
Nurturing Self, Nutritional Alkalinity and Live Foods
Yoga for Relaxation & Stress Relief
Your Back at Work: Releasing Stress in the Office Environment
Dance of the Sexes, the Polarity of Attraction and Magnetism
Secrets of Communication for Relationship Success
Dream Vision, Co-Creating Our Future Reality
Dolphin Magic, Healing & Playing with our Dolphriends
Amakua in Nature, Understanding Animal Guidance

Call or email Sundae for availability for seminars, retreats, professional speaking engagements and book signings.

Other Services:

Sundae is also available for personal consultations, psychic readings, regressions and healing sessions.

Past Life Regression/Intuitive Spiritual Counseling

Together, we will journey into the unconscious mind in a deep state of relaxation and identify situations and experiences from the past that cause problems in the present. Discover the basis for low self-esteem, poor self-image and any other attitude that keeps us small. Bring yourself into alignment with your Higher Self and know how to heal and evolve with more harmony.

Insightful Astrological & Psychic Guidance

Know your challenging patterns and take responsibility for healing them for your heart and soul's evolution. Understand your life cycles, and those of your loved ones so you can make more conscious, wise choices in your career, relationships and health. Be more productive with your time and your resources and know when to invest and when to take time off. Please submit your name, birth date, time and place beforehand.

Polarity Therapy

The balance and flow of energy in the body is the underlying foundation of health. With this energy therapy, you can experience less tension as we open your body's energy circuits for more health, vitality, harmony, and evolution in your life. Have your three major currents and the five elements balanced and reconnected fully. Experience the bliss and deep relaxation when these three main currents are flowing; the harmony, creative and bipolar currents. Discover integration when your elemental lines are open and filled with life force.

Call or email Sundae for availability.

"Wisdom of the Ages" Book Series:

BOOK I: Divine Reason & Rhyme, Access Higher Guidance and Nature's Wisdom. A "Nature's Wisdom" Chart called can be purchased with all the Guidance Groups.

BOOK II: Mind Heart Harmony, Freeing Ourselves from Self-limiting Patterns.

BOOK III: Get Healthy Before You Die, A Healing Guide.

CD: Relaxation & Empowerment

Progressive Relaxation through the Body: 10 minutes
Journey through the Energy Centers for Clearing & Healing: 20 minutes
Combination of both: 30 minutes
This CD assists us in creating an alpha brain wave state that encourages, relaxation and receptivity to Guidance.

DVD's: Get Healthy Yoga

An Award Winning TV Series: 16 one-hour shows presenting health & holistic education, relaxing yoga in nature, the complete breath, deep gentle stretching and meditation with affirmations for health and wellbeing accompanied by beautiful music and exquisite Hawaii nature scenes. These shows encourage our harmony current by releasing the tension, relaxing the muscles and opening to our intuition.

Part One: Yoga in Nature, 4 Shows

Part Two: Mind Heart Harmony, 4 Shows

Part Three: Inner Guidance, 4 Shows

Part Four: A Healing Guide, 4 Shows

Health & Healing Affirmations, 1 Show

35 minutes of affirmations for health and wellbeing, with beautiful music and exquisite hawaii nature scenes obtained and combined from several shows. Great for background ambiance and programming positive health and healing messages.

All products can be ordered by phone: 1 (888) 811-7161 or (808) 262-4404

Printed in the United States
By Bookmasters